Hot & Spicy
Southeast
Asian Dishes

Also by Dave DeWitt, Mary Jane Wilan, and Melissa T. Stock

Hot & Spicy Latin Dishes

Hot & Spicy & Meatless

Hot & Spicy Chili

Hot & Spicy Southeast Asian Dishes

Dave DeWitt

Mary Jane Wilan

Melissa T. Stock

PRIMA is a trademark of Prima Publishing, a division of Prima Communications, Inc.

Portions of this book first appeared in *Chile Pepper* magazine. Used by permission.

Illustrations by Lois Bergthold

Library of Congress Cataloging-in-Publication Data

DeWitt, Dave.
    Hot & Spicy Southeast Asian dishes : the best fiery food from the Pacific rim / Dave DeWitt, Mary Jane Wilan, and Melissa T. Stock.
       p.   cm.
    Includes index.
    ISBN 1-55958-577-3
    1. Cookery, Southeast Asian. 2. Cookery (Hot peppers) I. Wilan, Mary Jane.
II. Stock, Melissa T. III. Title. IV. Title: Hot and spicy Southeast Asian dishes.
TX724.5.S68D49 1995
641.5959—dc20   94-37126
                                                   CIP

95 96 97 98 99 AA 10 9 8 7 6 5 4 3 2 1

Printed in the United States of America

How to Order:
Single copies may be ordered from Prima Publishing, P.O. Box 1260, Rocklin, CA 95677; telephone (916) 632-4400. Quantity discounts are also available. On your letterhead, include information concerning the intended use of the books and the number of books you wish to purchase.

Acknowledgments

Thanks to the following people for their help on this project:

Peter Aiken, Jeff Corydon, Binh Duong, Linda Gant, Nancy Gerlach, Kat Hardy, David Karp, Ellie Leavitt, Daniel Lentz, Sue Louie, David Louie, Rosemary Ogilvie, Violet Oon, Devagi Shanmugam, Robert Spiegel, Richard Sterling, and Gloria Zimmerman.

Contents

Introduction

The smiling vendor in the Bangkok produce market had a black and white kitten sitting on a pile of green and red *prik khee nu* chiles and was surprised to see a *farangi* in front of her. Tourists were supposed to shop in the retail markets, not in the sprawling, riverside wholesale market, but we were on a search for chiles. And we found tons of them! Dried chiles were stacked in bales twenty feet high and fresh ones in all sizes were presented in basket after basket. It was a chilehead's fantasy come true, and Dave couldn't resist. He picked up one of the vendor's red chiles, but before he could pop it in his mouth, she shook her head negatively and made a discouraging gesture with her hands. Dave grinned at her and chewed up the chile without flinching, winning the admiration of the woman and the other nearby vendors, who, of course, had never heard of *Chile Pepper* magazine.

Later, on a trip to Johore Baru, Malaysia, we found even more evidence of the intense love for chiles in this part of the world. In a supermarket in a shopping mall, there was a display eight feet tall and fifty feet long that consisted of hundreds of brands of chile sauces stacked neatly on the shelves. Needless to say, we filled our basket with as many as we could—they were bound for Chuck Evans, our friend who has one of the largest collections of hot sauces in the world!

Although we were not able to travel to every country mentioned in this book, we have explored parts of Thailand, Singapore, and Malaysia. And we've been backed up by our contributors to *Chile Pepper* magazine, such as Richard Sterling, who has traveled to Vietnam and Cambodia to collect information on chile cuisines. We thank him and the others, who are listed in the acknowledgments.

This volume in the *Hot & Spicy* series is considerably easier on chileheads than our previous book, *Hot & Spicy Latin Dishes,* because the chiles used in these recipes—or nearly identical substitutes—are readily available. In *Hot & Spicy Latin Dishes,* most of the recipes called for approximate substitutions because the *ajís* and *rocotos* were available only to home gardeners or people who were able to shop in Mexican border town mercados. Nearly all the Southeast Asian chiles are of the *Capsicum annuum* species, so very similar varieties are readily available in North America. The flavor of the dishes will not be affected by the substitutions suggested.

However, the adventuresome shopper will find fresh and dried Southeast Asian chiles in Asian markets, and to assist with that search, we have listed the varieties of Southeast Asian chiles by their transliterated names in the Glossary. Because of the vagaries of the Anglicized spellings of Thai, Malay, Vietnamese, and Burmese words, we have settled on the spellings used by a standard reference work, *The Letts Companion to Asian Food and Cooking*, by Jacki Passmore. The recipe titles are our own descriptions of the dishes; if the title of the recipe is known in its original language, we give it in parentheses. Since English is a primary language in Singapore and a second language in Thailand, sometimes the title of the recipe is given only in English.

There are a number of unfamiliar ingredients in many of the recipes, and we have described them in the glossary. We strongly suggest visiting Asian markets to find them. In Albuquerque, New Mexico, for example, we can choose among eight Asian markets that carry nearly every ingredient mentioned in the glossary. Such ingredients can also be ordered (see Mail-Order Sources, pages 289–290).

We continue to use the same Heat Scale that we devised for *Chile Pepper* magazine and the other books in the *Hot & Spicy* series: Mild, Medium, Hot, and Extremely Hot. Each rating takes into consideration the type of chiles in the dish, the number of chiles used in the recipe, and the degree of dilution. The relative heat of each recipe can be easily adjusted.

We hope you enjoy our hot and spicy trek east. For more coverage of Southeast Asian and other hot and spicy cuisines, subscribe to *Chile Pepper* magazine, P.O. Box 80780, Albuquerque, NM 87198, (800) 359-1483.

Chiles in
Southeast Asia

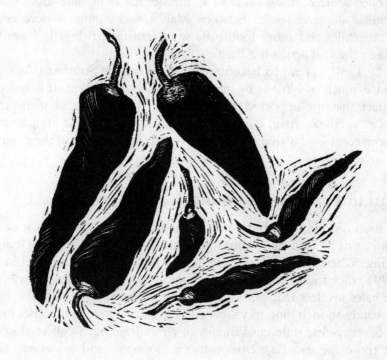

As everyone knows by now, chiles are not indigenous to Asia but were transferred there through trade. Although hard evidence is lacking, ethnobotanists theorize that either Arab, Hindu, or Portuguese traders—or some combination—carried chiles from India to Malacca, on the Malay Peninsula across from Sumatra, between 1510 and the late 1520s. From there, Portuguese traders introduced the fiery fruits into Thailand, and numerous trading groups took them to Java, Sumatra, New Guinea, Macao, and the Philippines.

From the varieties present today in the region, it appears that the *Capsicum annuum* and *frutescens* species were the primary chiles transferred to the region. Whatever their species, they quickly became a very important element in the cuisines of all the countries in the region. As Thai food expert Jennifer Brennan described the process, chile peppers were "adopted by the Thai with a fervor normally associated with the return of a long-lost child."

In 1529, a treaty between Spain and Portugal gave the Spanish control of the Philippines and the Portuguese control of Malaysia. Since the Spanish also controlled Mexico, it was easier to administer the Philippines from that colony, so regular shipping routes between Manila and Acapulco were established. Mexican chiles and other foodstuffs were transferred directly from the New World to the Old across the Pacific.

By 1550, chiles had become well established in Southeast Asia, probably spread as much by birds as by human trade and cultivation. It is an ironic culinary fact that the imported chiles became as important as many traditional spices in Southeast Asian cuisines, thus illustrating how the pungency of chiles has been combined with indigenous flavors to fire up most of the cuisines of the region.

Thailand and Its Neighbors

Thai food is extensively spiced with chiles but, contrary to popular belief, there is not just one "Thai chile," but rather many different varieties that are used in cooking. When Dave and Mary Jane toured the wholesale market in Bangkok in 1991, they found literally tons of both fresh-dried chiles in baskets and in huge bales five feet tall. The chiles ranged in size from piquin-like, thin green pods barely an inch long to yellow and red pods about four inches long.

Seventy-nine different varieties of chiles have been collected in Thailand from three species: *Capsicum annuum, chinense,* and *frutescens.* Given the volatile state of chile nomenclature, it is not surprising that some confusion exists concerning the terms for Thai chiles. For example, one reference book states that *prik khee nu* is a New Mexican pod type, while the general consensus is that it is the tiny, elongated "bird pepper" so associated with Thai cooking. *Prik khee nu* translates, inelegantly, as "mouse dropping chile." The chiles that resemble the New Mexican type are called *prik num*, "banana peppers," and *Kashmiri*, because they are grown extensively in Kashmir, India.

Confusion exists here, too, because the *Kashmiri* chiles are also called *sriracha*, or *siracha* chiles. They are so named because a sauce made from these chiles originated in the Thai seaside town of Sriracha as an accompaniment to fish, and it became so popular that it has been bottled and sold around the world. However, the chiles used in *sriracha* sauce now are red serranos. *Prik khee fah* is a term used to refer to cayenne chiles, while *prik yuak* is the yellow wax hot variety.

In agricultural terminology, the two types of chiles grown commercially in Thailand are "bird pepper" (*prik khee nu*) and "chili" (*prik khee fah*). Chiles accounted for about 12 percent of the total agricultural land in Thailand in 1985 (the most recent year for which we have statistics), and about 100,000 acres were planted in "bird pepper" and 45,000 acres in "chili." For comparison, the approximate number of acres devoted to chiles in New Mexico, the number one chile-producing state in the United States, varies between 35,000 and 40,000 acres. The Thai chiles are grown on terraces on hillsides and in irrigated paddy fields after the rice season is over.

The same trade routes that introduced the chile pepper into Thailand also spread the concept of curries from India to all parts of the globe. Consequently, Thailand is a perfect example of a culinary collision of cultures: Indian curry spices were combined with the latest exotic import—chile peppers—to create some of the hottest curries on earth.

Most commonly in Thailand, fresh chiles are ground up with other ingredients to make the famous Thai curry pastes (see Chapter 2) that are staples in Thai cooking and take several forms. *Kaeng* (often spelled *gaeng*) is the term for a bewildering variety of Thai curries. Some *kaengs* resemble liquid Indian curry sauces and are abundant with traditional curry spices such as turmeric, coriander, and cardamom. Another type of *kaeng* curry omits these curry spices and substitutes herbs such as cilantro, but the chiles are still there. This second group of *kaeng* curries is said to be the original Thai curries, invented long before they were influenced by Indian spices. As with the curries of Sri Lanka, these *kaeng* curries are multicolored; depending on the color of the chiles and other spices and the amount of coconut milk added, they range from light yellow to green to pale red. *Kaeng kari* is yellow-colored because it contains most of the curry spices, including turmeric, and is fairly mild. One of the more pungent of these *kaeng* curries, *kaeng phed,* is made with tiny red chiles, coconut milk, and basil leaves, and is served with seafood.

Chiles are also important to another aspect of Thai cuisine: the presentation of the meal. "The Thais are as interested in beautiful presentation as the Japanese are," writes Jennifer Brennan. "The contrasts of color and texture, of hot and cold, of spicy and mild are as important here as in any cuisine in the world." Considering the emphasis on both heat and presentation in their cuisine, it is not surprising that the Thais love to garnish their hot meals with—what else?—hot chiles. Their adoration for the chile pepper extends to elaborately carved chile pod flowers. They use multicolored, small chiles for the best flower effect, with colors ranging from green to yellow to red to purple. The procedure for creating chile pod flowers is quite simple. Hold the chile by the stem on a cutting board and use a sharp knife to slice the chile in half, lengthwise, starting one-eighth inch from the stem down to the point (or apex, for the botanically minded). Rotate the chile 180 degrees and repeat the procedure until the chile is divided into sixteenths or more.

The thinner the "petals," the more convincing the chiles will be as flowers when the chiles are soaked in water containing ice cubes, which is the next step. Immerse the chiles in ice water until the slices curl—a few hours—and then remove the seeds with the tip of a knife. The chile flowers can then be arranged artistically on the platter and later devoured as a spicy salad condiment, which accompanies the traditional Thai curries.

Hot and spicy curries also appear commonly in the cuisine of Myanmar (formerly Burma), Thailand's neighbor to the west. There, chiles are known as *nga yut thee,* and they are used to make *balachuang,* a spicy relish that not only accompanies curries, it is served at every meal. To make a Burmese curry, the cooks make a curry paste out of their five basic ingredients: onions, garlic, chiles, ginger, and turmeric. Burmese cooks add other spices as well, including an occasional prepared curry powder. But the hallmark of the Burmese curry is its oiliness. The cooks use a combination of peanut oil and sesame oil, about a cup of each in a wok, and heat it until it smokes—this is called "cooking the oil." The curry paste is added, the heat is reduced, and the paste is cooked for fifteen minutes. Then meat is added, cooked, and eventually the oil rises to the top. This state is called *see byan,* "the return of the oil." When the oil floats on top, the dish is done. The oil is not skimmed off the top, but rather is absorbed by the side dish of rice when it is served. Surprisingly, the curries do not taste greasy—probably as a result of the light oil used.

In Laos, which borders Thailand to the northeast, chiles are known collectively as *mak phet*. There are many characterizations of *mak phet* chiles in the Laotian language, such as by color and size. *Mak phet dip* are fresh green chiles while *mak phet deng* are fresh red chiles. *Mak phet nyai* are large chiles, *mak phet kuntsi* are small chiles, and *mak phet kinou* are the tiny, "rat dropping" chiles— undoubtedly a variety similar to the Thai *prik khee nu,* as they share the same terminal word. Other characterizations of Laotian chiles are *mak phet haeng,* dried red chiles, and *mak phet pung,* ground red chiles.

Fresh small red and green chiles are used extensively in a number of chile pastes in Laos. Jalapeño- and serrano-like chiles are beaten with pestles in huge mortars, and locally available spices are added. Larger chiles are stuffed, as with a favorite Laotian creation called *mawk mak phet*. It features poblano or New Mexican chiles that are stuffed with vegetables, spices, and white fish, and then steamed.

Fish combined with chiles also provides the essential flavor of another nearby country. In Vietnam, where the heart of the chile cuisine coincides with the center of the country, principally in the city of Hue, a fish and chile sauce called *nuac cham* reigns supreme. It consists of fish sauce, lime, sugar, garlic, and fresh, small, red serrano-like chiles called *ot,* which is the generic Vietnamese term for chile peppers. Dried chiles are *ot kho,* chile sauces are *tuong ot,* and chile pastes are *tuong tuoi.*

According to Richard Sterling, who has traveled extensively in the region, chiles are ubiquitous in Cambodia, Thailand's neighbor to the southeast. "Every grand market and merchant's corner of Phnom Penh offers them in baskets, piles, and bags," he wrote in *Chile Pepper* (May–June, 1993). "We don't know precisely when or by whom the chile was introduced to this part of the world, but it was certainly by the Spanish or Portuguese in the late sixteenth century." Sterling referred to the first documented official contact between what is now Cambodia and Europeans, which occurred in 1596 when the Portuguese governor of Manila sent an official expedition to the king of Angkor in 1596. "We don't know what the expeditions' supplies, provisions, and gifts for the king included," adds Sterling, "but one hundred years after Columbus, the Portuguese were well supplied with *Capsicums* from the New World. It is delicious to speculate that though the military missions came to naught, a chile culinary mission enjoyed great success."

The Spiciest Islands

In Indonesia, Malaysia, and Singapore, the words for rice (*nasi*), chicken (*ayam*), hot sauce (*sambal*), and many other food terms are often identical from region to region, so it is difficult to separate the Malaysian and Indonesian elements of the food of the spiciest islands. After the Portuguese won control of the Malacca Strait in 1511, it is probable that chile peppers were imported soon afterward by traders sailing to and from the Portuguese colony of Goa, India. The spice trade was one of the primary motivating factors in European exploration of the rest of the world, so it is not surprising that many countries sought to control the output of the "Spice Islands." These islands, which now comprise parts of the countries of Indonesia and Malaysia, produced cinnamon, cloves, nutmeg, black pepper, and many other spices. What *is* surprising about the Spice Islands is that they were infiltrated and "conquered" by a New World spice—chile peppers.

Asian food authority Copeland Marks observed, in a *Gourmet* article, that the cuisine of the region would be "unthinkable without them. . . . When the chile arrived in Indonesia it was welcomed enthusiastically and now may be considered an addiction." An addiction they may be, but their nomenclature is as confusing as ever. They have a common term in the region, *cabe* (also spelled *cabai*). *Cabe hijau* refers to green chiles while *cabe merah* means red chiles and *cabe rawit* are the notoriously hot bird chiles (*Capsicum frutescens*). But another word for chiles in Java and other parts of Indonesia is *lombok,* while *cili* is the operative alternate in Malaysia. *Cili padi* are apparently the same as *cabe rawit,* the small bird chiles, while dried red chiles are *cili kering.*

The nomenclature gets even more muddled when the chilihead travels to Bali, a Hindu outpost in predominantly Muslim Indonesia. There, chiles are *tabia. Tabia lombok* (sometimes called *tabia jawa*) is finger-length and resembles cayenne, while *tabia Bali* is about an inch long and is the most popular chile on the island. *Tabia kerinyi* are the "bird's eye" chiles, or piquins, and *tabia gede* is the bell pepper.

Chiles are the number one vegetable crop in Indonesia, occupying 18 percent of the total acreage with an astonishing 500,000 acres under cultivation. That figure placed Indonesia third in world chile production in 1986, after India and Mexico. In agricultural terminology, there are two varieties under cultivation: *cabe rawit* ("chili pepper" or "bird pepper"), a variety of *Capsicum frutescens,* and *cabe merah,* or "cayenne." The Indonesian chiles are planted in alternating rows with shallots and sometimes with rice.

In Indonesia, chiles are used in a wide variety of dishes and are often combined with coconut cream or milk. On the island of Java, sugar is added, making that cuisine a mixture of sweet, sour, and fiery hot. Some cooks there believe that the addition of sugar keeps the power of the chiles and other spices under control.

Perhaps the principal use of chiles in this part of Asia is in sauces called *sambals* that are spread over rice or are used as a dip for *satay*, barbecued small chunks of meat. Chiles are often combined with peanuts for the *satay* dips. One word in particular frequently comes up in discussions of Indonesian food, and that is *rijsttafel*, which means "rice table" in Dutch. It is not a dish, but rather a feast of many dishes, including curries. The term derives from the Dutch settlers, who staged elaborate dinner parties in an attempt to upstage one another. It was up to the creative chef never to duplicate flavors, types of meat, or cooking styles, and for every dish that was spicy hot, there had to be a bland dish to offset it. Likewise, sweet dishes were offset by sour, warm dishes by cold dishes, wet by dry, and firm-textured by soft-textured.

Often, as many as fifty or sixty dishes were served, but despite such attention to detail, the food was not as important as the spectacle in a *rijsttafel*, and the quality of the party was judged by the number of servants it took to produce the affair. If fifty servants were required, the party was known as a "fifty-boy *rijsttafel*," which the Indonesians naturally found offensive. Today the term is considered to be a degrading holdover from colonial times; however, scaled-down *rijsttafels* are still staged for tourists—but without all the servants. Some of the curry dishes included in early *rijsttafels* were the *gulais*, curried stews, and the *rendangs* (sometimes spelled *randang*), which are meat dishes cooked in coconut milk and spices.

By comparison with the Indonesian figures, chiles are grown on a scant 2,500 acres in Malaysia—but still are the most important vegetables grown in the country in terms of total acreage, value, and per-capita consumption. There are two main varieties of *Capsicum annuum* under cultivation, 'Kulai' and 'Langkap'. They are grown by themselves or are intercropped with coconut, rubber, or pineapple. Malaysia provides more than 90 percent of Singapore's needs for fresh chile, with the remainder coming from Thailand.

In Malaysia, too, chiles play an important role in curries. For example, *lemak kuning* is a coconut-based sauce made with most of the regional curry ingredients; *kerabu kerisik* is made with fried, pounded coconut, lime juice, dried shrimp, shallots, and chiles; and *kacang* blends together the flavors of peanuts, lemongrass, galangal, chiles, and coconut milk.

Similarly, the famous *sambals* range from simple chile sauces to curry-like pastes and are primarily used to spice up other dishes, such as mild curries. The basis for most *sambals* is chiles, onions (or shallots or garlic), and citrus, but many other ingredients are used, including lemongrass, *blacan*, ginger, galangal, candlenuts, kaffir lime leaves, and coconut milk. Thus the *sambals* resemble a curry paste, but with a much greater amount of chiles.

In the nearby Philippine Islands, *sili* and *siling* are the Filipino (Tagalog) words for *Capsicums* in general. *Siling bilog* is bell pepper while *siling haba* is the long green or red chile. *Siling labuyo* is the bird pepper, which is very small and very hot. For years, *siling labuyo* appeared as the hottest chile in the world in *The Guinness Book of World Records,* but it was eventually replaced by the habanero, the true world's heat champion.

The chiles are primarily used by Muslims in the southern islands of the Philippines. The fiery *siling labuyo* is often crushed in vinegar to make a dipping sauce called *sawsawan.* A particularly hot region is Bicol, especially considering the fact that there was no Mexican influence there. It is said that the Bicolanos put the *siling labuyos* into everything they eat. "Half a vegetable dish could easily be ground chiles," writes Filipino food expert Irene Pineda Roces in *The Culinary Culture of the Philippines,* her tongue slightly in cheek. "A common joke is that the Bicolano ties down his chile plants first upon the approach of a typhoon before he looks after his wife."

Although Filipino food in general cannot be described as fiery, we have uncovered a few hot and spicy dishes from the islands. *Puerco en Adobo,* or Pork in Adobo (page 154), is one of them, and it's probably the closest food there is to a national dish of the Philippines. As with the Mexican version of the same dish, chiles are added according to the cook's taste.

In the Markets of Singapore

Singapore is the melting pot (or maybe the tossed salad) of Southeast Asia, so it's not surprising that ethnic influences from all over the region are found there. Originally, this tiny island nation—smaller than New York City—was part of what is now Malaysia, which means that its original cuisine was Malay.

In 1819, Sir Thomas Stamford Raffles colonized Singapore for the British, and soon the small fishing village became the leading port east of the Suez Canal. The British influence accounts for the fact that the principal language of Singapore is English (other official languages are Tamil, Malay, and Cantonese), but the impact of the Brits on food was not so great. Nowadays, about the only surviving British culinary heritage involves drinks; the hotels and restaurants serve high tea in the afternoon, excellent Singapore-brewed beers and stouts, and plenty of gin drinks.

The expansion of Singapore as a major trading center led to settlement by other ethnic groups. By 1821, the population was over 5,000 and included, besides Malays and Europeans, numerous Chinese and Indian settlers. Under British control, the settlers were kept in their own ethnic enclaves so they could not easily unite and rebel. These enclaves—such as Chinatown, Arab Street, and Little India—although unofficial now, still exist to this day.

We took a trip to the markets of these ethnic neighborhoods to get a true appreciation of the myriad ingredients found in the ethnic foods of Singapore. In Little India, we first visited the "dry" markets selling the various spices that comprise the curries: chiles, cloves, turmeric, star anise, peppercorns, cinnamon, coriander, and more. It was a vivid sensory assault on the eyes and nose. As Mary Jane put it, "I've never been any place that smelled so wonderful and exotic." We watched Indian cooks prepare the *chapatti* flat bread and tasted a wide variety of "chips" made from various flours.

Food abounded in the Indian wet market, so named because of the water on the floor from the cleaning of seafood and meats. It was a huge, warehouse-like affair with the sides open to the air. It was neatly divided into sections: fruits, vegetables, meats, seafood, groceries, and food vendors. Lamb and mutton were hanging to age, every type of tropical fruit was available for sale except the notorious durian, which was out of season, and there were tiger prawns seven to eight inches long. The fresh chiles for sale looked just like the ones we had seen the week before in Bangkok, and we soon found out why: they were imported because Singapore does not have much of an agriculture industry.

We took a break to sample Indian rose milk and tea and then pushed on to the Chinatown wet market. Despite the noise and crowded conditions, we were surprised by how clean everything was. All of the vendors touching meats or seafood wore plastic gloves and everyone was low-key and very friendly—even urging us on occasion to photograph them cleaving the heads off of fish. We found out later what the fish heads were used for—fish head curry, of course.

We were surprised by the number of live animals for sale. There were large fish swimming in aquariums—the freshest imaginable—and huge crabs crawling around in cages. During one memorable transaction, the vendor removed several frogs from a cage to show a customer how fresh they were. The woman shopper chose the one that jumped the farthest and the vendor quickly killed and skinned it on the spot. We were relieved to note that there were no live pigs for sale in the market.

The influence of the Chinese, which now comprise about three-quarters of the population of Singapore, has been vast. The major Chinese immigrants were Hokkiens (from Fujian Province), Teochews, Cantonese, and Hainanese. All brought their own regional cultures and food traditions to Singapore and settled in their own enclaves. Many of the earliest Chinese settlers were men, and because of the lack of Chinese women in Singapore, they married Malay women. Thus a distinct subculture was born, known in Malay as *Peranakan* (meaning "to be born here"). The women of that subculture were known as *Nonyas,* Malay for "ladies." The intermarriage of Chinese and Malay ended once the population of Singapore grew large enough to include Chinese women, and *Nonyas* soon became part of the mainstream of Singapore culture. But one *Nonya* tradition—cooking—lives on. The necessity of using Malaysian rather than Chinese produce resulted in the addition of chile peppers to the recipes.

Examples of hot and spicy *Nonya* dishes are Sautéed Pork in Tamarind Sauce (page 136), Prawns in Chile-Garlic Sauce (page 205), and neither recipe stints on the chiles. *Nonya* cuisine is an excellent example of a culinary collision of cultures, as it combines the subtlety and relative blandness of Chinese cooking with the spiciness of Malay food. It has been said that "in one meal, you get a perfect balance of opposing flavors, textures, and colors." And what more could we ask from any hot and spicy Southeast Asian meal?

Recipes follow for coconut milk and tamarind sauce, two basic ingredients that are used again and again in the recipes in this book.

Coconut Milk Substitutes

One cup of coconut milk contains—depending on its thickness—about 45 to 60 grams of fat—quite a bit in today's world of low-fat diets. Fortunately, a low-fat coconut milk is now available that reduces the fat level to about 12 1/2 grams. To lower the level even further, we suggest using a coconut flavoring. Several companies manufacture coconut flavoring, or extract, which concentrates the flavor while removing nearly all of the fat. Two brands of coconut extract on the market are Nielsen–Massey Coconut Extract and Wagner's Coconut Flavor—they are available at gourmet shops and by mail order. By combining such extracts with whole milk, the amount of fat is decreased to 8 grams; when combined with low-fat milk, that figure is further reduced to 5 grams. These substitutes may not be perfect, but they are a lot healthier. Since the consistency of coconut-flavored milk is thinner than that of canned coconut milk, cooks may need to add more of the substitute to a recipe and cook it a bit longer to achieve good results. Yogurt can also be combined with coconut extract; the consistency will be thicker, the taste will be different and interesting, but the fat count will be even lower, about 3 grams.

1 cup milk (whole or low fat)
1/2 teaspoon coconut extract

Combine the ingredients in a bowl and stir.

Yield: 1 cup

Coconut Milk and Cream

Both coconut milk and cream are extracts from coconut and it is important to differentiate them from the highly sweetened, canned coconut cream (or syrup) that is used to make drinks called piña coladas. The sweetened, canned cream is not a substitute and should not be used in any recipe in this book. Coconut milk is used extensively in Southeast Asian dishes and it is best when made from freshly grated coconut meat. But if that is not available, use desiccated, unsweetened coconut flakes and substitute cow's milk for the water. Coconut milk powder, now available in some specialty markets, mixes well with water to make coconut milk. Canned coconut milk is also commonly available, but cooks should check the label to make certain that sugar has not been added. New, low-fat canned coconut milk is now on the market.

Coconuts are widely available in Asian markets and large supermarkets across America. Look for a coconut without cracks or any sign of mold. The fresher the coconut, the more liquid it has. To break a coconut open, heat the oven to 350 degrees. Puncture a hole through one of the "eyes" and drain the liquid. This coconut water makes an excellent drink and can be consumed straight or mixed with rum or scotch. Place the coconut in the oven for 20 minutes, then remove it and allow it to cool. Break it open with a hammer, and the meat should fall away from the shell. If some meat still clings to the shell, carve it out using a small knife. Use a vegetable peeler to remove the thin brown skin from the meat, and then grate the meat on a metal grater, or carefully chop it in a food processor using the "pulse" mode.

4 cups grated coconut
2 1/2 cups boiling water or hot milk

In a bowl, cover the grated coconut with the boiling water (or milk for a thicker coconut "cream") and let it steep for 15 minutes. Using a strainer, drain the coconut and reserve the "milk." The coconut meat may be squeezed through muslin cloth or a double layer of cheesecloth to collect the rest of the "milk."

Store the "milk" in the refrigerator (it has about the same shelf life as whole milk), and the "cream" will rise to the top.

Variation: For a thicker milk, approaching cream, instead of steeping the grated coconut in hot water, puree it in a blender with the water and then strain it through cloth.

Yield: 2 cups

Tamarind Sauce

Tamarind is available commercially in many forms. When you find pods, as we easily can at our local supermarket, this is the way to make a simple sauce for use in other recipes.

6 tamarind pods
3 cups water
2 teaspoons sugar (or more or less depending on taste)

Shell the tamarind pods and remove the seeds from the pulp. Bring the water to a boil in a saucepan, add the pulp, and simmer until the liquid is reduced to about 1 cup. Add the sugar and simmer for an additional 5 minutes. Strain the sauce through a piece of muslin and squeeze as much liquid as possible from the pulp.

Yield: 1 cup

Sambals and More

Hot Sauces
and
Condiments

*S*ambals—those unique, chile-infused sauces—play a huge role in Southeast Asian cooking, as often one will make its appearance at the beginning of the meal as an ingredient and another during the meal as a condiment. The essence of chile heat in the region lies in the hot sauces and condiments, as even the British realized. "The most common seasoning to give a relish to their insipid food is the *lombock* (i.e. red pepper)," wrote Sir Thomas Stamford Raffles in 1817 in *The History of Java*. "Titurated with salt, it is called *sambel* both by the Malayans and the Javans, and this condiment is indispensable and universal. It is of different kinds, according to the substances added to increase or diversify its strength and pungency. . . ."

An Indonesian legend holds: "Even an ugly girl will find a husband if she can create a great *sambal*." And any beauty-challenged female will succeed in marriage if she chooses one of our six *sambals!* The most basic *sambal* is named after the *ulek-ulek*, the Indonesian pestle used to crush fresh chiles in a *cobek*, or mortar. *Sambal ulek* is so simple that we have not included a recipe here; simply puree fresh red jalapeños in a food processor with salt and add tamarind liquid and fish or shrimp paste to taste.

Sambals can be served hot or cold with boiled or fried potatoes, baked breadfruit or yams, hard-boiled eggs, fried fish and prawns, stir-fried meats and noodles, and, of course, curries. All of our *sambals* can be stored for weeks in a jar in the refrigerator. For the serious *sambal* addict, they can all be served on crackers or in sandwiches!

Sambalan, which we translate as Basic Spice Islands Chile Paste (page 18), is the next step up from *sambal ulek,* combining onions with two varieties of chiles. Chile and Nut Relish (*sambal badjak*) has the flavor of tropical nuts, while *sambal matah,* Hot Shallot and Lemongrass Sambal (page 20), has citrus and shallot overtones. Pineapple, Cucumber, and Chile Condiment (page 21), or *sambal timun* from Singapore, is more of a relish than an ingredient, as is *sambal kelapa,* Spicy Coconut Relish (page 22), a dry *sambal*. We conclude our examination of *sambals* with Malaysian Tomato Sambal (page 23) or *sambal buah tomat,* another relish—but one that uses a close relative of chiles: tomatoes.

Related sauces from Indonesia and Malaysia are Indonesian Peanut–Chile Sauce (page 24), which is served with grilled meats, and two additional relishes: *petjili nanas,* or Sweet–Hot Indonesian Pineapple Relish (page 25), and *atjar tjampur kuning,* Pickled Spicy Mixed Vegetable Relish (page 26).

Sambals and relishes are hardly the only hot condiments in Southeast Asia. Laos is well represented by Laotian Garlic–Shallot Hot Sauce (page 27), which is used at the table, and by *jaew som mak nao,* Lime and Garlic-Chile Sauce with

Pork (page 28), which is primarily served over rice or noodles. The latter is unusual because it contains ground pork.

From Myanmar come two very strong hot fish sauces, *ngapi ye*, Hot Anchovy Sauce (page 29), and Burmese Ginger–Chile Shrimp Paste (page 30), which is commonly served as an accompaniment to curries. The classic *nuoc cham*, or Vietnamese Dipping Sauce (page 31), is our sole sauce selection from Vietnam, but Cambodia is represented by Three Cambodian Condiments (page 32), as recommended by Richard Sterling, and by two curries: Lemongrass Curry Sauce (page 34) and Red Curry Cambogee (page 35).

As might be expected from one of the spiciest countries in the world, Thailand has a wide variety of hot sauces ranging from simple, like *nam prik* (Pepper Water Sauce, page 36), to the more complex curry pastes. Nam Prik Egg Sauce (page 37) really spices up soups, while two red chile dips, Red Chile and Tomato Dip (page 38) and Red Chile and Green Mango Dip (page 39), are served with raw vegetables.

Last but not least are three classic chile pastes from Thailand; they are the basis for the famous Thai curries. These pastes are easily made fresh, keep well for at least a month in the refrigerator, and add a terrific zing to curries. Green Curry Paste (page 40) is usually made with fresh serranos, although jalapeños make a good substitute. We make the Red Curry Paste (page 41) out of two varieties of red chile, New Mexican and piquin.

The Muslim Curry Paste (page 42) is so named after Muslim traders (or perhaps for Muslim harbor officials in the port of Bangkok) who first imported it from India. This paste is unique in that it uses curry spices most Thai dishes avoid, such as coriander, cloves, and cinnamon. It was first prepared in the court of King Rama I in the nineteenth century.

Basic Spice Islands Chile Paste

(*Sambalan*)

This Malaysian paste is the culinary equivalent of *harissa* in North Africa and *berbere* in Ethiopia. Its most common use is in making quick main dishes. About 1 tablespoon of the *sambalan* is stir-fried with every 8 ounces of the already-cooked meat, such as chicken or beef. Coconut milk is added to make a gravy, the mixture is reduced, and the dish is served over rice.

20 dried red New Mexican chiles, seeds and stems removed, soaked in hot water for 20 minutes

8 dried chiltepins, piquins, or Thai chiles, seeds and stems removed, soaked in hot water for 20 minutes (optional for a hotter paste)

3 onions, chopped

7 cloves garlic

2 teaspoons fish paste

1/2 cup peanut oil (or more if needed)

1/4 cup peanut oil

1 cup tamarind water (see Glossary)

2 teaspoons salt

2 tablespoons brown sugar

Combine the chiles, chiltepins (if using), onions, garlic, fish paste, and 1/2 cup peanut oil in a food processor and puree to a smooth paste. Heat the 1/4 cup peanut oil in a wok or skillet to high heat, add the paste, and fry until it is dark in color and the oil starts to separate. Add the tamarind water, salt, and brown sugar and simmer for 5 minutes, stirring occasionally. Store in bottles in the refrigerator for up to a week.

Yield: About 2 cups

Heat Scale: Medium to Hot

Chile and Nut Relish

(*Sambal Badjak*)

Badjak is one of the most commonly served of the Indonesian *sambals* and is usally made with candlenuts, which are hard to find in North America. We recommend substituting macadamia nuts or cashews. Serve this *sambal* with grilled meats.

7 fresh red serrano or jalapeño
    chiles, seeds and stems removed,
    chopped
1 tablespoon shrimp paste
1 medium onion, chopped
4 cloves garlic, chopped

½ cup chopped macadamia nuts
Salt to taste
1 tablespoon brown sugar
½ cup water
½ cup coconut milk
3 tablespoons vegetable oil

Combine the chiles, shrimp paste, onion, garlic, and nuts in a food processor and puree to a coarse paste. Transfer to a bowl and add the salt, brown sugar, water, and coconut milk. Mix well.

Heat the oil in a skillet and add the chile mixture to it. Sauté the mixture for 20 minutes, stirring constantly.

Yield: About 2 cups

Heat Scale: Hot

Hot Shallot and Lemongrass Sambal

(*Sambal Matah*)

Here is a Balinese *sambal* that features lemongrass and the "bird's eye" chiles, those tiny but incredibly fiery pods that are known as chiltepins in Mexico and the United States. It can be served on the side to add heat to any Asian dish, particularly those with rice, fish, or chicken.

10 shallots, peeled and diced

4 cloves garlic, peeled and minced

10 fresh chiltepin, piquin, or Thai chiles, stems removed, minced with the seeds, or substitute 5 red serranos

4 kaffir lime leaves, minced as finely as possible

1 teaspoon shrimp paste

4 two-inch stalks lemongrass, minced

1/2 teaspoon salt

1/4 teaspoon crushed black peppercorns

2 tablespoons lime juice

1/3 cup peanut oil

Combine all ingredients in a bowl, stir well, and allow to sit for 1 hour at room temperature to blend the flavors.

Yield: About 2 cups

Heat Scale: Hot

Pineapple, Cucumber, and Chile Condiment

(*Sambal Timun*)

This typical relish from Singapore includes Malaysian fruit and Chinese dried shrimp. Serve this Oriental "salsa" with rice and curry dishes or any dish to which you want to add a sweet and hot flavor.

4 fresh serrano or jalapeño chiles,
    seeds and stems removed,
    chopped
1/2 cup dried shrimp
1/4 cup lime juice, fresh preferred
1/4 cup vinegar
3 teaspoons sugar

1 cucumber, peeled and diced
1/2 cup diced pineapple chunks,
    fresh preferred
4 green onions, chopped, including
    some of the green
Salt to taste

Combine the chiles, shrimp, lime juice, vinegar, and sugar in a blender and puree until smooth. Toss the remaining ingredients with the dressing and let sit for 2 to 3 hours to blend the flavors before serving.

Yield: About 2 cups

Heat Scale: Medium

Spicy Coconut Relish

(*Sambal Kelapa*)

As with most *sambals,* this one is served on the side with a typical Indonesian meal to add even more heat to already spiced dishes. This *sambal* is drier than most.

1 cup grated fresh coconut

½ cup crushed red serrano or jalapeño chiles, stems removed, with seeds

1 tablespoon shrimp paste

1 medium onion, minced

2 teaspoons sugar

3 cloves garlic, minced

Salt to taste

Combine all ingredients in a wok and stir-fry, stirring constantly, for about 20 minutes, or until the mixture is brown and dry.

Yield: 2 cups

Heat Scale: Extremely Hot

Malaysian Tomato Sambal

(*Sambal Buah Tomat*)

This *sambal* is traditional, yet it is made with New World tomatoes. Serve it on the side with meat or rice dishes.

1/4 cup vegetable oil

3 fresh red serrano or jalapeño chiles, crushed in a mortar

1 teaspoon prepared prawn paste (or substitute shrimp paste)

1/2 teaspoon salt

2 teaspoons sugar

4 large ripe tomatoes, diced

1 onion, sliced and deep-fried until crisp, then crushed

Heat the oil in a wok and sauté the chiles, prawn paste, salt, and sugar over medium heat for about 5 minutes, stirring well. Add the tomatoes and stir-fry on high heat for 1 minute. Add the crushed onions and stir-fry for a minute more. Remove from the heat and serve cool.

Yield: 2 cups

Heat Scale: Medium

Indonesian Peanut–Chile Sauce

(*Katjang Saos*)

Hot and spicy peanut sauce is a standard condiment in Indonesia. This sauce is used not only with *satays* but as a basis for unusual curries and as a dipping sauce. It is traditionally prepared by pounding peanuts into a paste before using. We have simplified the recipe by substituting crunchy peanut butter.

4 green onions, chopped, white part only

4 cloves garlic, minced

1 teaspoon peeled and minced fresh ginger

1 three-inch stalk lemongrass, minced

1 tablespoon peanut oil

1 1/2 cups chicken stock

3 tablespoons crushed red chile, such as santaka (hot) or New Mexican (mild) or substitute Basic Spice Islands Chile Paste (see recipe, page 18)

1 tablespoon soy sauce

2 teaspoons dark brown sugar

1/4 teaspoon ground cumin

1 tablespoon lime juice

1 teaspoon prepared prawn paste (*blacan*)

1 teaspoon tamarind paste

2 cups crunchy peanut butter

Salt to taste

Sauté the onion, garlic, ginger, and lemongrass in the oil for 3 to 4 minutes until the onion is soft and transparent but not browned.

Add the chicken stock and bring to a boil. Reduce the heat and stir in the remaining ingredients. Simmer the sauce, uncovered, for 10 to 15 minutes until thickened.

Yield: 2 1/2 cups

Heat Scale: Varies

Sweet-Hot Indonesian Pineapple Relish

(*Petjili Nanas*)

Sweet relishes are called *petjili* in Indonesia, but the word "sweet" doesn't exclude chiles—it incorporates them. This relish is perfect to serve as an accompaniment to curries.

1 tablespoon vegetable oil
1 small onion, chopped
3 red serrano or jalapeño chiles, seeds and stems removed, chopped

1 whole pineapple, peeled and chopped
1 teaspoon ground cinnamon
2 tablespoons brown sugar
Salt to taste

Heat the oil in a wok and stir-fry the onion and chiles for 2 minutes, stirring constantly. Add the remaining ingredients and stir-fry for 10 minutes.

Variation: Replace the pineapple with 2 cups of chopped mangoes; then it is called *petjili mangaa*.

Yield: 6 servings

Heat Scale: Medium

Pickled Spicy Mixed Vegetable Relish

(*Atjar Tjampur Kuning*)

This is one of the more complex Indonesian condiments. The addition of turmeric is optional, but it indicates the influence of India on the cuisines of the East Indies. It is usually served with *satay* or curries.

1 cup julienned carrots
1 cup shredded cabbage
1 cup bean sprouts
1 tablespoon salt
2 cups vinegar
1 onion, sliced into thin rings
4 cloves garlic, coarsely chopped
2 tablespoons sugar

3 red serrano or jalapeño chiles, seeds and stems removed, minced
1 tablespoon peanut oil
1 tablespoon minced garlic
2 teaspoons turmeric (optional)
¼ cup ground macadamia nuts

Combine the carrots, cabbage, bean sprouts, and salt in a bowl and let sit for 30 minutes. Drain and reserve the vegetables. Heat the vinegar in a saucepan and add the onion, garlic, and sugar. Bring to a boil, reduce the heat, and simmer for 5 minutes. Remove from the heat, add the minced chiles, and cool.

Heat the peanut oil in a skillet and sauté the garlic, turmeric (if using), and macadamia nuts for 3 minutes. Add this mixture to the *atjar*, stir well, and serve.

Yield: 8 servings

Heat Scale: Medium

Laotian Garlic–Shallot Hot Sauce

(*Jaew Bong*)

Although *jaew bong* translates as "pickled sauce," that phrase is a misnomer as there is no vinegar in the recipe at all. Like many Southeast Asian sauces, this one is used as a table condiment to add heat to meat and rice dishes.

3 dried red New Mexican chiles, stems removed

2 small, hot, dried red chiles, such as Thai or piquin, stems removed

2 heads garlic, separated into cloves, unpeeled

2 shallots, unpeeled

1 tablespoon minced fresh ginger

1/4 teaspoon salt

1 tablespoon prepared fish sauce (*nam pla*)

Warm water

Place the chiles on a broiler pan and place under a gas broiler, about 3 or 4 inches from the flame. Turn them frequently and roast until brittle, about 2 minutes. Remove from the heat, crumble the chiles, removing as many seeds as possible, and reserve. (This can also be done in a saucepan over gas or electric heat.)

Place the garlic cloves on a broiler pan and place under the broiler, about 3 or 4 inches from the flame. Roast about 5 minutes, or until the garlic skins are lightly charred. Remove from the heat and cool. Repeat the process with the shallots.

Peel the garlic and shallots and chop them together coarsely. Add the crumbled chiles, ginger, salt, and fish sauce and transfer to a blender. Puree to a coarse paste. Remove and add warm water to make a thinner paste.

Yield: About 1/2 cup

Heat Scale: Medium to Hot

Lime and Garlic-Chile Sauce with Pork

(*Jaew Som Mak Nao*)

This unusual Laotian sauce is served primarily over rice, although it can be served over noodles, or—not suprisingly—over pork dishes such as *no non nang,* crisply fried pork rinds. Try this sauce as a dip for commercial pork rinds.

2 tablespoons ground pork
1 cup water
2 teaspoons prepared fish sauce (*nam pla*)
5 jalapeño chiles, roasted, peeled, stems removed, crushed in a mortar

5 shallots, peeled and crushed in a mortar
2 heads garlic, peeled, roasted in the oven until soft, and crushed in a mortar
Juice of 3 limes
1 tablespoon minced cilantro

Fashion the pork into a ball, place it in a saucepan, add the water and fish sauce, and bring to a boil. Cook until the pork is no longer pink, and remove the pork. Keep the pork broth in the pan.

Pound the pork in a mortar and remove to a bowl. Add the jalapeños, shallots, and garlic and mix well. Add this mixture back to the pork broth and add the lime juice. Cook over medium heat for 5 minutes, stirring well. Remove from the heat, allow to cool, and add the cilantro.

Yield: About 2 cups

Heat Scale: Hot

Hot Anchovy Sauce

(*Ngapi Ye*)

This highly aromatic Burmese sauce is commonly used in Southeast Asian curries. Shrimp or prawn paste may be substituted. Fermented dried fish can be found in Asian markets—or use canned anchovy fillets. The fishy aroma tends to dissipate during the cooking of the curry.

2 cups fermented dried fish or
    anchovies
½ cup water
¼ cup shrimp powder (available in
    Asian markets)

1 teaspoon cayenne powder
2 tablespoons lime juice
6 cloves garlic, minced

In a saucepan, bring the fish and water to a boil, then reduce the heat, simmer for 5 minutes, and mash the fish. Remove from the heat and when the mixture cools, add the remaining ingredients and stir well.

Yield: ¾ cup

Heat Scale: Hot

Burmese Ginger–Chile Shrimp Paste

(*Balachaung*)

Here is another intensely flavored, chile-intensive condiment that accompanies most dishes in Myanmar, especially curries. Western tastes may require a reduction in the shrimp and an increase in the green onions and garlic, so make adjustments accordingly.

1 3/4 cups peanut oil

1/4 cup minced garlic

3 tablespoons minced green onions, white part only

2 tablespoons minced fresh ginger

3 tablespoons minced jalapeño chile

1 pound dried shrimp, ground fine in a blender

1/2 teaspoon ground turmeric

2 teaspoons shrimp paste

Salt to taste

Heat the peanut oil until hot and fry the garlic, green onions, ginger, and chile for about 5 minutes, stirring constantly. Remove with a slotted spoon and reserve.

Add the dried shrimp and turmeric and fry for 2 minutes, stirring constantly. Add the shrimp paste and stir until well mixed. Add the reserved mixture, add salt to taste, and cook over low heat, uncovered, for 15 to 20 minutes. Use more peanut oil to adjust the consistency, if necessary.

Yield: 2 cups

Heat Scale: Medium

Vietnamese Dipping Sauce

(*Nuoc Cham*)

Richard Sterling collected this recipe in Hanoi. He wrote in *Chile Pepper:*
"No Vietnamese table is complete without a dish of *nuoc cham* for dipping
and drizzling over the dishes. It is as ubiquitous as rice."

1 or 2 cloves garlic

1 fresh red chile, such as serrano or
    jalapeño, seeds and stem
    removed

2 teaspoons sugar

1/4 fresh lime

2 tablespoons prepared fish sauce
    (*nam pla*)

2 1/2 tablespoons water

With a mortar and pestle, pound the garlic, chile, and sugar into a paste.
Squeeze in the lime juice. With a paring knife, remove the pulp from the lime
and pound it into the paste. Add the fish sauce and water and mix well.

Variations: For a real thrill, try this with a habanero! To make the traditional
Vietnamese sauce for roast beef, *nuac cham tuong gung,* omit the lime juice and
add 2 tablespoons minced fresh ginger.

Yield: 1/2 cup

Heat Scale: Varies with type of chile

Three Cambodian Condiments

Chile Pepper contributing editor Richard Sterling contributes these three popular Cambodian condiments. He says, "Condiments, for dipping, drizzling, and delighting, are critical to Khmer cookery. These are the ones I encountered most commonly."

Black Pepper Sauce

4 tablespoons lime juice
1 teaspoon freshly ground black
    pepper
1 teaspoon salt
Pinch of salt

Combine all the ingredients and allow to sit for 1 hour to blend the flavors. Use with any kind of shellfish or fried fowl.

Yield: ¼ cup

Lover Sauce

1 teaspoon Asian chile paste
2 tablespoons lime juice
½ teaspoon salt
½ teaspoon sugar

2 tablespoons prepared fish sauce
    (*nam pla*)
2 basil or mint leaves

Heat all but the leaves in a saucepan over medium high heat to thicken sauce to a syrupy consistency. Stir in leaves and serve. This makes a superior sauce for fried catfish.

Yield: ¼ cup

Heat Scale: Medium

Salt and Peppers for Fruit

1/2 teaspoon finely minced red chile,
     such as red jalapeño or Thai

1/2 teaspoon finely minced green
     chile such as serrano or Thai

2 tablespoons salt

Pinch of sugar

Combine all the ingredients and allow to sit for 1 hour to blend the flavors.
     Brush lightly on any kind of tart fruit: fresh pineapple, green apples,
gooseberries, green mangoes, or grapefruit.

Yield: 2 1/2 tablespoons

Heat Scale: Hot

Lemongrass Curry Sauce

Richard Sterling collected this recipe in Cambodia, of which he said, "There are as many curries as there are cooks. But all true Khmer curries have five constants: lemongrass, garlic, galangal, and coconut milk; the fifth constant is the cooking technique, dictated by the texture of lemongrass and the consistency of coconut milk. This is my personal all-purpose 4-cup curry, which is based on extensive observation and many trials. To prepare one portion, pour 1/2 cup of this curry sauce into a shallow vessel or a wok. Add 1/2 cup of meat or vegetables, bring to a medium boil and cook to desired degree. Try it with frog legs, as the Cambodians do."

1/3 cup sliced lemongrass

4 cloves garlic

1 teaspoon dried galangal

1 teaspoon ground turmeric

1 jalapeño chile, seeds and stem removed

3 shallots

3 1/2 cups coconut milk (made by soaking 4 cups grated coconut in a quart of water for an hour, then straining it)

3 kaffir lime leaves

Pinch of salt or shrimp paste

In a food processor, puree together the lemongrass, garlic, galangal, turmeric, jalapeño, and shallots.

Bring the coconut milk to a boil and add the pureed ingredients, lime leaves, and salt (or shrimp paste) and boil gently, stirring constantly, for about 5 minutes. Reduce the heat to low and simmer, stirring often, for about 30 minutes, or until the lime leaves are tender and the sauce is creamy. Remove the leaves.

Yield: 1 quart

Heat Scale: Mild

Red Curry Cambogee

Again from Richard Sterling, here is a variation on Cambodian sauces that adds even more intensity to Southeast Asian curries. Follow the instructions for use in the Lemongrass Curry Sauce recipe.

4 dried red New Mexican chiles,
   stems and seeds removed
1 cup boiling water

4 tablespoons paprika
2 to 3 tablespoons vegetable oil
4 cups Lemongrass Curry Sauce
   (see recipe, page 34)

Break the chiles into small pieces. Pour the boiling water over them to cover and let steep until they are soft, about 15 minutes. Combine the chiles, chile water, and the paprika in a blender to make a paste.

Heat the oil in a wok or skillet, add the chile paste, and stir-fry until it begins to darken. Reduce the heat, if necessary, to prevent burning.

Add the Lemongrass Curry Sauce, bring to a boil, then reduce the heat and simmer for 5 minutes.

Yield: 5 cups

Heat Scale: Medium

Pepper Water Sauce

(*Nam Prik*)

From *Chile Pepper* author Peter Aiken, who paddled to the floating markets in his kayak, here is a standard, basic Thai chile sauce. He comments: "I use *prik khee noo,* or 'mouse dropping' chiles grown by Thai friends." Use it to further spice up Thai main dishes, especially noodles and rice.

2 cloves garlic, sliced

3 fresh, small, Thai chiles, or substitute fresh chiltepins or piquins,
 stems removed, minced with the
 seeds

4 tablespoons lime juice

1/4 cup prepared fish sauce (*nam
 pla*)

2 cilantro leaves, chopped

Combine all the ingredients. Use immediately and seal and refrigerate the remaining sauce.

Yield: 1/2 cup

Heat Scale: Medium

Nam Prik Egg Sauce
(*Nam Prik Kai Gem*)

Nam prik literally means "pepper water" and that is a good description of this variation. Similar to *nuoc cham,* this sauce is found in many, many varieties on every table in Thailand. Serve this sauce with raw vegetables as a salad, with soup, rice, curries, or as a table sauce to add heat to any dish.

8 to 10 fresh serrano or jalapeño
   chiles
4 cloves garlic
4 green onions or shallots, chopped,
   white part only

4 hardcooked egg yolks
1 tablespoon prepared fish sauce
   (*nam pla*)
2 teaspoons sugar
3 tablespoons lime juice

Place all ingredients in a blender and puree to a smooth sauce. Add more lime juice if necessary.

Yield: ½ cup

Heat Scale: Hot

Red Chile and Tomato Dip
(*Nam Prik Num*)

Here is another sauce that is served as a dip for raw vegetables in Thailand or as a condiment for grilled or roasted meats—but this one has a traditional, slightly burned flavor. To make this sauce milder, substitute fresh New Mexican red chiles for the jalapeños. With the exception of the fish sauce, this recipe is virtually identical to the *salsas* served in northern Mexico that are made with grilled vegetables. This dip will store for about a week covered in the refrigerator.

3 fresh red jalapeño chiles, stems removed

3 shallots, peeled and halved

5 cloves garlic, peeled

2 ripe tomatoes

1 1/2 tablespoons freshly minced cilantro

1 tablespoon prepared fish sauce (*nam pla*)

1 tablespoon fresh lime juice

Heat a skillet very hot and roast the chiles, turning occasionally, until the skins blacken. Remove to a bowl. Add the shallots and garlic and roast over high heat, stirring occasionally, for 5 minutes. Remove to a bowl. Add the tomatoes to the skillet and roast, turning occasionally, until the skins blacken. Remove to a bowl and cut into quarters.

Combine the chiles (skins on), shallots, garlic, and tomatoes (skins on) in a food processor and process on "pulse" to make a coarsely chopped texture. Transfer this mixture to a bowl, add the cilantro, fish sauce, and lime juice, and mix well.

Yield: About 2 cups

Heat Scale: Medium

Red Chile and Green Mango Dip

(*Nam Prik Ma Muang*)

This intense Thai sauce is the dip of choice for raw vegetables such as string beans, zucchini, cucumbers, and carrots; and for fried eggplant or squash.

1/2 cup chopped unripe mango
1 tablespoon shrimp paste
2 cloves garlic, peeled and chopped
3 fresh red jalapeño chiles, seeds
    and stems removed

1 1/2 tablespoons lime juice
1/4 teaspoon sugar
2 tablespoons hot water
1/2 teaspoon prepared fish sauce
    (*nam pla*)

In a food processor, combine the mango, shrimp paste, garlic, chiles, lime juice, sugar, and hot water and puree to a fine paste, adding more water if necessary. Remove to a bowl, stir in the fish sauce, and serve.

Yield: About 1 cup

Heat Scale: Hot

Green Curry Paste

(*Kreung Kaeng Kiow Wahn*)

This standard Thai green curry paste has dozens of uses. Just add 1 teaspoon of this paste to make other curry concoctions more flavorsome, more zesty, and more pungent. Marinate a dozen shrimp in this paste, stir-fry them quickly in olive oil, and the result is an instant lunch or dinner.

1 tablespoon coriander seeds

1 tablespoon cumin seeds

6 whole peppercorns

3 stalks lemongrass, bulb included, chopped

1/2 cup cilantro

1 two-inch piece of galangal or ginger, peeled

1 teaspoon lime zest

8 cloves garlic

4 shallots, coarsely chopped

12 green chiles such as serranos, seeds and stems removed, halved

1/4 cup water

1 teaspoon salt

1 teaspoon shrimp paste

Roast the coriander and cumin seeds for about 2 minutes in a dry skillet. When they are cooled, grind them to a fine powder in a spice mill.

Combine all ingredients in a food processor or blender and puree until a fine paste is formed.

Pour the paste into an airtight jar and refrigerate. It will keep in the refrigerator for about a month.

Yield: About 1 1/4 cups

Heat Scale: Hot

Red Curry Paste

(*Nam Prik Gaeng Ped*)

A popular ingredient in Thailand, this curry paste can be added to any dish to enhance its flavor. It is, of course, a primary ingredient in many of the famous Thai curries. Traditionally, it is patiently pounded by hand with a heavy mortar and pestle, but a food processor does the job quickly and efficiently. It will keep in the refrigerator for about a month.

5 New Mexican dried red chiles, seeds and stems removed

10 small dried red chiles, such as piquins, seeds and stems removed and enough water to cover

2 teaspoons ground cumin

2 teaspoons ground coriander

2 small onions

1 teaspoon black peppercorns

1/2 cup fresh cilantro

1/4 cup fresh basil or mint leaves

1 teaspoon salt

3 two-inch stalks lemongrass, including the bulb

1 one-inch piece of galangal, peeled

1 tablespoon chopped garlic

1 tablespoon shrimp paste

1 tablespoon corn or peanut oil

1 tablespoon lime zest

1/4 cup water

Soak all the chiles in enough water to cover for 20 minutes to soften, then remove and drain. Roast the coriander and cumin seeds for about 2 minutes in a dry skillet, and when they are cooled, grind to a fine powder in a spice mill.

Combine all ingredients in a food processor or blender and puree into a fine paste. Store it in a tightly sealed jar in the refrigerator.

Yield: About 1 cup

Heat Scale: Hot

Muslim Curry Paste

(*Kaeng Mussaman*)

Muslim curry paste is a relatively recent curry for Thailand—it is only about 250 years old. Food historians say that Muslim traders from India introduced this curry to King Rama I, and the royal cooks perfected it. Initially, the story goes, the cooks were not keen on using cinnamon, but once they tasted their preparation, they fell in love with the new curry. It is commonly combined with beef, potatoes, tamarind, and coconut milk to make a curry served at wedding feasts.

12 dried red chiles, such as Thai or piquins, seeds and stems removed

1 cup warm water

2 tablespoons cumin seeds

1 teaspoon coriander seeds

1 teaspoon black peppercorns

1 teaspoon whole cloves

1 teaspoon cinnamon powder

1 teaspoon mace powder

1 teaspoon nutmeg powder

1 teaspoon cardamom powder

3 stalks fresh lemongrass, including the bulb

1 two-inch piece of galangal or ginger, peeled

2 teaspoons salt

6 shallots, finely chopped

1 tablespoon shrimp paste

Soak the chiles in warm water for 20 minutes, then remove and drain.

Meanwhile, in a frying pan, roast the cumin, coriander, peppercorns, and cloves in a dry skillet for 2 minutes, then remove from the heat. Roast the cinnamon, mace, nutmeg, and cardamom powders in the skillet for 1 minute, then remove from the heat. Grind the cumin, coriander, peppercorns, and cloves in a spice mill and then combine them with the other roasted spice powders. Set aside.

In a food processor or blender, combine all the ingredients and puree into a fine paste.

Transfer to a clean, airtight jar and refrigerate. The paste keeps for about one month in the refrigerator.

Yield: About 1 1/4 cups

Heat Scale: Hot

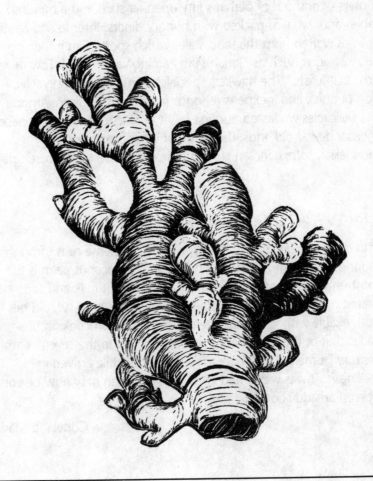

At a Hawker Centre

"We're off to the Newton Circus Hawker Centre," announced Jeanne Seah, our culinary guide for our first evening in Singapore. Within minutes, we were sampling barbecued stingray—and other strange but delicious foods.

The Newton Circus Food Centre, with its hawkers—so named because in the past the cooks would "hawk" their food to customers—consisted of perhaps fifty open-air stalls and a hundred tables and was jam-packed with hungry diners. Intense and exotic aromas wafted from the food stalls, which sported an intriquing array of signs, such as "Juriah Nasi Padang" and "Rojak Tow Kua Pow Cuttlefish." The hawkers specialized in a bewildering selection of quick and inexpensive foods from many cuisines. Among the delicacies we tasted our first night in Singapore were Chinese thousand-year-old eggs, the famous Singapore chile crab, Indonesian *satays,* Indian curried dishes, and the Malayan stingray.

The Two "C"s Indonesian Cuisine

❝ In spite of regional differences, a unifying theme runs through Indonesian cooking: coconut and chile. The coconut palm is the most universal plant in the islands, and coconut milk and the grated meat pervade the cuisine. Indonesian cookery would be unthinkable without them. The use of coconut in cooking precedes that of the chile, which was introduced in the seventeenth century [some say the sixteenth]. When the chile arrived in Indonesia, it was welcomed enthusiastically and may now be considered an addiction. **❞**

Copeland Marks

Durian Quotes, Part 1

❝ It is a big fruit, about the size and shape of an over-inflated rugby football, set all over with pyramidal spines that give it, with its khaki-green colouring, the look of something that might go off at any moment. ❞

Sri Owen

❝ Of all fruits, at first the most intolerable but said by those who have smothered their prejudices, to be of all fruits, at last, the most dispensable. When it is brought to you at first, you clamor till it is removed; if there are durians in the next room, you cannot sleep. Chloride of lime and disinfectants seem to be its necessary remedy. To eat it, seems to be the sacrifice of self-respect; but endure it for a while, with closed nostrils, taste it once or twice, and you will cry for durians thenceforth, even—I blush to write it—even before the glorious mangosteen. ❞

Bayard Taylor, 1982.

❝ It's like eating a garlic custard over a London sewer. ❞

Sir James Scott, a Victorian traveler

Chiles Are Undoubtedly "Heaty"

❝ Some foods are considered more healthy and 'cooling,' others rich and 'heaty.' Like the Yin and Yang of the Chinese: 'heaty' and 'cooling' are balancing opposites. One must learn how to combine them within a meal. Crabs, lobsters, and oysters, for example, are heaty foods, as is garlic; they inflame the body and the passions, they say. White marrow (squash), lettuce, cucumber, and milk are cooling. Pineapples and mangos are heaty whereas limes and lemons are cooling. Yams and potatoes are heaty. Durian inflames; mangosteens cool. It is always wise to follow a meal of the former group with a balancing amount of the latter. Many of the injunctions turn out to be surprisingly accurate. Drink milk out of the shell of the durian whose flesh you have eaten and you will never have any durian breath—a social disaster far worse than garlic breath.**

Sharmini Tiruchelvam

How to Ulek Sumatran Chiles

Lovingly crushed, seeds and all, with a stone mortar called an *ulekan* and pestle (*ulek-ulek*), homemade Sumatran *sambal ulek* is what heats up the country's hottest cuisine. One expert on Indonesian cooking says if you're serious about it you'll always crush ingredients using a mortar and pestle. With Padang-style cuisine, I'd say this makes sense only if you crave exercise, or if, once in a red pepper, you want to try doing things as they do in Padang! The amount of processing that Sumatran dishes call for is best left to a food processor or blender. Otherwise, besides much tedious work, you actually risk burns to hands, eyes, or whatever else the *sambal* touches.

Jeff Corydon

Meet the Enemy and Eat Him

The use of chiles in cooking is limited, and as a result, Cambodian food is quite mild. However, says Cambodian Yann Ker, his countrymen are fond of using sliced chiles as a table condiment, and that is where the heat comes in. Mrs. Pheng Chu adds that one variety of Cambodian chile is so hot that its name, *mateh khamang,* means 'enemy.'

Alexandra Greeley

Rojak and Satays

Salads and Appetizers

It's a fact; people love to snack. And not just at a party—before meals, in between meals, and after meals. Appetizers fit right into this munching mania, and in Southeast Asia we certainly found no exception to this taste for treats.

The salads and appetizers you will find in this chapter are a sizzling sampling of the best tasting—not to mention most representative—finger foods and veggies of each country. One of the things we found to be most stimulating about the incredible foods we discovered was that literally all the cuisines have one thing in common—chile peppers. Even the salads and their pungent partners the dressings contain heaps of hots. Experience this yourself with our first of nine salad recipes, Bean Curd, Vegetable, and Peanut Salad with Hot Chile Dressing (page 50)

Southeast Asia is blessed with many wonderful attributes, but one of the most outstanding we found was the abundance of exotic fruits. We have taken full advantage of the recipe possibilities this has produced, with five salads that feature fruits. From Cambodia (Green Mango Salad, page 54) to Bali (Gado Gado, page 52), the salads offer the perfect blending of heat and sweet. Thai salads often incorporate fresh or cooked vegetables, seafoods, and fruit. This combination works well in *som tam* (Shrimp and Papaya Salad, page 55).

The next two recipes are definitely a double delight. Choose your own level of adventure with our two fruit salads from neighboring Indonesia and Malaysia. The Malaysian Mixed Salad (page 56) offers a wilder taste through the use of New Mexico red chile (an appropriate substitute for Asian chiles), while the Padang Spicy Fruit Salad (page 58) mixes four different fruits with a more mild heat level. And the last of our fruit salads, Spicy Coconut and Grapefruit Salad (page 57), could certainly be a large part of an Asian meal. This salad is an excellent palate cleanser—and thus will prepare your mouth for the next interesting entrée!

We're certain "Eat your vegetables!" is a well-documented cry heard from mothers around the world. We've made it easy to accommodate this command with the next-to-last of our salad samplings. The Cambodian Hot Cucumber Salad (page 60) offers twice the treat, as it uses both New Mexico green chiles and Thai chiles. And who says vegetables are boring? Give the Vegetable Salad with Spiced Coconut Dressing (page 61) or Pickled Mixed Vegetables (page 62) from Thailand a try if you need to add a little zing to your life. And last, but certainly not least, is our recipe for Spiced-Out Seafood Salad (page 63). Rest assured you will not find this chile, garlic, and ginger-laden salad in your local grocery store!

Everything's gone afoul—or is that everything goes with fowl? We vote for the second phrase and with that have come up with some pretty delicious poultry-based appetizers. If you want to win friends and influence neighbors, serve the Spicy Duck Appetizer for Six (page 64) at your next party. The sauce cooks down to a curry of sorts and is truly wonderful. And why not throw a little craziness into your next barbecue and grill up a few *satays* instead of hot dogs? Our Indonesian Chicken, Shrimp, and Pineapple Satay (page 66) will make you a star!

Get your sea legs ready for our next set of appetizers. Seafood is abundant in Southeast Asia, so we've put together a scintillating selection.

The eggroll is representative world wide as the food of Asian cuisine. In Vietnam, the Westerners love the Fried Crab and Pork Rolls (page 65). If you're feeling adventurous, make a variety of the dipping sauces in Chapter 2 to go with them. Our Fiery Shrimp Toast (page 68) puts a nice twist on the usual ingredients one sees served on toast points. And we suggest mixing things up even more with the Fancy Burmese Shrimp Puffs (page 70) and Sweet Potato and Shrimp Squash Cakes (page 72) and the Lime Oysters with Garlic (page 69). Your Aunt Nelda will think something is *definitely* up with you.

Our last four recipes are probably the most unusual in this chapter. We begin with Curried Frogs' Legs (page 74), which requires a bit of work but will be well worth it once you taste this unique appetizer. Street vendors in Singapore hawk Singapore Meat Dumplings daily. If you're lucky enough to get to Singapore, we say go for it. If not, we suggest the recipe on page 76. The Fried Coconut Triangles (page 77) and Tempeh Pancakes (page 78) round out this chapter. Whether by land or by sea, the ingredients in these salads and appetizers are the key to fantastic Asian cuisine.

Bean Curd, Vegetable, and Peanut Salad with Hot Chile Dressing

This salad is from West Java, and is the perfect addition to any vegetarian meal. Serve the Tempeh Pancakes (page 78) with this for a terrific combination of flavors.

Hot Chile Dressing

1/4 cup finely chopped fresh santaka chiles (or substitute serranos or jalapeños

1/2 teaspoon finely grated fresh ginger root

1 teaspoon minced garlic

1/4 cup distilled white vinegar

2 cups cold water

2 tablespoons sugar

1/2 teaspoon *trassi* (shrimp paste)

1 teaspoon salt

The Salad

1 cup fresh bean sprouts

3 fresh bean curd cakes, cut into 1/2-inch cubes

1 cup thinly shredded purple cabbage

1 cup thinly sliced radishes

1 cup chopped sauerkraut

1 cup shelled peanuts

In a food processor, combine the chiles, ginger root, garlic, and vinegar and blend for 30 seconds. Scrape off the sides of the processor bowl with a rubber spatula. Blend again until the mixture is smooth.

Add the 2 cups of water, sugar, *trassi,* and salt to the chile mixture and blend for a few seconds longer. Taste for seasonings and set aside.

Steam the bean sprouts for 12 to 15 minutes, then cool. Next, arrange the sprouts, bean curd cakes, cabbage, radishes, sauerkraut, and peanuts in layered mounds on a large platter. Pour the sauce evenly over the vegetables and serve immediately.

Serves: 4

Heat Scale: Medium

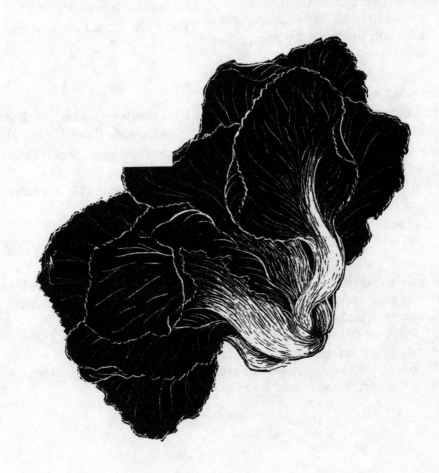

Gado Gado

This popular salad from Bali is a meal in itself. Traditionally, the salad is composed of a wide array of raw and parboiled ingredients, arranged in layers, and is served with the spicy peanut dressing.

Peanut Dressing

1 cup peanut butter, smooth or crunchy

1/2 cup water

1 to 2 bird's eye chiles (chiltepins), stems removed, finely minced or substitute piquin or cayenne chiles

3/4 teaspoon garlic powder

2 teaspoons brown sugar

2 tablespoons dark soy sauce

1 tablespoon lemon or lime juice

1/2 to 1 cup canned coconut milk

The Salad

1/2 pound mung bean sprouts, brown ends pinched off

1/2 pound green beans, cut into 2-inch pieces

2 large carrots, julienned (cut into matchstick-size pieces)

1 small head cauliflower, separated into small florets

3 large potatoes, boiled and sliced into rounds about 1/4-inch thick

3 hardcooked eggs, peeled and quartered

1 large cucumber, skin scored and sliced very thinly

To make the dressing, place the peanut butter and water into a saucepan and stir over gentle heat until mixed. Remove from the heat and add all other ingredients to make a thick dressing with a pouring consistency.

Drop the mung bean sprouts into boiling water and immediately remove, drain, and rinse under a cold tap.

Boil, steam, or microwave the green beans, carrots, and cauliflower until only just tender. Rinse in cold water to cool.

Arrange the vegetables in separate sections on a large platter, with wedges of egg and potatoes in the center and cucumber around the edge of the platter.

Serve cold, accompanied by the peanut dressing, which is spooned over the individual servings.

Serves: 8

Heat Scale: Medium

Green Mango Salad

Chile Pepper magazine Contributing Editor Richard Sterling collected this Cambodian recipe on one of his many adventures. He suggests that if you can't find green mangoes, adequate substitutes are green papaya or white Chinese cabbage. The Cambodians use any number of dried or smoked fish products in this recipe: Thai fish sauce, smoked white fish, dried shrimp, and so on. If you don't have access to any of these, try dark meat tuna.

1 tablespoon Basic Spice Islands
　　Chile Paste (page 18) or substi-
　　tute commercial chile paste
1 tablespoon chunky peanut butter
Juice of 1 lime
4 teaspoons fish sauce (*nam pla*), or
　　to taste
1 green tomato, sliced thin
1 green mango, peeled and
　　julienned very fine

2 shallots, sliced thin
1 pickling cucumber, sliced thin
Salt and pepper to taste
1 green onion, chopped
2 red bell peppers, stems and seeds
　　removed, sliced
Chopped fresh basil or mint

Combine the chile paste, peanut butter, lime juice, and fish sauce. Toss with the tomato, mango, shallots, and cucumber. Add salt and pepper to taste.
　　Garnish with the green onion, peppers, and basil or mint, and serve.

Serves: 6

Heat Scale: Mild

Shrimp and Papaya Salad

(*Som Tam*)

This Thai recipe incorporates the highly aromatic flavor of lemongrass with those of robust, sweet papaya and succulent shrimp. Traditionally, an unripe papaya is used in this dish. However, since a green papaya may be difficult to find, a ripe papaya offers a slightly different, but tasty, alternative.

1 head of lettuce, washed, with leaves separated and gently dried

1/2 purple cabbage, shredded

2 one-inch stalks lemongrass, minced

2 papayas, peeled, seeded, and thinly sliced

2 firm tomatoes, sliced into thin rounds

1/2 pound cooked shrimp

2 1/2 tablespoons roasted peanuts, crushed

2 serrano or jalapeño chiles, seeded and cut into slivers

Juice of 2 limes

Juice of 1 lemon

2 tablespoons fish sauce (*nam pla*)

1 tablespoon sugar

2 green onions, finely chopped

On a medium platter, arrange the lettuce leaves and set aside. In a bowl, combine the cabbage and lemongrass. Setting a few slices aside for garnish, add the papayas and tomatoes to the bowl. Arrange the mixture on the platter, adding the shrimp and peanuts to cover. Garnish with the remaining papaya, tomatoes, and chiles. In a separate bowl, mix the lime juice, lemon juice, fish sauce, sugar, and green onions together, stirring until the sugar dissolves. Pour the dressing evenly over the salad and refrigerate until served.

Serves: 6

Heat Scale: Medium

Malaysian Mixed Salad

(*Rojak* No. 1)

We've found that fruit salad of some type is a favorite in almost every culture around the world. This Malaysian variation offers a sweet taste with a powerful chile zing!

The Dressing

2 teaspoons Hot Shallot and Lemongrass *Sambal* (page 20) or substitute any prepared *sambal*

1/2 teaspoon dried shrimp paste
1 tablespoon sugar
1 tablespoon vinegar
1 tablespoon lemon juice

The Salad

1/2 cucumber, diced
1/2 pineapple. peeled, cored, and diced

1 green mango, peeled, pitted, and diced
2 dried New Mexican red chiles, seeded and crumbled

Combine all of the dressing ingredients in a food processor and blend until the mixture is smooth. In a shallow bowl, combine the cucumber, pineapple, and mango. Next, pour the dressing over the fruit. Top with the crumbled red chiles and serve.

Serves: 6

Heat Scale: Medium

Spicy Coconut and Grapefruit Salad

If you're feeling adventurous and have access to fresh, exotic fruit, substitute pomelos for the grapefruit, as they do in Thailand.

1 cup shredded fresh coconut

1 teaspoon sugar

2 teaspoons soy sauce

1 tablespoon lemon juice

1 tablespoon lime juice

2 tablespoons water

2 teaspoons vegetable oil

2 cloves garlic, crushed

1 serrano or jalapeño chile, stem and seeds removed, chopped

2 tablespoons finely diced onion

2 large grapefruit, peeled and sectioned

Place the coconut in a frying pan and roast until it just turns brown. Remove the coconut from the heat and place it in a mixing bowl. Add the sugar, soy sauce, lemon and lime juices, and water. Pour the oil in the frying pan and sauté the garlic, chile, and onion until brown. Add this to the coconut mixture, stirring well. Arrange equal amounts of the grapefruit segments on four plates, then pour some of the coconut dressing over each. Refrigerate for at least 15 minutes and serve.

Serves: 4

Heat Scale: Medium

Padang Spicy Fruit Salad

(*Rojak* No. 2)

Padang Spicy Fruit Salad is the second of our *rojak* fruit salads, this time from Padang, Indonesia. *Chile Pepper* magazine contributor Jeff Corydon says that the secret of this recipe is in the sauce, which includes crushed peanuts and lots of chile. Please note that this recipe requires preparation in advance.

1 quart water

1 teaspoon salt

1 pomelo or tart pink grapefruit, sectioned

2 mangoes, a bit underripe, peeled and cut into bite-sized pieces

2 tart apples, peeled and cut into bite-sized pieces

1 pineapple, peeled and cut into bite-sized pieces

4 serrano or jalapeño chiles, stems and seeds removed, chopped

1/4 teaspoon shrimp paste (*trassi*)

1/2 teaspoon salt

2 tablespoons dried tamarind pulp

1/4 cup dark brown sugar

1/4 cup crunchy peanut butter

Mix 1 quart of water with 1 teaspoon of salt and soak the pomelo, mangoes, apples, and pineapple overnight in the refrigerator.

Place the chiles, *trassi*, and 1/2 teaspoon of salt in a food processor and blend until smooth.

Make the tamarind water by mashing the dried tamarind in 2 table-spoons of hot water until it softens and dissolves. Strain the mixture to remove any seeds or debris.

Combine the brown sugar in a pan with the 1 cup of water, and melt over low heat until the sugar dissolves, about 5 to 10 minutes. Add the peanut butter, chile pepper mixture, and tamarind water, and simmer for 5 minutes more, stirring often, until a fairly thick, sticky syrup forms. Put the syrup in the refrigerator to chill.

When ready to serve, drain the water from the fruit. Pour the syrup over the fruit, and toss with a spoon to coat evenly. Serve at once.

Serves: 8

Heat Scale: Medium

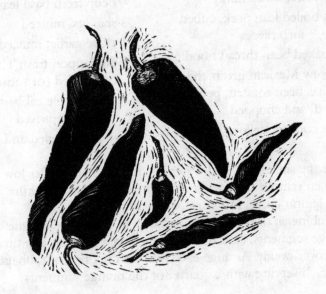

Cambodian Hot Cucumber Salad

(*Nuom Trosot*)

This spicy dish features *Cucumis sativus,* or the cucumber, along with fresh herbs and scallops. The addition of two types of chiles makes this Cambodian recipe twice as good!

The Dressing

4 tablespoons sugar

1 1/2 tablespoons salt

6 tablespoons water

4 tablespoons lime juice

1 tablespoon lemon juice

4 tablespoons fish sauce (*nam pla*)

3 cloves garlic, minced

The Salad

8 medium-sized cucumbers, peeled lengthwise, sliced thinly

7 ounces boiled lean pork, cubed into 1/2-inch pieces

2 cups soaked bean thread noodles

1/2 cup New Mexican green chile that has been roasted, peeled, seeded, and chopped

2 pounds cooked scallops

1/4 cup fresh mint leaves

1/4 cup fresh basil leaves

3 shallots, minced

1 clove garlic, minced

1 tablespoon fresh Thai chiles, chopped (or substitute piquins)

1 large purple cabbage, washed, leaves removed

1 orange, peeled and quartered

Combine the sugar, salt, and water in a saucepan. Stir over low heat until dissolved, then remove the pan from the heat. When the mixture is cool, add the lime and lemon juices, fish sauce, and garlic.

Combine all of the salad ingredients in a bowl except the cabbage leaves and orange segments. Add the salad dressing a little bit at a time, tossing the salad to cover evenly. Arrange each portion on a bed of cabbage leaves. Garnish each serving with a quarter of the orange segments.

Serves: 4

Heat Scale: Hot

Vegetable Salad with Spiced Coconut Dressing

(*Urab*)

One of the keys to authentic Indonesian cooking is to use the freshest ingredients possible. To find a "young" coconut, shake it and make sure it has lots of liquid—the more liquid, the fresher the fruit.

The Dressing

5 tablespoons Tamarind Sauce (page 14)

4 teaspoons Spicy Coconut Relish (*sambal kelapa;* page 22)

1/2 teaspoon crushed fresh ginger

2 teaspoons salt

1 young coconut, shelled and coarsely grated

The Salad

1/2 pound fresh bean sprouts, washed

2 cups shredded purple cabbage

1/2 pound fresh spinach, coarsely chopped

1/2 pound string beans, washed and broken into 1-inch strips

2 limes, sliced into rounds

In a bowl, combine the tamarind sauce, *sambal kelapa,* ginger, and salt, mixing well. Add the coconut last, gently tossing it into the dressing.

Steam the bean sprouts, purple cabbage, spinach, and string beans separately, until they are cooked *al dente.* When all of the vegetables have completed steaming, set them aside in a bowl and allow them to cool to room temperature.

Combine the vegetables with the dressing, and serve immediately at room temperature. Garnish each plate with sliced limes.

Serves: 6

Heat Scale: Hot

Pickled Mixed Vegetables

This recipe hails from Thailand, where pickled vegetables are often served warm. This dish works well served with meat, poultry, or fish dishes.

1 pint rice vinegar

1 tablespoon white sugar

1 teaspoon salt

1/4 cup cucumbers, sliced into rounds

1/4 cup cauliflower florets

1/4 cup red bell pepper, cut into bite-sized pieces

1/4 cup green bell pepper, cut into bite-sized pieces

1/4 cup carrots, cut into bite-sized pieces

1/4 cup broccoli florets

1/4 cup celery, cut into bite-sized pieces

1/4 cup jicama, cut into bite-sized pieces

6 cloves garlic, finely chopped

6 fresh santaka chiles, seeded and finely chopped, or substitute piquins or 10 serranos

3 shallots, finely chopped

1/2 white onion, finely chopped

3/4 cup peanut oil

1/3 cup sesame seeds, roasted in a dry skillet

Heat the vinegar, sugar, and salt in a saucepan large enough to hold all of the vegetables. Cook each vegetable separately in the mixture, until they are slightly cooked but still crunchy. Set each of the vegetables aside after they are cooked. Place the garlic, chiles, and shallots in a food processor and blend until the ingredients make a paste. Blend in a tablespoon of oil if the paste seems too thick. Place the remaining oil in a wok and fry the paste for 2 to 3 minutes. Turn the wok on high and add the vegetables, stir-frying for 30 seconds. Place the vegetables on a platter and sprinkle with the toasted sesame seeds. Serve immediately, or store in air-tight jars in the refrigerator.

Serves: 4

Heat Scale: Hot

Spiced-Out Seafood Salad

(*Pla Talay*)

Fish is plentiful in Southeast Asia, especially in Bangkok, a city near the Gulf of Thailand. This recipe also utilizes kaffir lime leaves, whose fragrance is thought to ward off evil spirits.

3 tablespoons lime juice

2 tablespoons fish sauce (*nam pla*)

5 dried Thai chiles, crushed, or substitute piquins

1 tablespoon minced garlic

1 tablespoon minced ginger

2 tablespoons finely sliced lemongrass

2 tablespoons finely minced shallots

1/4 cup diced, boiled, and shelled prawns or shrimp

1/4 cup diced boiled fish

1/4 cup boiled scallops

1/4 cup baby squid, sliced

1/4 cup boiled and shelled clams

1/4 cup fresh mint leaves

1/4 cup cilantro

1/4 cup shredded kaffir lime leaves

3 serrano or jalapeño chiles, seeded and thinly sliced

In a large bowl combine the lime juice, fish sauce, and the crushed chiles. Gently mix in the garlic, ginger, lemongrass, and shallots, and set aside. In another large bowl, combine the seafood. Pour the first mixture on top of the seafood, turning and tossing well. Garnish with the mint leaves, cilantro, lime leaves, and sliced chiles.

Serves: 4

Heat Scale: Hot

Spicy Duck Appetizer for Six
(*Be Sipyan*)

In parts of Burma, the meat of the duck is a prized delicacy. This recipe combines the heat of jalapeño chiles with the sweetness of curry. For the best results, serve this appetizer warm.

1 duck, 4 to 5 pounds, with giblets
4 cloves garlic, sliced thin
1 teaspoon curry powder
1 jalapeño chile, stemmed, seeded, and minced
1/2 teaspoon salt
1 teaspoon lemon juice
1 teaspoon lime juice

1 teaspoon shrimp paste
1 tablespoon peanut oil
1/2 inch fresh ginger, sliced thin
1 cup sliced onions
1 tablespoon soy sauce
1/4 teaspoon ground turmeric
2 1/2 cups water

Cut the duck into 8 pieces, removing the loose skin and fat. Dry the duck pieces on paper towels, and set aside. In a large mixing bowl, combine the garlic, curry powder, jalapeño, salt, lemon juice, lime juice, shrimp paste, peanut oil, ginger, onions, soy sauce, and turmeric. Add the duck pieces to the mixture, making sure each piece is completely coated with the marinade. Place the bowl in the refrigerator, marinating the duck for 30 minutes.

Transfer the duck and marinade to a large pan, and cook over moderate heat for 5 minutes, then reduce the heat to low. Add 1 cup of water and stir the duck mixture well. Cover the pan and cook the duck for 30 minutes.

When the 30 minutes is completed, add the remaining 1 1/2 cups of water and continue to cook the duck on low heat for about 45 minutes. When the duck is done, the meat should be tender and the water will have evaporated, leaving a thick, spicy sauce. Pour off any excess oil, transfer to a platter, and serve.

Serves: 6

Heat Scale: Mild

Fried Crab and Pork Rolls

(*Cha Gio*)

This snack is very popular in Vietnam, especially with many Westerners, as tourism picks up in this part of Southeast Asia. Traditionally, the rolls are made with Vietnamese rice paper; however, since we have found these difficult to locate, we have substituted Chinese spring roll wrappers.

8 ounces cellophane noodles
1 small onion, minced
6 green onions, minced
7 ounces minced pork
7 ounces flaky crab meat
1/2 teaspoon salt
1 tablespoon fish sauce (*nam pla*)
1/4 teaspoon ground black pepper

1 teaspoon cayenne powder
Half packet Chinese spring roll wrappers
Vegetable oil for deep frying, peanut preferred
Vietnamese Dipping Sauce (page 31)

First, make the filling: soak the cellophane noodles in water for 10 minutes, then drain and measure out 1/2 cup of the noodles. Cut the noodles into 1-inch lengths. In a mixing bowl, combine the noodles, onions, pork, crab meat, salt, fish sauce, ground pepper, and cayenne powder. Stir well and set aside.

Next, fill the wrappers: cut each spring roll wrapper in half. Put 2 teaspoons of filling at the end of each wrapper. Roll up each wrapper, turning in the sides so that the filling is completely enclosed. Moisten the edge of each wrapper with a little water to make it stick.

When all of the rolls are prepared, heat the oil in a wok and fry a few at a time on medium heat until they are crisp and light brown. Make sure that the oil is quite hot, or the filling will not cook through. Put paper towels on a platter and place each roll on the platter to drain off the excess oil. Place the Vietnamese Dipping Sauce in small bowls and serve with the spring rolls.

Yield: 24

Heat Scale: Medium

Indonesian Chicken, Shrimp, and Pineapple Satay

Our friends from the Golden Dragon Restaurant in Colorado Springs, Colorado sent us this excellent appetizer recipe. Sue Louie also runs the AiKan Company, which produces and markets spicy Asian sauces.

Satay

8 ounces chicken breast, cut into cubes

8 ounces shrimp, shelled and deveined

2 tablespoons AiKan Spicy Soy Master Sauce

2 tablespoons AiKan Ultimate Stir-Fry Sauce

2 tablespoons lime juice

1 cup fresh pineapple, cut into chunks

1 cup red bell pepper, cut into cube

Peanut Sauce

1 cup chicken stock

1/2 cup peanut butter

1/4 cup shredded coconut

1/2 teaspoon ground cumin

1/2 teaspoon ground coriander

1/2 teaspoon instant minced garlic

1/2 teaspoon hot red chile powder

Place the chicken, shrimp, and AiKan sauces (or, if AiKan sauces are not available, the soy sauce, molasses, curry powder, cayenne, and instant minced garlic) in a bowl. Mix in the lime juice, add the pineapple and bell pepper, and marinate for 15 minutes in the refrigerator.

In a bowl, combine all of the peanut sauce ingredients. Place the mixture in a saucepan and heat until it thickens, stirring often.

Thread the chicken, shrimp, pineapple, and bell pepper onto skewers and grill or broil until browned and done.

Serve the *satay* with the peanut sauce for dipping.

Note: If AiKan sauces are not available in your area, they can be ordered (see Mail-Order Sources), or use this substitution:

1 tablespoon soy sauce
1 tablespoon molasses
1 tablespoon curry powder
1 teaspoon cayenne powder
1 teaspoon instant minced garlic

Serves: 4

Heat Scale: Medium

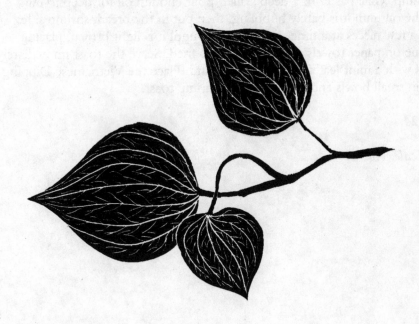

Fiery Shrimp Toast

(*Bahn Mi Chien Tom*)

No matter the culture, just about everyone is glad to have a technique to turn not-so-fresh bread into something wonderful. This Vietnamese appetizer is best when made with 2-day-old bread.

12 slices stale bread
½ cup shrimp paste
3 fresh piquin chiles, seeded and
　　minced, or substitute any small,
　　hot chile
Vegetable oil for deep frying
　　(peanut preferred)

Fresh mint leaves
2 small cucumbers, peeled and
　　sliced into small rounds
Vietnamese Dipping Sauce
　　(page 31)

Trim off the crusts and cut each piece of bread lengthwise. Place the shrimp paste in a small bowl and mix in the piquins. Spread each piece of bread with the shrimp/chile paste. In a deep skillet, pour enough oil for deep frying. Heat the oil until it is barely bubbling, then put in the bread, shrimp side down, a few pieces at a time. Fry the bread until it is light brown, placing each one on paper towels to drain after it is fried. Serve the toast immediately, topped with a mint leaf and cucumber round. Place the Vietnamese Dipping Sauce in small bowls and serve with the shrimp toast.

Yield: 24

Heat Scale: Hot

Lime Oysters with Garlic

This Cambodian delicacy is one of many oyster-based recipes from Southeast Asia. The oysters are served in soups, simmered in miso and sake, and in a variety of other delicious ways. The meat of pearl oysters is said to be exceptionally tasty.

36 large fresh oysters, in the shell
1 ¹/₂ tablespoons vegetable oil
3 teaspoons minced garlic
1 teaspoon minced fresh piquin
    chiles, or substitute any small,
    hot chiles
1 teaspoon minced fresh ginger
1 teaspoon turmeric
2 teaspoons minced lemongrass

¹/₄ cup lime juice
¹/₄ cup lemon juice
¹/₂ cup fish sauce (*nam pla*)
¹/₂ teaspoon salt
¹/₂ teaspoon black pepper
1 teaspoon sugar
3 teaspoons finely minced mint
    leaves

Open the oysters over a dish to save their liquid. Remove the top shells and discard, loosening the oysters. Keep the bottom shells. Heat the oil in a small pan and add the garlic, chiles, ginger, turmeric, and lemongrass and fry gently for 3 minutes in the oil, stirring often. In a separate pan, mix together the lime juice, lemon juice, fish sauce, salt, pepper, and sugar. Add the reserved oyster liquid and cook until hot, stirring frequently. Place the oysters in the mixture and poach for 30 seconds. Return the oysters to their shells with some of the sauce and the fried ingredients. Garnish each oyster with the chopped mint.

Serves: 6

Heat Scale: Medium

Fancy Burmese Shrimp Puffs

(*Pazoon Lone-Jaun*)

These Burmese shrimp balls may seem similar to the Chinese version, but they are much more delicate and moist, and thus we think better! A traditional fritter-type snack, these may be made with just about any kind of fish you enjoy.

½ cup lightly salted butter, at room temperature

2 onions, quartered

2 pounds raw medium shrimp, shelled and deveined

¼ cup cornstarch

¼ cup chopped fresh cilantro

2 tablespoons dry vermouth

3 jalapeño chiles, stemmed, seeded, and minced

2 tablespoons chopped red bell pepper

¼ teaspoon cayenne powder

¼ teaspoon kosher salt

4 egg whites, at room temperature

Peanut oil for frying

Place the butter and onions in a food processor, and process until the onions are finely minced. Add the shrimp, a few at a time, and process until the mixture becomes a paste. Be careful not to overprocess. Scrape the paste into a small mixing bowl and stir in the cornstarch, cilantro, vermouth, jalapeños, red bell pepper, cayenne powder, and salt, mixing well. Set the paste aside.

Place the egg whites in a small mixing bowl and beat them with an electric mixer until small peaks form. Gently fold the egg whites into the shrimp mixture. Place the mixture in the refrigerator, covered, until you are ready to use it. Place a platter in the refrigerator to chill.

Pour oil into a large, heavy saucepan, to a depth of about 2½ inches. Heat the oil to 350 degrees. Remove the shrimp mixture from the refrigerator. Fill a small bowl with cold water. Dip a teaspoon into the cold water, then scoop out a heaping spoonful of the shrimp mixture. Remove the platter from the refrigerator, and place each shrimp ball on the platter as you make it. Make sure to dip the teaspoon into the cold water between scoopings.

Using a slotted spoon, gently place the balls into the oil, making sure they do not touch each other. Fry the puffs until they are golden brown—check them after 2 minutes, and turn them to make sure each side is browned. Carefully remove each puff to a plate covered with paper towels to drain off any excess oil. Transfer the drained puffs to a cookie sheet. Loosely cover the sheet with foil, and place the shrimp puffs in the oven (set at a low temperature) to keep warm. Continue the frying and draining process until all of the shrimp mixture is used.

Serves: 12

Heat Scale: Medium

Sweet Potato and Shrimp Squash Cakes

(*Ukoy*)

Fried cakes are a staple appetizer in the Philippines. For a veritable taste explosion, serve the cakes with the Pineapple, Cucumber, and Chile Condiment (*sambal timun*, page 21).

1/2 cup hot water

11 medium-size raw shrimp in their shells

1 teaspoon annatto seeds

1 teaspoon salt

1 cup flour

1 cup cornstarch

2 cloves garlic, minced

3 fresh piquin chiles, seeded and minced, or substitute any small, hot chile

1 large sweet potato, peeled and grated

1 medium-sized acorn squash, peeled, halved, seeded, and coarsely grated

2 cups vegetable oil

1/4 cup finely chopped green onions

Pineapple, Cucumber, and Chile Condiment (page 21)

Combine the water, shrimp, annatto seeds, and salt in a heavy saucepan. Over high heat, bring the mixture to a boil, stirring well. Reduce the heat to a low simmer and cook for 2 to 3 minutes, or until the shrimp turn pink. With a slotted spoon, place the shrimp onto paper towels to drain, and then pour the cooking liquid through a sieve and into a bowl. Measure the liquid, and add enough water to make 1 1/4 cups. Set aside. Shell and devein the shrimp.

In a deep mixing bowl, combine the flour and the cornstarch. Pour in the reserved liquid, and beat until it is absorbed. Next add the garlic, chiles, sweet potato, and squash, and beat vigorously until the mixture is well combined.

Pour the oil into a heavy skillet. Heat the oil until it is very hot, but not smoking. To make each cake, spoon about 1/3 cup of the vegetable mixture onto a saucer. Next, sprinkle a teaspoon or two of the chopped green onion on top, and lightly press a shrimp into the center. Then, holding the saucer

close to the surface of the hot oil, slide the cake into it with the aid of a
spoon. Fry the cakes, three or four at a time, for about 3 minutes, spooning
the oil over each cake, then turning them carefully with a spatula. Repeat the
same process on the other side. Once each cake is browned on both sides,
transfer to a paper towel to drain off the excess oil. Arrange the cakes, shrimp
side up, on a platter. Serve immediately with the dipping sauce (Pineapple,
Cucumber, and Chile Condiment, page 21).

Yield: About 10 cakes

Heat Scale: Medium

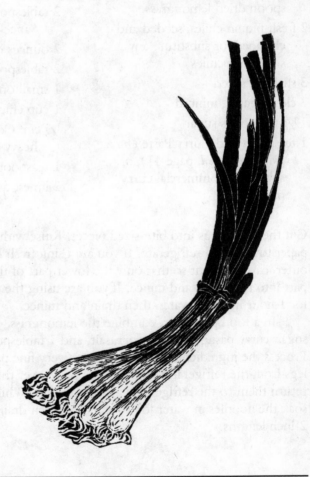

Curried Frogs' Legs

(*Ech Nau Ca-Ri*)

This Vietnamese recipe is sure to get any party hopping. All frog jokes aside, this dish is both spicy and smooth, and doesn't taste like chicken! If you're watching your calories, substitute light coconut milk or half-and-half for the heavy cream.

4 pairs of large frogs' legs, trimmed

1 stalk fresh lemongrass or 1 table-spoon dried lemongrass

2 fresh piquin chiles, seeded and chopped, or substitute any small, hot chiles

3 shallots, sliced

3 cloves garlic, minced

1 1/2 teaspoons sugar

1 teaspoon Red Curry Paste (*nam prik gaeng ped*, page 41), or substitute commercial curry paste

2 teaspoons curry powder

1/4 teaspoon salt

2 tablespoons Vietnamese Dipping Sauce (*nuoc cham*, page 31)

2 ounces cellophane noodles

2 tablespoons peanut oil

1 small onion, chopped

1 cup chicken broth

1/2 cup Coconut Milk (page 12) or heavy cream

1 teaspoon cornstarch

2 limes, quartered

Cut the frogs' legs into bite-sized pieces. Rinse with cold water, pat dry with paper towels, and refrigerate. If you are using fresh lemongrass, peel away the outer leaves and cut so that only the lower part of the stalk remains. Cut this part into thin slices and mince. If you are using the dried lemongrass, soak it for 1 hour in warm water, then drain and mince.

In a food processor, combine the lemongrass, chiles, shallots, garlic, sugar, curry paste, curry powder, salt, and 1 tablespoon of the *nuac cham*. Process the ingredients until they form a very fine paste. Remove the frogs' legs from the refrigerator, and rub the paste over them. Cover the legs and return them to the refrigerator for 30 minutes. While the legs are marinating, soak the noodles in water for 30 minutes, then drain them and cut into 2-inch lengths.

Heat the oil in a large skillet over moderate heat. Place the onion in the oil and sauté until it is translucent. Add the frogs' legs to the oil, and brown well on all sides, for 3 to 4 minutes. Add the chicken broth and bring to a boil. Reduce the heat, and cover and simmer for 15 minutes.

Next, add the coconut milk, leaving the lid off. In a separate bowl, add 1 tablespoon of cold water and the remaining *nuoc cham* to the cornstarch, and stir well. Add the cornstarch mixture to the skillet, and cook, stirring, until the mixture thickens. Add the cellophane noodles and bring the mixture to a boil. Remove from the heat and place on a platter and garnish with lime wedges. This dish is also great when served over rice.

Serves: 4

Heat Scale: Mild

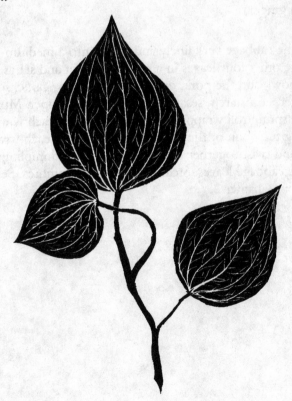

Singapore Meat Dumplings

These dumplings are a festive touch to any gathering. They are especially good when presented with a variety of dipping sauces from Chapter 2.

8 purple cabbage leaves, blanched

9 ounces ground lean pork

1 tablespoon minced green onions

2 red jalapeño chiles, stemmed, seeded, and minced

1/2 teaspoon minced garlic

1 tablespoon light soy sauce

1 tablespoon ginger juice (squeezed from fresh ginger)

1/8 teaspoon minced ginger

1 tablespoon cornstarch

2 tablespoons sesame oil

1 teaspoon sugar

1/2 teaspoon ground black pepper

1 package commercial spring roll wrappers

Chop half of the cabbage very finely and put it into a medium-sized mixing bowl. Place the other four leaves in a steamer basket and set aside. In the same mixing bowl, add the pork, green onions, chiles, garlic, soy sauce, ginger juice, ginger, cornstarch, sesame oil, sugar, and pepper. Mix well.

Place the spring roll wrappers on a plate and cut each wrapper in half. Place a heaping teaspoon of the filling in the center of each wrapper; gather up the edges and twist together to a point. Place the dumplings in the steamer on the cabbage leaves. Steam for about 18 minutes. Serve with dipping sauces from Chapter 2.

Yield: 24 dumplings

Heat Scale: Hot

Fried Coconut Triangles

(*Tempa Tempa*)

Padang, Sumatra is where you'll find these sweet, meaty treats. Make sure you use heavy duty foil in the preparation of this recipe, as the triangles must be firmly packed.

5 shallots, peeled and sliced
1/2 teaspoon turmeric
2 piquin chiles, seeded and minced, or substitute any small, hot chiles
1 teaspoon fresh, minced ginger
1 clove garlic, sliced

1 teaspoon salt
1/4 teaspoon black pepper
1 tablespoon dried shrimp
2 cups grated coconut
1 tablespoon rice flour
Corn oil for deep frying

In a food processor, blend three of the shallots, the turmeric, chiles, ginger, garlic, salt, pepper, and dried shrimp into a paste. Place the paste in a mixing bowl and mix in the remaining 2 shallots, coconut, and rice flour.

Cut out eight 3 1/2-inch squares of aluminum foil, and fold each in half diagonally (forming a triangle). Fold each triangle in half again, forming a smaller triangle. Pinch the edges together along one of the open sides of each triangle, forming pockets with one open side. Fill each triangle with about 1/3 cup of the coconut mixture and press the sides together firmly between the palms, so that the mix will stick together when removed from the foil pouch. Refrigerate until ready to use.

Heat the oil in a wok to moderate heat. Carefully remove the coconut triangles from the foil, and fry them in batches. Turn them over to brown on all sides, then remove and drain on paper towels.

Yield: 8 triangles

Heat Scale: Medium

Tempeh Pancakes

(*Mendoan*)

This dish is a cocktail hour appetizer in Indonesia. These fried squares offer an interesting texture, as they are soft and not crispy. Tempeh is a soybean product. The soybean is combined with Koji, a fermented rice. Tempeh comes in small squares and is sold in the freezer section in one pound packages or it is available in Asian markets.

6 macadamia nuts

5 shallots, sliced

3 serrano or jalapeño chiles, seeded and minced

2 cloves garlic, sliced

1/8 teaspoon turmeric

1/2 teaspoon salt

1 teaspoon ground coriander

2 cups rice flour

4 cups Coconut Milk (page 12)

1 egg, beaten

5 green onion tops, sliced thinly

2 pounds tempeh

Peanut oil for deep frying

In a food processor, finely chop the nuts, then blend them with the shallots, jalapeños, garlic, turmeric, salt, and coriander to form a smooth paste.

In a large mixing bowl, mix the rice flour, coconut milk, and egg together until the mixture is smooth. Add the paste and the green onion tops, and mix the batter well. Cut the tempeh into slices 2 inches by 3 inches, and 1/8 inch thick. In a deep skillet, heat the oil. Dip the tempeh into the batter (it should be thin) and fry it in batches, until the batter is firm but not brown.

Serves: 12

Heat Scale: Medium

The Truth about Thai Heat

"For many *farangis,* Thai food is synonymous with the incendiary heat of chiles, and one of the most frequent comments about the cuisine is that it's very hot, if not at times too hot. Chalie is sensitive to this complaint and insists that well-prepared Thai dishes should be balanced, so that the spiciness of hot peppers is offset by the sweetness of coconut milk or palm sugar, the pungency of fresh herbs, the sourness of lime juice or tamarind, or the saltiness of *nam pla.* Too often in Thai restaurants in the West that balance is out of whack. In traditional home-style cooking, Chalie explained, the mother spiced the dishes mildly and offered small bowls of hot sauce on the side so that each person could fire up his or her serving to taste. Only when she thought she didn't have enough food for a meal would the heat be increased to keep the family from eating too much.**"**

> Kemp M. Minifie, writing about the Thai Cooking School
> and its director, Chalie Amatyakul

All Chopped Up

" The most elaborate Balinese dishes are prepared only on special occasions: weddings, tooth filings, and cremations, when many guests must be fed. And special food is usually prepared on important religious occasions, the most important of which is *Galungan,* occurring once every 210 days, and the anniversary of the local temple. The special meal that is most loved by the Balinese and least known to foreigners is called *ebat,* meaning 'chopped up.' The preparation of *ebat* is truly a Herculean task, often involving dozens of men, unlike the simple daily meals that are always cooked by women. Since there is no refrigeration, the food, especially meat, spoils quickly in the hot, humid climate. So, cooking usually begins shortly after midnight, is finished by dawn, and the food is eaten before noon."

Fred B. Eiseman, Jr.

Indonesian Food Etiquette

"As is the custom throughout Indonesia, you eat with your right hand by compressing a bit of rice, meat, and curry together with the tips of your fingers and pushing it into your mouth. Forks and spoons are also often provided, but it is very bad form to stick the spoon for eating into the dishes of curry. Use a separate spoon for this!"

Yohanni Johns

Java Idyll

"But the real poetry of Java is found outside Djakarta. For a while I lived in the hills of Java. From the bungalow I could look down on paddy fields; patchwork quilt done predominantly in green. There in the mornings, sitting on the veranda, I could see the awakening of the *kampong.* There was the smell of fish frying in oil and the sight of a young girl walking slowly, gracefully to the pool, where the water was fresh and clean and bamboo groves gave shelter from the peering eyes of a water buffalo."

Marie Kozslik Donovan

Street Food in Hanoi, 1994

"The level of street stall fare has evolved to such a degree that entire small streets are now jam-packed with vendors, with each individual vendor or proprietor brandishing something different. You may end up sitting down at a table in front of someone preparing strips of beef grilled in *la lot* leaves, but that doesn't mean you must play musical chairs to sample other vendors' offerings too. Simply walk up and down the street, perhaps choosing to order a plate of chicken salad with *rau ram,* a bowl of duck and bamboo soup, and/or a plate of tiny rice-flour dumplings stuffed with shallots, shrimp, and shredded pork. The dishes are then prepared and brought to you where you are sitting. If you're with a group of people getting together for lunch or dinner, with everyone ordering from up and down the street, a simple meal instantly becomes a fabulous feast, all to be enjoyed while sitting out in the open air."

                                                    Jeffrey Alford

At the Floating Market

"In the floating markets—particularly Damnern Saduak, about an hour's drive outside Bangkok—I can glimpse the still-active waterborne life of Thailand. Hundreds of long-tailed boats loaded with freshly picked fruits and vegetables, dried fish, rice, and other products are paddled by attractive women wearing broad-brimmed lampshade-style hats. In other boats vendors stir-fry tasty noodle dishes, prepare delicious fried bananas, and sell thirst-quenching fresh coconut milk and tasty sweets. The scenes and smells are colorful and exotic."

                                                    Ruth Law

From Furr to Pho
Soups and Stews

The Thais, like many other Southeast Asian peoples, are very fond of soup. Thai soup may be enjoyed as a snack, as a meal in itself, or as an accompaniment to a full Thai dinner. Unlike the Western cuisines, soup is not served as a separate course; it accompanies the meal itself, and certain combinations of food are complemented by the judicious choice of what soup to serve along with the dinner.

Such pairings of soups with main dishes typify the cuisine of Thailand, which is one of the most culturally coherent cuisines compared to those of other Southeast Asian countries. The major reason for this is that Thailand has never been subject to European rule and consequently has developed its own cuisine, undisturbed by European influences.

Thai soups are delicately balanced in terms of flavor, texture, and ingredients. Some of the ingredients that typify Thai soups are lemongrass, kaffir lime leaves, cilantro, fish sauce, coconut milk, and last, but not least, the famous (or infamous) red hot Thai chiles, which add fiery fuel to the soups.

Thai soups are nothing short of magnificent, and when we were in Thailand, even strolling down a side street, we would be surrounded with the tantalizing aromas of soups cooking. Soup is always simmering—in the restaurants, in the homes, and even in the markets. A hot bowl of spicy soup on the hottest day can be a wonderful, refreshing experience. Because Thailand is such a popular tourist destination, it is no wonder that so many Thai restaurants—and Thai soups, in particular—are popular in North America.

The first recipe, Hot and Sour Shrimp and Mushroom Soup (page 87), from central Thailand, combines two very Thai ingredients—lime leaves and lemongrass—for a palate-pleasing combination. Tamarind Soup with Fish and Vegetables (page 88) is considered a clear soup, and the vegetables add an unexpected crunch. The heavy use of cilantro and fresh ginger along with lemongrass in Spicy Lemongrass and Prawn Soup (page 90) adds a unique and unexpected flavor. Coconut milk somewhat tempers the heat in the Herbed Soup of Crab in Coconut Milk (page 89) recipe, which calls for seven Thai chiles. Smoked Whitefish Soup (page 92) has an unusual flavor because of the smoked fish; however, it is surprisingly delicate. Seafood, chiles, and fresh mint make Scallop and Chile Soup (page 93) taste both hot and cool! Spiced Soup of Prawns (page 94), from the Thai Cooking School at Bangkok's Oriental Hotel, doesn't stint on the use of chiles; however, the heat is tempered by the addition of lemongrass and fresh lime juice.

The next two recipes, Herbed Soup of Chicken in Coconut Milk (page 95) and Spicy Coconut Milk and Chicken Soup (page 96), are variations of a classic recipe. Both soups, like many Thai recipes, present a balance between heat and cool citrus overtones. The substantial and filling Thai Chicken and Mushroom Soup (page 97) can be found throughout the country, with subtle variations depending on the cook.

Like the Thais, the people of Burma (now called Myanmar) do not consider soup a separate course, with the exception of Burmese Fish Soup with Garnishes, or *mohinga* (page 98), a flavorful soup reminiscent of the curries of India. There is even an old Burmese saying, "Eat hot curry, drink hot soup, burn your lips, and remember my dinner." Burmese Spicy Lentil Soup (page 100) is thinner than Western versions of lentil soup, and is kept hot and served throughout the meal. The heat of the chiles is balanced by the tang of the tamarind.

The Laotian Breakfast Soup (page 101) included here is representative of the many similar soups served in Laos; our research suggests that many Southeast Asian countries have their own versions. Chiles are a favorite seasoning, vegetables abound in the soups, and tart flavors and aromatic leaves reign supreme. There is no real substitute for the "Laotian leaf" in this recipe, as marijuana is illegal in North America, but we have suggested one: *rau ram*, a Vietnamese herb available in Asian markets.

Soup stalls abound in Vietnam; one can even custom order a *pho* in the soup stall by including different noodles, meat, fish, and condiments. Soup is considered a fast breakfast food. Try the Vietnamese Sweet and Sour Snapper Soup (page 102) to get you moving in the morning, or any other time of day.

Soups are popular in Singapore all day long, from the popular Newton Circus Hawker Centre to the most elegant restaurants. Cook the Hot Chile and Seafood Soup (page 103) to clear your palate and sinuses. Another soup from the region that will clear your head is the Green Papaya Red Soup (page 106) from Bali. This Balinese soup is rich with red chile paste and the tart flavor of lemongrass. The recipe, Spicy Sumatran Vegetable Stew (page 104), is rich with chiles, vegetables, and coconut milk. It is definitely an entrée rather than something you would have for breakfast! The Hot Coconut Vegetable Soup (page 107) from Indonesia is sometimes served as an introduction to a complete Indonesian meal. The vegetables, meat, and the spicy seasonings make it a meal in itself! Indonesian Mutton Soup (page 108) is another recipe that can hold its own as a meal in itself. Don't let the word "mutton" put you off; lamb or goat meat can be used, and it is delicious.

Another substantial meal in a bowl is the Pork Soup with Chile Leaves (page 110) from the Philippines. The unique sour-salty taste comes from the use of guavas and fish sauce. The shrimp paste and chiles add just the right amount of spice to this dish.

Since Cambodia is bounded by Thailand and Vietnam, it is influenced by both cuisines. Elephant Walk Spicy Chicken Soup (page 110), from Cambodia, once again illustrates the use of balanced flavors—lemongrass (tart), fish sauce (salty), and chiles (fiery)—to create a delicious soup that can be served as an entrée. The Royal Khmer Sour Chicken Soup (page 112) is a stewlike soup that is both hot and spicy and is tempered with a little coconut milk. Sidewalk soup restaurants abound in Cambodia, as in many other Southeast Asian countries, and the Angkor Vegetable Soup (page 114) is a classic example of how a basic recipe can be enhanced by the addition of different vegetables and condiments. Using this recipe, the diner's particular taste determines what he adds to his soup. Be sure to add enough chiles!

Hot and Sour Shrimp and Mushroom Soup

This soup is most frequently served in central Thailand, and can be made either with shrimp or chicken. It is fast to prepare and makes a spicy, satisfying meal. Serve the soup very hot and accompany it with hot, cooked rice.

4 cups fresh chicken stock, preferably homemade

2 cups sliced oyster mushrooms

1/2 cup straw mushrooms, halved

2 to 4 fresh serrano or jalapeño chiles, stems and seeds removed, cut into thin rings

12 medium shrimp, shelled, deveined, tails removed, and cut in half

2 fresh kaffir lime leaves, or substitute 1/2 teaspoon freshly grated lime zest

2 large stalks lemongrass, the white bulb slightly pounded

3 tablespoons fresh lime juice

Freshly ground black pepper to taste

2 tablespoons fish sauce (*nam pla*)

Bring the stock to a boil in a large saucepan, then add the mushrooms and the chiles. Add the shrimp, lime leaves, and lemongrass and simmer over medium heat for 6 minutes, or until the mushrooms are tender and the shrimp is cooked.

Reduce the heat to a simmer and stir in the lime juice, black pepper, and fish sauce.

Remove the lemongrass stalks and the lime leaves before serving.

Serves: 4 to 6

Heat Scale: Mild to Medium, depending on the number of chiles added

Tamarind Soup with Fish and Vegetables

(*Tom Som Pla*)

This Thai soup is clear, hot, spicy, refreshing, and delicious. Do we need to add any more adjectives? The vegetables added at the end of the cooking process add some crunch to this flavorful soup.

3 cloves garlic

2 shallots

1/2-inch piece of fresh ginger, peeled

1/2 teaspoon powdered turmeric

2 teaspoons shrimp paste

8 whole black peppercorns

1/4 teaspoon salt

2 teaspoons minced cilantro root (or stems)

2 tablespoons vegetable oil

1/2 pound mild white fish fillets, chopped into 1/2-inch pieces

6 1/2 cups clear fish stock (or clam juice)

1/3 cup Tamarind Sauce (page 14)

2 tablespoons palm sugar

1 cup fresh green beans, cut into 1/4-inch sections

2 small fresh red chiles, serrano or jalapeño, stems and seeds removed, cut into thin rings

1 1/2 cups shredded cabbage

3 green onions, cut into 1/2-inch sections

3 tablespoons chopped cilantro for garnish

Place the first eight ingredients in a blender or food processor and blend into a smooth paste.

Heat the oil in a deep saucepan. When the oil is hot, add the paste and stir-fry for 4 minutes, stirring so that the mixture doesn't burn.

Add the fish, fish stock, tamarind sauce, and palm sugar and bring the mixture to a boil. Reduce the heat, cover, and simmer for 40 minutes.

Add the green beans and simmer for 5 minutes.

Then, add the chiles, cabbage, and green onions and simmer for 2 to 3 minutes.

Ladle the soup into warm bowls and garnish with the cilantro.

Serves: 6

Heat Scale: Medium

Herbed Soup of Crab in Coconut Milk

(*Tom Poo Gathi*)

We thank the Thai Cooking School at the Oriental Hotel in Bangkok for this crab soup recipe. There is a prodigious amount of chiles in this recipe; however, the heat is tempered somewhat by the addition of coconut milk. If you have all of the ingredients ready before starting, this soup takes only a few minutes to prepare and cook.

3 cups Coconut Milk, medium thickness (page 12)

5 shallots, crushed

2 stalks lemongrass, finely sliced, white part only

1 cup cooked crab meat

3 tablespoons fish sauce (*nam pla*)

1 teaspoon sugar

1 tablespoon fresh lime juice

2 tablespoons Tamarind Sauce (page 14)

2 tablespoons shredded kaffir lime leaves

7 dried Thai chiles, seeded and crushed, or substitute any small, hot red chiles

2 tablespoons chopped, fresh cilantro for garnish

Bring 1 cup of the coconut milk almost to a boil (be careful not to let it curdle) and then add the shallots, lemongrass, and crab.

Add the fish sauce, sugar, and lime juice and bring to a light boil. Then add the remaining 2 cups of coconut milk and once again bring to a light boil. Lower the heat to simmer and stir in the tamarind sauce, lime leaves, and chiles.

Serve hot and garnish with chopped, fresh cilantro.

Serves: 4

Heat Scale: Hot

Spicy Lemongrass and Prawn Soup

(*Tom Yaam Goong*)

This Thai recipe is a clear, hot soup, and it's rich in flavor and texture. This soup is perfect to serve with the hot and spicy Thai banquet that you have been promising to prepare for years.

1 pound medium prawns or shrimp, shelled, deveined, and cleaned— reserve the shells

1/3 cup vegetable oil

4 cups water

2 cups chicken stock

2 cloves garlic

5 black peppercorns

3 tablespoons chopped cilantro root

3 stalks lemongrass, pounded with a mallet or flat side of knife

2 tablespoons freshly grated ginger

5 kaffir lime leaves, shredded

2 tablespoons fish sauce (*nam pla*)

2 tablespoons fresh lime juice

3 fresh red serrano or jalapeño chiles, seeds and stems removed, sliced into thin rings

4 fresh green serrano or jalapeño chiles, seeds and stems removed, sliced into thin rings

3 green onions, cut into 1/2-inch diagonals, white part only

1 cup straw mushrooms, sliced; optional

3 tablespoons chopped, fresh cilantro for garnish

Shell and devein the prawns (or shrimp), but leave the tails on. Reserve the shells.

Heat the oil in a large, heavy casserole and add the shells, sautéing them for 4 to 5 minutes. Add the water and the chicken stock and bring the mixture to a boil. Reduce the heat, cover the pan, and simmer for 15 minutes. Then pour the stock through a fine strainer into another casserole and bring the strained stock to a boil.

Place the garlic, peppercorns, and cilantro root in a mortar or blender and pound or blend the ingredients to a smooth paste.

Add the pounded paste mixture to the boiling stock and add the lemongrass, ginger, lime leaves, and prawns (or shrimp). Bring the mixture back to a boil and then reduce the heat to a simmer and cook the mixture for 3 to 4 minutes.

Then, add the fish sauce, lime juice, chiles, and green onions. Stir to blend the ingredients. (Add the optional straw mushrooms at this point.)

Serve the soup in large, warmed bowls and garnish with chopped, fresh cilantro.

Serves: 6

Heat Scale: Hot

Smoked Whitefish Soup

(*Nam Yar Pa*)

This Thai recipe is more robust and richer than the traditional version because of the large quantity of coconut milk. It can be served as a soup, or as a curry-like main dish over cooked rice. We found this dish to have an interesting taste because of the addition of "kippers," or smoked whitefish.

8 cups Coconut Milk (page 12)

4 green serrano or jalapeño chiles, seeded and finely sliced

2 stalks lemongrass, minced, white part only

8 cloves garlic, thinly sliced

4 pieces dried galangal

1 tablespoon freshly grated ginger

1 teaspoon shrimp paste

5 shallots, cut into thin, lengthwise slices

2 boned kipper fillets (4 ounces), flaked, or substitute any other smoked whitefish

1 pound cooked small shrimp

1/2 cup bean sprouts

2 hardboiled eggs, quartered

8 fresh, sweet basil leaves

In a large, heavy casserole, bring the coconut milk and the chiles to a boil. Add the lemongrass, garlic, galangal, ginger, shrimp paste, shallots, and kippers. Bring the mixture back to a boil and stir it until the fish has been thoroughly incorporated, about 6 minutes.

Add the shrimp and cook for 2 minutes.

Turn off the heat, stir in the remaining ingredients, and cover for 3 to 4 minutes.

Serves: 6

Heat Scale: Medium

Scallop and Chile Soup

This refreshing soup from Thailand is redolent with the ingredients that make Thai cooking so distinctive and unique: lime leaves, lemongrass, chiles, and the famous Thai fish sauce. Serve this soup anytime, but it is particularly refreshing when the temperature is up and you can perspire your way to coolness!

6 cups chicken stock

2 cloves garlic, chopped

4 lime leaves

2 stalks lemongrass

2 tablespoons Thai fish sauce (*nam pla*)

1 teaspoon crushed red Thai chiles, or other small, hot, red chiles

1/2 teaspoon salt

1 pound scallops, washed

1 pound shrimp, peeled, deveined, and shelled

1 cup straw mushrooms

2 serrano or jalapeño chiles, seeds and stems removed, cut into rings

1/3 cup freshly chopped mint

6 green onions, finely chopped

Combine the first seven ingredients in a heavy soup pot, bring to a boil, and allow the mixture to boil for 2 minutes.

Add the scallops, shrimp, mushrooms, and chiles, and let the mixture come to a boil. Then reduce the heat to a simmer and cook until the scallops and shrimp are done, about 3 to 5 minutes. Stir in the mint and the green onions and serve immediately.

Serves: 6 to 8

Heat Scale: Hot

Spiced Soup of Prawns

Here is one more great recipe from the Thai Cooking School at the Oriental Hotel, and this one is considerably spicier than the Herbed Soup of Crab in Coconut Milk. This soup is pure flavor and pure heat—just the thing to cool you down on a hot summer day, or heat you up on a cold winter night!

4 to 5 cups chicken broth

2 garlic cloves

3 cilantro roots

3 black peppercorns

3 slices of fresh galangal, or substitute ginger

3 stalks lemongrass, sliced

2 cups prawns, shelled and cleaned

3 to 4 tablespoons fresh lime juice

3 to 4 tablespoons fish sauce (*nam pla*)

5 dried red Thai chiles, crushed, or substitute piquins

2 tablespoons chopped, fresh cilantro

7 kaffir lime leaves, shredded

Bring 2 cups of the chicken broth to a boil.

While the broth is heating, make a paste of the garlic, cilantro, and peppercorns. Add the paste to the broth when it reaches the boiling point. Boil for a minute and then add the galangal slices, lemongrass, and prawns.

Add the remaining broth and bring to a boil again.

Season to taste with the lime juice, fish sauce, and chiles.

Ladle the soup into bowls and sprinkle with chopped, fresh cilantro and lime leaves.

Serves: 4 to 6

Heat Scale: Hot

Herbed Chicken Soup with Coconut Milk

(*Gai Tom Kha* No. 1)

This recipe was given to us when we visited the Thai Cooking School at the Oriental Hotel in Bangkok. The chef had just finished a class, and the aromas from the cooking school were nothing short of fabulous! The soup is fast and easy to prepare and will give your guests a true taste of the subtleties of Thai cuisine.

1 cup sliced galangal, or substitute ginger

7 cloves garlic

3 black peppercorns

7 cilantro roots (or stems)

2 fresh lemongrass stalks, finely sliced

3 shallots, sliced

4 cups Coconut Milk, medium thickness (page 12)

2 cups thinly sliced raw chicken

3 to 4 tablespoons fish sauce (*nam pla*)

3 to 4 tablespoons fresh lime juice

5 dried Thai chiles, crushed, or substitute piquins

7 kaffir lime leaves, shredded

3 sprigs fresh cilantro, chopped

Using a food processor, puree together one-half of the galangal or ginger, the garlic, peppercorns, cilantro, lemongrass, and shallots. Set aside.

Pour 1 cup of the coconut milk into a large, heavy soup pot, and bring it to a boil. Add the reserved puree and stir well. Add the chicken and keep stirring.

Add the remaining galangal or ginger and the 3 remaining cups of coconut milk. Bring the mixture to a boil, then reduce the heat to simmer and check to see if the chicken is cooked through.

Season to taste with the fish sauce, lime juice, and crushed chiles.

Sprinkle the soup with the shredded lime leaves and the chopped cilantro before serving.

Yield: 4 to 6 servings

Heat Scale: Medium

Spicy Coconut Milk and Chicken Soup

(*Gai Tom Kha* No. 2)

When we were in Thailand, we sampled this soup as often as we could, at a variety of shops and restaurants, and collected recipes and ingredients as we went along our merry way. We think the following combination of ingredients works quite well in our second version of *gai tom kha*.

5 cups chicken stock (preferably homemade)

3 fresh serrano or jalapeño chiles, stems and seeds removed, thinly sliced

2 1/2 cups unsweetened Coconut Milk (page 12)

10 quarter-sized slices galangal, or 5 quarter-sized slices fresh ginger

2 tablespoons fish sauce (*nam pla*)

3 tablespoons fresh lime juice

4 lemon leaves, or 2 teaspoons grated lemon zest

2 stalks fresh lemongrass, finely minced, or 2 teaspoons dried lemongrass

8 ounces straw mushrooms, sliced lengthwise; or 1 cup sliced button mushrooms

2 whole chicken breasts, skinned, deboned, and sliced into 1-inch pieces

1/2 teaspoon sugar

Heat the chicken broth in a large pot with the chiles. When it starts to simmer, stir in the coconut milk and continue stirring until the mixture is thoroughly blended.

Add the galangal or ginger, fish sauce, lime juice, lemon leaves, lemongrass, mushrooms, and chicken and simmer for 15 to 20 minutes, until the chicken is cooked. Stir in the sugar and serve hot.

Serves: 4 to 6

Heat Scale: Medium

Thai Chicken and Mushroom Soup

(*Kaeng Chud Kai Hed*)

This filling chicken and mushroom soup, and variations of it, are found in most parts of Thailand. Because the chicken is cooked in chicken stock rather than water, it is a richer than usual base for the soup. The vegetables and the dash of fish sauce make this soup a crunchy and tasty main-course meal.

1 four-pound whole chicken, chopped in large pieces

6 cups chicken stock, preferably homemade

1/2 teaspoon salt

8 green onions, finely chopped

2 tablespoons vegetable oil

2 serrano or jalapeño chiles, stems and seeds removed, thinly sliced

1 tablespoon fish sauce (*nam pla*)

4 dried mushrooms, Black or Champignon mushrooms soaked in warm water for 30 minutes, drained, rinsed, and finely chopped

3 cloves garlic, crushed

3 tablespoons chopped cilantro

3/4 cup bean sprouts

3/4 cup chopped cucumber; reserve several small swirls of the skin for the garnish

Wash the chicken under cold water and then place it in a heavy Dutch oven casserole. Add the stock, salt, and green onions and bring the mixture to a boil. Reduce the heat to a simmer, cover, and simmer for 1 1/2 hours or until the chicken is thoroughly cooked. Transfer the chicken to a platter and reserve the stock. When the chicken is cool, shred the meat and set the meat aside.

Heat the oil in a large wok or saucepan and, when it is hot, add the sliced chiles, fish sauce, mushrooms, garlic, cilantro, bean sprouts, and the shredded chicken. Stir-fry for 3 minutes and then add the reserved chicken stock. Reduce the heat to a simmer and cook for 3 to 4 minutes.

Just before serving, add the cucumber and the reserved swirls of cucumber skin.

Serves: 4 to 6

Heat Scale: Medium

Burmese Fish Soup with Garnishes

(*Mohinga*)

This is one of Burma's classic dishes. Tourists who visited Burma before the country closed its doors to the outside world in the 1960s remember how the Rangoon streets used to swarm with *mohinga* sellers. The dish, cooked the previous night, was available in the streets in the early mornings. The hawkers carried it on their shoulders on a long bamboo pole that held two evenly balanced containers. True *mohinga* contains the outer bark of the banana tree— which is difficult to find in the United States. It still tastes great even without the bark.

1 cup *moong dal* (lentils)

2 cups water

3 pounds catfish (or other white fish), cut into bite-size pieces

1 teaspoon salt

1 teaspoon turmeric

3 stalks lemongrass, including the bulb

1/2 cup roasted peanuts

1/2 cup long-grained rice

1 cup peanut or corn oil

5 medium-sized onions, finely chopped

6 cloves garlic, chopped

1 two-inch piece of ginger, peeled and minced

1 tablespoon paprika

1 teaspoon freshly ground black pepper

1/4 cup fish sauce (*nam pla*)

2 cups Coconut Milk (page 12)

4 cups water

1 cup bamboo shoots

12 shallots, chopped

4 cups water

1/2 teaspoon salt

1 tablespoon olive oil

1 pound rice noodles

Garnishes

6 hardboiled eggs, halved

1 cup cilantro leaves

1 large green onion, finely chopped

6 limes, quartered

2 tablespoons fish sauce (*nam pla*)

1 teaspoon cayenne powder

Boil the *moong dal* in 2 cups of water for 12 minutes over low heat. Set aside.

Toss the fish with salt and turmeric and marinate at room temperature for 15 minutes.

Pound the lemongrass lightly. Put the peanuts in a spice mill and pulverize for a minute; set aside. In a dry skillet, heat the rice, stirring continuously for about 5 minutes. Powder the rice in a mortar, blender, or spice mill.

Heat the oil in a large skillet for 1 minute. Add the onions and fry over low heat until they turn golden, about 5 minutes. Add the marinated fish, garlic, lemongrass, ginger, paprika, black pepper, and fish sauce and cook, uncovered, over medium heat for 5 minutes.

Add the coconut milk, water, peanuts, rice powder, bamboo shoots, and shallots and stir well. Bring to a boil, lower the heat, cover, and simmer for 12 minutes.

Meanwhile, heat the other 4 cups of water in a large pot; add the salt and olive oil as the water starts boiling. Add the noodles and cook, covered, for about 5 minutes. Drain and set aside.

To serve, place the curry, the garnishes, and the rice noodles in separate bowls in the center of the table. Guests should fill their soup bowls first with noodles, then with fish curry, and then select whatever garnishes they wish.

Serves: 4 to 6

Heat Scale: Mild

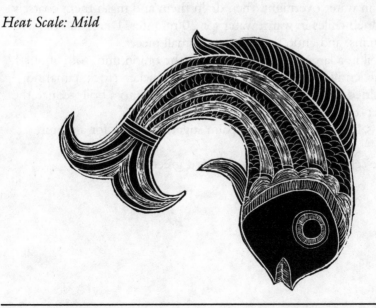

Burmese Spicy Lentil Soup

Burma, now called Myanmar, is a country that doesn't stint on the use of chiles. Although many Southeastern Asian dishes are served at room temperature, soup is always served hot. If it is a light soup, it (instead of a drink) is sipped throughout the meal. Burmese Spicy Lentil Soup is too hearty for sipping, however, and would be eaten throughout the meal instead of being a separate course, as in Western cuisines.

3/4 cup dried lentils, washed

2 dried red chiles, piquin or Thai

2 fresh serrano or jalapeño chiles,
    seeds and stems removed,
    chopped

2 tablespoons vegetable oil

2 cups diced onion

1 1/2 tablespoons curry powder
    (preferably imported)

2 small bay leaves

5 cups chicken stock

3 tablespoons Tamarind Sauce
    (page 14)

1/2 teaspoon salt

1 teaspoon cracked whole black
    pepper

1 teaspoon palm sugar

5 tablespoons chopped green
    onions for garnish

Soak the lentils in water overnight, then drain them and mash them coarsely.

Soak the dried chiles in warm water for 20 minutes. Drain and remove the seeds and stems, and chop the chiles into small pieces.

Heat the oil in a large saucepan and sauté the onion until soft, about 1 minute. Add the lentils, curry powder, bay leaves, chicken stock, tamarind sauce, and the dried and fresh chiles. Bring the mixture to a boil, reduce the heat to a simmer, cover, and cook for 15 minutes.

Stir in the salt, black pepper, and palm sugar and cook for a minute longer.

Just before serving, garnish with chopped green onions.

Serves: 5

Heat Scale: Hot

Laotian Breakfast Soup

(*Furr*)

This soup is a very popular breakfast dish and usually has noodles, bits of pork, garlic, and marijuana leaves. In Laos, marijuana is just another herb. Other Southeast Asian countries have their own versions and recipes for *furr.* In Laos, when a *furr* shop gets very busy and full of people, one can only suspect that the cook is adding more marijuana to the noodles than his competitor!

2 tablespoons vegetable oil

3/4 cup minced raw pork

2 cloves garlic, minced

1 cup chopped onion

1/2 cup pumpkin, cut into 1/2-inch cubes

1 cup long beans, cut into 3/4-inch pieces (or substitute green beans)

2 red serrano or jalapeño chiles, stems and seeds removed, minced

1/2 cup sliced mushrooms

1 quart beef or chicken stock

1 handful Laotian leaf (marijuana), or substitute *rau ram,* a Vietnamese herb

1/4 pound rice vermicelli

Heat the oil in a heavy saucepan and sauté the pork. Push the pork to one side and sauté the garlic and onion. Then add the pumpkin, beans, chiles, and mushrooms and sauté the vegetables for 30 seconds.

Pour in the stock and bring the mixture to a boil, then reduce the heat to a simmer and add the Laotian leaf (or *rau ram*) and the vermicelli. Simmer the soup for 30 minutes, or until the vermicelli is cooked.

Serves: 4

Heat Scale: Medium

Vietnamese Sweet and Sour Snapper Soup

(*Canh Chua Ca*)

This soup is typical of many of the soups of Vietnam. It is delicately seasoned, and no single ingredient overwhelms the others; instead, all the ingredients present a balanced taste in this easy and quick-to-prepare recipe.

1 pound snapper or other delicate white fish fillets

3 tablespoons frozen orange juice

1 1/2 tablespoons apple cider vinegar

1 medium onion, thinly sliced

1 quart water

3 medium tomatoes, skins removed, sliced

1 1/2 cups mung bean sprouts

1 1/3 cups thinly sliced celery

1 teaspoon soy sauce

Freshly ground black pepper to taste

1/4 teaspoon ground cayenne

2 tablespoons chopped, fresh cilantro

Fresh red serrano or jalapeño chile slices, to taste

Rinse the fish fillets with cold water and dry with paper towels. Cut the fish into 1-inch pieces and set aside.

In a large saucepan, combine the orange juice, vinegar, onion, and water and bring to a boil. Cover the pot and simmer gently for 15 minutes.

Add the tomatoes to the simmering water and continue to cook for 3 to 4 minutes, or until the tomatoes begin to soften.

Stir in the remaining ingredients and simmer for 2 minutes.

Serves: 4

Heat Scale: Varies, Medium to Hot

Hot Chile and Seafood Soup

(*Masak Kuah Pedas*)

This soup hails from Singapore, a place where the chefs don't stint on the heat. As with many of these soups, substitutions can easily be made. If you don't want to use shrimp or prawns in this recipe, substitute firm, white fish fillets.

6 candlenuts or macadamia nuts

1/2 teaspoon turmeric

2 tablespoons grated fresh ginger

1/2 cup peeled and sliced shallots

1 tablespoon shrimp paste

4 fresh red serrano or jalapeño chiles, stems and seeds removed

4 cups water, or 2 cups water and 2 cups chicken stock

6 pieces dried tamarind seed

1/2 teaspoon salt, or to taste

1 1/2 pounds cleaned, shelled prawns, or substitute a firm, mild white fish

1 teaspoon Basic Spice Islands Chile Paste (*sambalan,* page 18)

2 teaspoons butter or margarine

1 1/2 teaspoons sugar

1 tablespoon fresh lime juice

Place the nuts, turmeric, ginger, shallots, shrimp paste, and chiles in a blender and blend to form a paste.

Pour the water (or the water/broth combination) in a saucepan with the paste and the tamarind and bring to a boil. Lower the heat to a simmer and cook for 30 minutes, adding the salt.

Add the prawns or fish to the simmering mixture and cook for 8 minutes, or until done.

Mix the *sambalan,* butter or margarine, sugar, and lime juice together. Just before serving the soup, remove the saucepan from the heat and stir in the *sambalan* mixture.

Serves: 4

Heat Scale: Medium

Spicy Sumatran Vegetable Stew
(*Sayur Lodeh*)

This recipe was collected by Jeff Corydon for *Chile Pepper* magazine in Padang, Sumatra. Jeff says that the spiciest cooking in Indonesia comes from Sumatra and, more specifically, around Padang. The fiery *bumbu,* or blend of chiles and spices, gives this dish its spicy reputation. Don't let the long list of ingredients prevent you from making this dish; there are only three ingredients that you'll have to purchase from an Asian market.

1 small eggplant, coarsely chopped

Salt

6 red serrano or jalapeño chiles, stems and seeds removed, chopped

1 large onion, chopped

2 cloves garlic, chopped

3 macadamia nuts

1/2 teaspoon shrimp paste

1 teaspoon salt

1 teaspoon ground coriander

4 tablespoons vegetable oil

1/2 cup cooked tiny shrimp

1/2 cup thinly sliced bamboo shoots

1/2 cup chopped green beans, fresh or frozen

1 red bell pepper, stem and seeds removed, chopped

2 zucchini squash, chopped

6 large cabbage leaves, chopped

2 cups chicken broth

1 tomato, coarsely chopped

1 stalk lemongrass

2 lime leaves, or substitute one bay leaf

1 cup Coconut Milk (page 12)

Salt and sugar to taste

Sprinkle the eggplant with salt, and let it sit for 30 minutes. Squeeze out the moisture, rinse the eggplant, and roll it up in paper towels to absorb any excess moisture.

Place the chiles, onion, garlic, nuts, shrimp paste, salt, and coriander in a blender, add a little water, and puree until the mixture is smooth.

Heat the oil in a wok or large skillet, add the chile–spice puree, and cook for 2 to 3 minutes over medium heat. Add the shrimp, and then the bamboo shoots, green beans, red bell pepper, zucchini, and cabbage leaves, a handful at a time.

Pour in the broth, cover, and simmer gently for about 10 minutes to partially cook the vegetables.

Add the chopped tomato. Put the lemongrass and lime leaves or bay leaf in a piece of cheesecloth, then add to the stew. Stir in the coconut milk and simmer for an additional 3 minutes, stirring constantly.

Remove the packet of lemongrass and lime leaves or bay leaf and discard. Adjust the sugar and salt to taste and serve.

Yield: 6 servings

Heat Scale: Mild

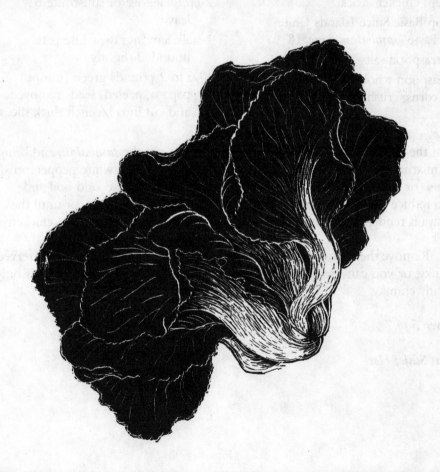

Green Papaya Red Soup

(*Gedang Mekuah*)

Make this soup, pretend you're in Bali, and prepare to get heated up! The Balinese do not skimp on the chile heat, as this recipe demonstrates. Many Southeast Asian cuisines use unripened or green papaya as a vegetable; check your local Asian (or Latin American) grocery stores to see if they have them. If green papayas are not available, substitute summer squash or Chinese winter melon.

5 cups chicken stock

1 cup Basic Spice Islands Chile Paste (*sambalan*, page 18)

1/2 teaspoon salt

1 teaspoon whole white peppercorns, crushed and ground

2 *salam* leaves; or substitute bay leaves

1 stalk lemongrass, white part pounded slightly

1 1/2 to 2 pounds green (unripe) papaya, peeled, seeds removed, and cut into 1/4-inch thick slices

Heat the chicken stock in a heavy Dutch oven, stir in the *sambalan,* and bring the mixture to a boil. Boil for a minute, then add the salt, white peppercorns, *salam* (or bay) leaves, lemongrass, and papaya. Bring to a second boil and then reduce the heat to simmer and cook for 12 to 15 minutes, or until the papaya is tender. If the mixture becomes too thick, add a little more chicken stock.

Remove the stalk of lemongrass and serve. This papaya soup can be served chunky, or you can use a potato masher and mash the mixture until it is only slightly chunky.

Serves: 5 to 7

Heat Scale: Hot

Hot Coconut Vegetable Soup

(*Sajoer*)

In Indonesia, *sajoer* frequently begins the meal. It can be served over boiled rice in soup bowls or by itself. This recipe takes little time to prepare and will add zest to the beginning of any meal. The vegetables can be varied, with whatever is in season, but do not use many leafy ones. For example, the cabbage can be replaced with kale or bok choy, but don't use both.

1 1/2 teaspoons coriander seeds

1/2 teaspoon cumin seed

2 bay leaves

1 dried lemon leaf

3 cloves garlic, peeled

2 tablespoons coarsely chopped fresh ginger

2 tablespoons peanut oil (or vegetable oil)

4 Brussels sprouts, washed and cut into eighths

2 carrots, thinly sliced

3/4 cup fresh green beans, cut into 1/2-inch pieces

1/2 cup green peas (fresh or frozen)

2 cabbage leaves, shredded

2 medium onions, chopped

1 green bell pepper, seeded and diced

1 or 2 fresh red chiles (such as serranos or jalapeños), seeds and stems removed, diced

4 cups Coconut Milk (page 12)

2 cups water or chicken stock

3/4 pound fresh shrimp, shelled and deveined

Crush the first six ingredients in a small food processor or a mortar to create a smooth paste.

Heat the oil in a small, heavy sauté or frying pan, add the spice mixture, and fry it for 2 to 3 minutes, stirring constantly.

In a large, heavy soup pot, add all of the vegetables to the coconut milk and water (or chicken stock) and bring to a boil. Turn the heat down and simmer, uncovered, for 15 minutes. Add the shrimp and simmer for an additional 5 to 6 minutes more.

Serve hot in soup bowls.

Serves: 6 to 8

Heat Scale: Medium

Indonesian Mutton Soup

Indonesia raises goats rather than sheep; yet "mutton" was the meat of choice in the wet market of Little India in Singapore, so we can only assume that this delicious, curry-like soup can be made with either lamb or goat meat. The recipe is provided by courtesy of Mrs. Devagi Shanmugam of the Thomson Cooking Studio in Singapore.

2 pounds lamb or goat meat, cubed

3 quarts water

5 fresh green serrano or jalapeño chiles, stems removed

5 fresh red serrano or jalapeño chiles, stems removed

1 two-inch piece fresh ginger, peeled

2 teaspoons black peppercorns

2 teaspoons anise seed

2 teaspoons cumin seed

5 cardamom pods, or 2 tablespoons cardamom powder

3 whole cloves

3 tablespoons coriander seed

1 stick cinnamon

1 whole star anise

5 bay leaves

1 cup fresh mint leaves

4 stalks lemongrass, crushed

1 teaspoon ground turmeric

4 curry leaves (optional)

1 cup water

4 medium tomatoes, diced

2 sticks cinnamon

3 cardamoms

5 whole cloves

5 tablespoons vegetable oil

3 teaspoons rice flour for thickening (optional)

3 green onions, chopped, for garnish

Put the meat and the 3 quarts of water in a large pot.

In a food processor or blender, coarsely grind together the next 16 ingredients (from the chiles through the curry leaves), along with the 1 cup of water. Strain this mixture into the pot with the meat. Save the residue, tie it securely in a muslin or cotton cloth, and add it to the pot.

Fry the tomatoes, cinnamon, cardamoms, and cloves in the oil until the tomatoes are soft, and add the mixture to the pot.

Bring the pot to a boil, lower the heat to simmer, and cook (covered) until the meat is tender and nearly falls apart, about 1 ½ to 2 hours. Remove the spice bundle, thicken the soup with the rice flour, if necessary, and garnish with the green onions.

Serves: 6 to 8

Heat Scale: Medium

Pork Soup with Chile Leaves

(*Bulanglang*)

Filipinos generally prefer their soups to have some sour overtones, and this distinctive taste is achieved by the addition of sour fruits such as tamarind, green mango, or (as in this recipe) guava. The *patis*, Phillipine fish sauce, is added at the end of the cooking and is used much as Westerners use salt. The combination of sour and salty tastes is a very popular one.

10 ripe guavas, peeled and quartered

6 to 7 cups of water

2 1/4 pounds pork with bones, cut into serving pieces

1 garlic clove, minced

1 onion, chopped

1 tablespoon shrimp paste

2 fresh piquin chiles, seeds and stems removed, diced; or substitute 1/2 teaspoon cayenne powder

1 bunch pepper or chile leaves, washed

Patis (Phillipine fish sauce) to taste; or substitute *nam pla*

Boil the guavas in the water until they are tender, about 10 minutes. Reserving the water, remove the guavas; remove their seeds and mash the guavas with a wooden spoon. Return the mashed guavas to the boiling water and add the pork, garlic, onion, and shrimp paste. Cover and simmer gently for 1 hour, or until the meat is tender, checking occasionally to see that the water still covers the meat.

    Add the chiles or cayenne pepper and the pepper or chile leaves and stir through the soup for 3 minutes. Season to taste with *patis*.

Serves: 4

Heat Scale: Medium

Elephant Walk Spicy Chicken Soup

(*S'ngao Mouan Hao*)

This spicy Cambodian soup recipe was given to us by the owners of the Elephant Walk Restaurant in Somerville, Massachusetts and was originally published in *Chile Pepper* magazine. It is hearty enough to be served as an entrée for lunch, accompanied with jasmine rice and fish sauce.

4 whole chicken breasts, skinned, but with bone left in

6 cups water

1 stalk lemongrass, white bulb split open with knife or cleaver

2 teaspoons salt, to taste

2 teaspoons sugar

2 cloves garlic, minced

2 tablespoons fish sauce

Juice of 2 limes

2 green onions, angle-cut into 1-inch lengths

1 tablespoon minced fresh piquin chiles; or substitute 2 tablespoons minced serranos or jalapeños

1 to 2 tablespoons chopped fresh basil

Wash the chicken breasts under running water.

Bring the water to a boil in a medium stock pot and add the chicken breasts, lemongrass, salt, sugar, garlic, and fish sauce. When the stock reaches a boil again, skim the surface thoroughly. Next, reduce the heat to a simmer, cover, and cook for 1 hour.

Remove the chicken breasts from the pot and let them cool slightly; then shred the meat from the bone and return the meat to the pot. When the shredded chicken is heated through, turn off the heat, add the remaining ingredients, stir, and serve immediately.

Serves: 4

Heat Scale: Hot

Royal Khmer Sour Chicken Soup

(*Somlah Machou Sdaik*)

The recipe for this delicious Cambodian soup was collected by David Karp from the Elephant Walk Restaurant in Somerville, Massachusetts. A. Kenthao de Monteiro was the creator of this *somlah*, a thick, stewlike soup, which is a staple of Cambodian cuisine. *Somlah machou*, sour soup, is often made with fish or shrimp, but this version features chicken.

Paste

1 tablespoon minced lemongrass

3 thin slices peeled galangal; or substitute ginger

2 medium shallots, peeled

5 cloves garlic

1/2 teaspoon turmeric

4 New Mexican dried red chiles, deveined, seeded, and soaked 10 minutes in lukewarm water

4 kaffir lime leaves

1 teaspoon shrimp paste

Soup

1 cup pea eggplants

2 teaspoons oil

2 tablespoons oil

1 pound sliced chicken

4 cups chicken broth

1 teaspoon fish sauce

1 teaspoon *prahok* (preserved fish juice, called *padek* by the Thai)

1 teaspoon salt

2 teaspoons sugar

4 tablespoons coconut milk

1 cup water

2 cups small, round Asian eggplants, cut in half

1/4 cup Tamarind Sauce (page 14) or substitute 4 tablespoons fresh lime juice

1 handful Asian basil for garnish

Combine all of the paste ingredients in a food processor, puree until smooth, and set aside.

Sauté the pea eggplants over high heat with 2 teaspoons of oil and set aside.

In a stock pot, add the paste and 2 tablespoons of oil and cook over medium heat for 2 minutes, stirring constantly, until the aroma of the paste is released.

Add the chicken and stir for 5 minutes. Then add the remaining ingredients, except for the Asian eggplants and tamarind sauce. Once the stock has reached a boil, add the eggplants and tamarind sauce. Allow the mixture to boil gently for 10 minutes.

Serve in a soup tureen with a platter of cooked jasmine rice and fresh sliced chiles on the side. Garnish with the fresh basil leaves.

Serves: 4

Heat Scale: Mild

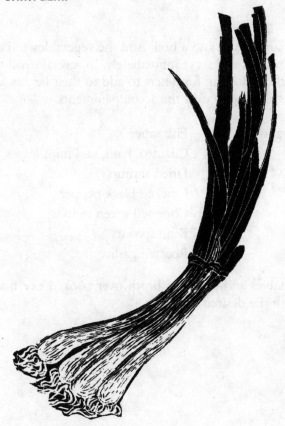

Angkor Vegetable Soup

This recipe is from Richard Sterling, who observed: "On nearly all of the streets in all of the towns in Cambodia, there are sidewalk soup restaurants. People stop at any time of day for a bowl of vegetable soup or noodle soup called *pho*. Though originally from Vietnam, it has become, like pizza in the U.S.A., a national dish. To be authentic, the soup stock should be clarified, so it's best to make 'skeleton soup' from last night's roast chicken or 'fish bone soup' from your fish fry or good old marrow bone soup."

8 cups clear broth
4 cups chopped vegetables, any
    number, any kind

In a large pot, bring the clarified stock to a boil. Add the vegetables and cook to the desired degree of firmness and serve immediately. In several small dishes, serve any or all of the following for diners to add to their large soup bowl, and then ladle the boiling soup over the accompaniments.

Chopped fresh chiles (serranos or
    jalapeños work fine)
Paper-thin slices of raw beef (the
    broth will cook them)
Minced raw shrimp or fish
Crab meat
Lime wedges

Fish sauce
Cilantro, basil, and mint leaves
Dried shrimp
Cracked black pepper
Chopped green onions
Bean sprouts
Roasted garlic

Variation: Omit the vegetables and pour the broth over cooked rice noodles that have been dressed with the desired garnishes.

Serves: 6

Heat Scale: Varies

Nothing Beats a Bug

❝At that moment we heard a friendly sizzle and smelled our favorite aromas: chile and garlic. We followed our noses to a food stall where a well-fed merchant smiled a greeting. Before him were two huge woks filled with dancing hot oil, one redolent of garlic, the other breathing ginger. Bowls of sliced garlic, crushed red chile, sliced green serranos, and whole flaming-looking little orange peppers lay about. A large basket covered with a cloth mesh held the merchant's meat: giant locusts.

The merchant reached under the mesh and grabbed a large handful of the squirming giants and dropped them into the hot, garlic-scented oil. They sizzled and hissed and turned from green to golden brown. He put them in a bag and sprinkled them with soy sauce and crushed chile.

I broke the body into halves, gave Bruce one, and in unspoken agreement, we ate them simultaneously. No guts gushed.

"You know," Bruce said, "I've seen jumbo prawns smaller than these."

"Let's get the garlic flavor."

"With chile!"

"Yeah!"

"You know, these are like chips and salsa," I noted for the record.

"Or nachos."

Taking another one from the bag and sniffing its pungent garlicky-chile goodness, I said, "I wonder what they'll have for us at our next stop, in Burma."

Then we strolled about the bazaar, chatting with vendors, joking with children, and eating the food of Nero and John the Baptist. ❞

Richard Sterling, in Thailand at the Cholburi Provincial Bazaar

Thai Culinary Influences

"What has long intrigued me about Thai food is its reflection of the unique way in which influences from neighboring countries have been adapted. As we tasted our way through five days of classes these culinary borrowings became clearer. From India came the curries, but, whereas Indian curries are based on spices, Thai curries are predominantly herbal, with the prevailing flavors of coriander root, lemongrass, chiles, and basil and only the occasional use of cumin, coriander seed, and cardamom. Reminiscent of Chinese cuisine are the stir-fried meats and poultry and the noodle dishes, but the addition of such seasonings as shrimp paste, lime juice, tamarind, and basil makes them distant relations. The Thais adopted *sates,* the skewers of grilled meats served with a peanut sauce, from the Malaysians, but instead of a dry marinade the Thais often combine the spices with coconut milk and let the meat marinate in the mixture before grilling it.**"**

         Kemp M. Minifie, writing about the Thai Cooking School

Nation of Foodies

"As I quickly discovered upon my arrival in this gleaming, steaming island nation, Singaporeans are downright obsessed with food. With the second-highest standard of living in Asia next to Japan, they support countless hawker stands peddling everything from grilled stingray on banana leaves and frogs' legs with ginger to fried rice with squid and clay-pot prawn noodles.**"**

         John Watson

New World Foods in Indonesia

❝The Dutch experience also brought into the Indonesian kitchen the extraordinary foods of Mexico that came to Europe via the Spanish conquests. It was the Spanish, who more than anyone else, were responsible for making available to Europe and Asia the important foods from Mexico that launched the development of the cuisines of Europe. Tomatoes, squash, corn, cocoa, avocados, potatoes, and the indispensable hot chile pepper ushered in an era of experimentation in the kitchens of France and Italy and the ultimate establishment of cooking as an aesthetic experience. The Dutch brought all this to Indonesia. Awaiting them was the Indonesian genius for adapting imported culinary influences and fusing them with the unique agricultural products of the islands.❞

Copeland Marks

Take 5,000 of Your Closest Friends to Dinner

A Bangkok restaurant that makes Circus Circus look like a petting zoo is *Mang Gorn Luang* (Royal Dragon Seafood Restaurant), where some of the waiters must don roller skates to serve the 5,000 guests in the seven-story pagoda. Other waiters, bearing such delicacies as *yum yong* (sweet and salty banana-shoot salad) among their platters and dressed in traditional Thai costumes, are strapped into harnesses and are dropped from the roof—to the amazement of the diners in what is reputably the world's largest restaurant.

And Don't Talk with Your Mouth Full

"When visiting a Malay, the visitor bows and lifts the right hand to the forehead, saying: *'Assalam alaikum'* (Peace be with you). The host replies: *'Valaikum salaam'* (And with you). If the visitor is invited in, he removes his footwear outside before entering the house. Even before the guests are seated comfortably, there is a bustle to prepare a meal or a snack and drinks. The visitor is obliged to accept, even if he only takes a token amount. Malays generally eat with the fingers of their right hand only. Before any meal commences, the youngest member passes salt around and a pinch is placed on the tongue to refresh the mouth. No one rushes to gobble food.**"**

Rafi Fernandez

Rendang and Curries
Meat Dishes

In terms of meat consumption, Westerners are far more carnivorous than the peoples of Southest Asia. In Thailand, as in many other countries, a little meat goes a long way when it is combined with vegetables and sauces and served with vast quantities of rice. Meat is frequently reserved for special meals and holidays, and then it becomes the centerpiece of an extravagant meal. The majority of Thailand's population is Buddhist, so they are not allowed to butcher animals; thus, the slaughtering is all done by the Chinese and the Muslims.

Because meat is expensive, no part of the animal is wasted, as we found in the vast wholesale meat market in Bangkok. We saw all the parts of pigs and beef, actually water buffalo. There were stomachs, ears, heads, feet, and we knew that we had eaten some of them in the various dishes. However, prepared properly, even what would be considered a throw-away, or lowly, meat in North America can be turned into a tasty meal. And how about some stir-fried locusts with dried chiles? We never had the opportunity to try them but understand that they become very crunchy and are a little sweet.

The majority of the Thai recipes in this chapter are quick and easy to prepare, such as Spicy Sautéed Pork with Chiles and Basil (page 123). The basil in this recipe is vastly different from the garden variety; it can be found in Asian markets and is called holy basil or Oriental basil, and it imparts a unique flavor to this dish. The cilantro, peanuts, and chiles in Thai Minced Pork or Galloping Horses (page 124) really make this dish sparkle. Stir-Fried Mushroom–Chile Beef (page 126) is enlivened with fresh ginger, chiles, and fish sauce; it gives new meaning to tired, old stir-fry dishes! Fresh vegetables add interest to Thai Beef Salad (page 128), which is accompanied by a fish sauce dressing and even more chiles.

Since curries were transferred to Southeast Asia (from India), we have included a few interesting ones. Thai Muslim Curry (*gaeng mussamun*, page 130) had its origins in India, as the word *mussaman* is thought to be a corruption of the word "Muslim." This curry also uses spices that are not found in other, more traditional Thai dishes. Thai curries tend to be quite hot, and Hot Beef Curry with Lemongrass and Citrus (page 125) is no exception—six Thai chiles are included for your gustatory sweating pleasure. Beef in Red Curry Sauce (page 131) is also spicy and has a reddish hue because of the addition of red curry paste. Red curry is reserved mainly for beef dishes, to compensate for the strong taste of the meat. Another version of red curry sauce is found in Royal Thai Beef Curry (page 132), which includes spicy red curry paste, kaffir lime leaves, vegetables, and coconut milk.

Singapore is another food mecca of Southeast Asia, and with its meticulous hawker stalls and fine restaurants, almost any kind of cuisine can be found on this island city–country. It has one of the world's most famous hotels, Raffles, and it also has an incredible number of fine, diverse eating establishments. An interesting dish, Singapore Noodles (page 134), is rich with the diverse tastes of vegetables and spices. Sautéed Pork in Tamarind Sauce (page 136) is a spicy *Nonya* specialty that is literally rich with chiles, tamarind, and salted soybeans.

From another incendiary area, Bali, we include two recipes that are very tasty, but guaranteed to numb your taste buds. Spicy Mixed *Satays* (page 138) include bird's eye chiles, with just a little peanut butter. The recipe also includes chicken—which can be used on its own, because most people in Bali are Balinese Hindu and do not eat beef. For those who do eat beef, we include Balinese-Style Beef Strips (page 133), for which pork can be substituted, and its flavors of garlic, ginger, and chiles.

To continue this Indonesian taste tour, we offer the classic West Sumatran *Rendang* (page 137), in which beef or water buffalo is slowly simmered with chile-infused coconut milk. Hot and Spicy Fried Shredded Beef (page 140) is enhanced by the flavors of shrimp paste and coriander. Since much of Indonesia is predominantly Muslim, it would seem that pork would be hard to find. However, the big clue is to find a good Chinese butcher, who will always be happy to supply you with some good cuts. Spicy Pork in Eggplant (page 142) is another example of how a little meat goes a long way, with the addition of vegetables and the spice of chiles. It's also another example of how people of different religious beliefs can co-exist on the level of food and good old capitalism.

Indonesian Beef, Prawn, and Noodle Curry (page 143) covers all the bases because it also includes chicken. The curry powder, fresh vegetables, and chiles make this a real taste treat; the noodles make it a complete meal. West Sumatra Barbecue (page 144) uses beef hearts and tongue as part of its *satays*. Cooked properly, with all of the spices and chiles, this is truly a dish that should be tried. Since *satays* are so popular in Indonesia, we have included one more, Beef Satay with Spicy Sauce (page 146). It is redolent with peanuts, chile, ginger, and tamarind.

Water buffalo, a beef substitute in Laos, as well as in many other Southeast Asian countries, is extremely expensive. It is used raw, pounded to a paste; the skin is also dried and is a frequent ingredient in many Laotian recipes. The meat is also cooked in stews on special occasions. In the hands of a skillful cook, water buffalo meat can be made into delicious dishes that could pass as beef. Braised Water Buffalo Stew with Chiles (page 148) is a heady treat; garlic, as well as fresh vegetables, round out this spicy dish.

Many food writers observe that Vietnamese food is probably the healthiest in all of Southest Asia, with its emphasis on leaves, herbs, and uncooked or slightly cooked vegetables. The Vietnamese use chiles to a much lesser extent than do the cooks in nearby countries, notably Thailand. The cuisine is also more delicate than that of the other Southeast Asian countries. Beef is an expensive purchase for most Vietnamese, and it is always given special treatment, as demonstrated in the recipe for Vietnamese Roast Beef with Ginger Sauce (page 150). The use of fresh mint and raw green onions is very typical.

In Burma, beef is also a rare treat, and pork is by far the most popular meat used. Upper Burma has a large Chinese population, and they are very fond of pork; the Buddhists are also fond of pork, and it is only the Muslims who are prohibited from eating it. The recipe for Spiced Burmese Pork with Green Mango (page 152) demonstrates the Burmese ingenuity for combining unusual ingredients to create a special dish.

Much of Cambodian cuisine is spicy, a trait it shares with its neighbor, Thailand. The very hot and spicy Red Curry Cambogee with Meat and Peanuts (page 147) is frequently served at small, outdoor restaurants because of its ease of preparation. This recipe was collected at just such a place, and it was eaten with gusto, as the locals waited for a heat reaction! The Cambogee Beef (page 149) has a hint of sweetness and is similar to the *satays* of Indonesia; the grilled meat can also be wrapped with salad ingredients and dipped into a sauce, as is frequently done in Vietnam, Cambodia's neighbor to the east.

Unlike other Southeast Asian countries, whose cuisines have been influenced by the French, British, Chinese, and others, the cuisine of the Philippines has been heavily influenced by the Spanish. Adobo is considered to be the national dish of the country, and it can be made with pork, chicken, beef, or vegetables. Pork in Adobo (*adobong baboy*) (page 154) is a dish with numerous variations, giving full rein to the creativity of the cook. Sometimes the meat is cut up or left whole, as the roast is in this recipe. The dominant flavor, however, is always that of garlic and vinegar.

Spicy Sautéed Pork with Chiles and Basil

(*Moo Pad Bai Kra Pow*)

From Thailand comes this hot and spicy dish that is delicious and very easy to prepare. The *bai kra pow* or holy basil (also called purple basil or Oriental basil) used in this recipe is often available in Asian markets; if it is not, substitute fresh mint. Serve this dish with cooked rice noodles.

2 tablespoons vegetable oil

6 garlic cloves, finely minced

5 fresh green serrano or jalapeño chiles, seeds and stems removed, finely chopped

2 pounds ground pork

3 tablespoons fish sauce (*nam pla*)

2 tablespoons dark soy sauce

1/4 cup sugar

1/2 cup chopped, fresh *bai kra pow* (holy basil)

Heat the oil in a large wok or skillet, add the garlic and sauté it carefully, taking care not to burn it. Add the chiles and stir-fry over medium heat for 30 seconds; then add the pork and continue cooking, breaking up the meat, until all the pink is gone.

Stir in the remaining ingredients until the mixture is well blended and hot, about 1 minute.

Serves: 4 to 6

Heat Scale: Medium

Thai Minced Pork or Galloping Horses

(*Ma Ho or Mah Haw*)

We have found that *mah haw* translates literally as "horses of the Haw people," a tribal group that migrated to northern Thailand from Yunan, in China. Make this great recipe, and you'll create a history of your own. The combination of the pork, fish sauce, sugar, peanuts, and cilantro creates a unique taste sensation. Serve it over hot cooked rice. It is sometimes served as an appetizer over fruit.

2 tablespoons vegetable oil

5 cloves garlic, minced

4 fresh cilantro roots, crushed; or substitute 2 tablespoons chopped fresh cilantro leaves and stems

1 pound lean pork, coarsely ground or finely minced

4 tablespoons roasted peanuts, coarsely ground

3 tablespoons fish sauce (*nam pla*)

Freshly ground black pepper

3 tablespoons palm sugar or brown sugar

3 fresh jalapeño or serrano chiles, seeded, stems removed, and finely chopped

3 tablespoons chopped fresh cilantro

Hot cooked rice

Heat the vegetable oil in a wok or skillet. Add the garlic and cilantro and fry on low heat for a few seconds. Add the pork, the peanuts, fish sauce, ground black pepper, sugar, chiles, and the 3 tablespoons of chopped cilantro. Cook until the mixture is dark brown in color and the liquid starts to dissipate.

Serve the pork mixture over hot cooked rice.

Variation: Serve fresh, sliced mandarin oranges and fresh cubed pineapple along with this dish.

Serves: 4

Heat Scale: Medium

Hot Beef Curry with Lemongrass and Citrus

(*Gaeng Ped Korat*)

This spicy curry comes from Korat, northeast of Bangkok, and it is infused with freshly ground spices, chiles, and the palate pleaser, lemongrass. Remember, freshly ground spices add more flavor and freshness to the dish than do the bottled spices in your cupboard. Serve this dish with hot cooked rice.

6 dried red cayenne or Thai chiles, seeded, soaked in water, then chopped

Zest of 1 lime

1 tablespoon whole black pepper-corns

1 tablespoon coarsely chopped fresh ginger

1 teaspoon shrimp paste

2 stalks lemongrass, the white bulb slightly mashed

5 shallots, coarsely chopped

1 tablespoon fresh cilantro

2 teaspoons cumin seeds

2 tablespoons vegetable oil

1 pound lean ground beef; or 1 pound lean boneless beef cut into paper-thin strips

1 cup chicken stock

3 tablespoons fish sauce (*nam pla*)

Put the first nine ingredients in a food processor or blender and puree them, adding 1 or 2 teaspoons of the oil to make a paste. Scrape this mixture into a large bowl, add the beef, and mix until the beef is well coated.

Heat 1 tablespoon of the oil in a wok or large skillet and, over medium heat, stir-fry the beef-curry paste mixture for 1 minute, or until the beef loses its pink tinge. Add the chicken stock and bring the mixture to a boil. Cover and simmer for 30 minutes, or until the beef is cooked (or the strips are tender). Stir in the fish sauce and serve.

Serves: 4

Heat Scale: Hot

Stir-Fried Mushroom–Chile Beef

(*Neua Pad Prik*)

This stir-fry dish from Thailand contains some interesting ingredients that complement each other in taste and texture. It also contains bell peppers, as well as hot and spicy chile peppers, known as *prik* in Thailand. Because the flavors are so intense, we suggest serving it with hot cooked rice.

2-inch piece fresh ginger

1 tablespoon soy sauce

3 cloves garlic

1 tablespoon palm sugar, or substitute dark brown sugar

1 1/2 pounds tender beef fillet, thinly sliced

2 tablespoons vegetable oil

1 green bell pepper, seeded and cored and cut into 1/2 inch pieces

3 dried mushrooms, Chinese or shiitake, rehydrated in hot water, rinsed, and sliced; reserve the liquid

1 jar miniature (baby) corn, drained and rinsed

3 serrano or jalapeño chiles, seeds and stems removed, and cut into rings

4 scallions, white part and tender green, sliced

2/3 cup beef stock

2 tablespoons reserved mushroom liquid

1 tablespoon fish sauce (*nam pla*)

2 tablespoons oyster sauce

Put the first four ingredients in a miniblender and puree until the mixture is smooth. If it becomes too thick to mix, add a teaspoon or more of the soy sauce. Place the meat slices in a large bowl and cover with the pureed mixture, tossing to coat. Allow the beef to marinate for 30 minutes at room temperature.

    Heat the oil in a wok or large skillet. Add the beef strips and stir-fry at high heat until the pink color is gone. Lower the heat slightly, push the meat to one side of the pan, and add the bell pepper and mushrooms and sauté them for 30 seconds. Then add the corn, chiles, and scallions and combine with the other pan ingredients. Add the beef stock and the mushroom liquid and cook at medium low heat for 1 minute.

Stir in the fish sauce and the oyster sauce and serve hot.

Serves: 4 to 6

Heat Scale: Medium

Thai Beef Salad

(*Yam Neua*)

This recipe is from Gloria Zimmerman, who was one of the guest chefs and cookbook authors we met during the Hot & Spicy Asian Weekend at the Mohonk Mountain House. Gloria is co-author (with Bach Ngo) of *The Classic Cuisine of Vietnam*. She and the kitchen staff prepared this recipe for at least 100 people at the event, but (luckily for us) she has scaled it down here to serve the more manageable number of 4! The salad is substantial, delicious, and spicy, and makes a terrific luncheon entrée, preceded by one of the lighter soups from Chapter 4.

2 pounds sirloin steak, 1 inch thick

The Salad

1 small head of Boston (Bibb) lettuce

1 cucumber, peeled, seeded, and sliced

1 stalk lemongrass (bulb only), minced

2 tablespoons chopped fresh mint leaves

2 tablespoons chopped fresh cilantro

The Dressing

2 tablespoons fish sauce (*nam pla*)

4 tablespoons fresh lime juice

2 to 4 red serrano chiles, seeded, stems removed, finely chopped

1 teaspoon sugar

Garnish

1 red onion, peeled and thinly sliced

Broil the steak in the oven or over charcoal until it has reached the rare point. Cut the steak into 1-inch slices and place the slices on a platter.

Arrange the lettuce on a serving platter or on individual plates. Arrange the cucumber over the lettuce, followed by the lemongrass, mint, and cilantro.

In a small glass jar, combine all of the ingredients for the dressing and shake.
   Divide the steak between the 4 plates or arrange it on the platter with the salad. Arrange the sliced red onion over the steak and drizzle with the dressing.

Serves: 4

Heat Scale: Medium

Thai Muslim Curry

(*Gaeng Mussaman*)

The spices used in this curry indicate its Indian origins, as they are similar to those found in *garam masala*. This very festive and special curry is usually served on special occasions, such as weddings. The final result should have a taste that balances sweet and sour and salty; if it seems too sweet, add a little more lime juice.

4 cups Coconut Milk (page 12)

2 pounds beef, chuck roast or another inexpensive cut, with all fat cut off, and cut into 1½-inch chunks

1 cup dry-roasted peanuts

2 to 4 cups Muslim Curry Paste (page 42)

2 cups thick Coconut Cream (page 12, optional)

4 cinnamon sticks, 2 to 3 inches long

6 whole cardamom seeds

3 tablespoons fish sauce (*nam pla*)

2 tablespoons palm sugar; or substitute dark brown sugar

3 tablespoons Tamarind Sauce (page 14)

Juice of 1 lime, about 2 tablespoons

Pour the coconut milk into a large, heavy skillet and bring to a slow boil; add the beef chunks and the peanuts and simmer the mixture for 45 minutes to 1 hour, until the meat is tender. Remove the beef with a slotted spoon to another pan and keep warm.

Continue to boil the coconut liquid until it is reduced by about a half and stir in the curry paste and the coconut cream, if desired. Simmer the mixture for 1 minute, and then return the meat to the simmering mixture. Stir in the remaining ingredients and simmer for 5 more minutes.

Serve with hot cooked rice.

Serves: 6 to 8

Heat Scale: Medium to Hot

Beef in Red Curry Sauce

(*Gaeng Nuea*)

This is a classic hot and spicy Thai curry dish that is often prepared at home. Traditionally, one of the many kinds of Thai eggplants is used, *makeua poh* or *makeua peuang*, but they are sometimes difficult to find. The flavor won't be the same, but feel free to add cubes of Japanese eggplant, or for the look of a traditional Thai curry, add some green peas.

3 cups Coconut Milk (page 12)

5 tablespoons Red Curry Paste (page 41)

1½ pounds prepared chuck steak, thinly sliced

1 teaspoon lemon zest; or 2 crushed kaffir lime leaves

2 teaspoons salt

4 cups bamboo shoots

3 tablespoons fish sauce (*nam pla*)

2 teaspoons palm sugar or brown sugar

1 cup eggplant, zucchini, or yellow squash cut into 4-inch cubes

2 green serrano or jalapeño chiles, seeds and stems removed, and sliced into rings

2 cups coarsely chopped fresh basil leaves

Heat 1 cup of the coconut milk in a large, heavy Dutch oven. When it is hot, stir in the red curry paste and cook the mixture until small drops of oil appear on the surface. Continue to cook, stirring the mixture, for 1 minute.

Add the meat and simmer the mixture for 5 minutes, making sure there is some liquid in the pan. If the liquid starts to disappear before the meat is cooked, add a little more of the coconut milk. At the end of the 5 minutes, add the remaining coconut milk, lemon zest or lime leaves, salt, bamboo shoots, fish sauce, palm sugar, and eggplant and simmer for 10 minutes, or until the beef is tender.

Stir in the chiles and the basil and simmer for 2 minutes.

Serve with steamed rice.

Serves: 6

Heat Scale: Hot

Royal Thai Beef Curry

(*Gaeng Ped Neua*)

This recipe was a favorite of King Rama V, who reigned in Thailand from 1869 to 1910. It is tasty, rich, and very spicy and should be served with hot cooked rice or cooked Thai noodles.

1/2 cup Coconut Cream (page 12)

Red Curry Paste (page 41)

4 kaffir lime leaves, torn into small pieces

1 tablespoon fish sauce (*nam pla*)

2 teaspoons jaggery or palm sugar; or 1 tablespoon brown sugar

2 1/2 cups Coconut Milk (page 12)

1 1/2 pounds beef, sliced thinly across the grain into 1-inch pieces

1 cup cubed eggplant

1/3 cup fresh sweet basil leaves

2 fresh green serrano or jalapeño chiles, stems and seeds removed, thinly sliced

2 fresh red serrano or jalapeño chiles, stems and seeds removed, thinly sliced

In a small, heavy skillet, boil the coconut cream until it reaches the oily stage, then stir in the red curry paste. Add the lime leaves, fish sauce, and sugar. Set aside.

Pour the coconut milk into a saucepan and add the beef. Simmer for 8 to 10 minutes. Add the seasoned curry paste to the simmering beef, bring to a boil, and add the eggplant, basil, and chiles. Reduce the heat and simmer for 3 minutes.

Variation: Try this dish with Green Curry Paste (page 40).

Serves: 4 to 6

Heat Scale: Hot

Balinese-Style Beef Strips

(*Daging Masak Bali*)

Although most people on the island of Bali are Hindu, hot and tasty beef dishes are still to be found, perhaps at a snack food stall or a large feast. This Balinese dish is usually served with hot rice, cooked vegetables, and a selection of *sambals* from Chapter 2.

4 cloves garlic, minced

2 tablespoons chopped fresh ginger

6 red or green serrano or jalapeño chiles, seeded and chopped

1/2 teaspoon shrimp paste

1 1/2 cups chopped onion

3 tablespoons oil

1 1/2 pounds beef, thinly sliced

1 cup water

3 tablespoons Tamarind Sauce (page 14)

1 1/2 tablespoons soy sauce

2 teaspoons palm sugar; or substitute brown sugar

Salt to taste

Put the garlic, ginger, chiles, shrimp paste, and onion into a blender or food processor and blend until the mixture is smooth.

Heat the oil in a large, heavy skillet or a wok and add the blended mixture. Fry the mixture, stirring constantly, for 4 to 5 minutes until it no longer sticks to the pan. Add the beef strips and stir-fry them until the pink color disappears. Add the remaining ingredients and simmer the mixture until the beef is tender and most of the liquid has evaporated.

Serves: 6

Heat Scale: Hot

Singapore Noodles

This recipe comes from the Golden Dragon Restaurant in Colorado Springs, Colorado, the owners of which have traveled extensively. Donald Louie and his sisters Sue Louie and Linda Gant collected this recipe on their travels and have adapted it to use in their restaurant. As Sue Louie says of this recipe, "the first bite is a bit mild, but as you keep eating, the dish seems to get hotter and hotter." AiKan products are available at gourmet shops and through mail order.

1 cup rice stick noodles

Hot water

3 to 4 tablespoons vegetable oil

1 pound cooked or raw pork

1 cup bean sprouts

1 cup sliced *bok choy*

1 cup red and green bell peppers, chopped

1 cup chicken stock or water

4 teaspoons AiKan Sweet & Spicy Sauce (see note for substitution)

12 small shrimp, cleaned, cooked, and peeled

1/4 teaspoon curry powder

Pinch of salt and sugar, to cut the bitterness of the vegetables

Place the rice noodles in a bowl, add enough hot water to cover, and soak for 5 minutes. Drain the noodles and set aside.

In a wok or large skillet, heat the oil over medium high heat. Brown the pork and add the bean sprouts, bok choy, bell peppers, and chicken stock or water and bring to a boil. Add the drained rice noodles, AiKan sauce, shrimp, curry powder, and the pinch of salt and sugar. Toss well in the wok until all of the ingredients are hot and serve immediately.

Serves: 2

Heat Scale: Mild to Medium, depending on how much sauce you use

Note Here's a substitute if the AiKan Sweet & Spicy Sauce is not available. Combine all ingredients in a bowl.

1 teaspoon soy sauce

1/2 teaspoon Basic Spice Islands
    Chile Paste (page 18)

1/2 teaspoon *hoisin* sauce

1/2 teaspoon cooking sherry

1/2 teaspoon rice vinegar

1/2 teaspoon ground ginger

1/2 teaspoon minced garlic

1/2 teaspoon ground hot red chile
    powder

1 teaspoon Major Grey's Indian
    Curry

Sautéed Pork in Tamarind Sauce

(*Babi Assam*)

This dish is one hot and spicy *Nonya* specialty from Singapore. If you ever go to Singapore, make sure you get the taste buds tuned up; hot and spicy is a way of life, just as it is here in the Southwest—no exceptions. Serve this intense dish with hot, cooked white rice and a cool cucumber salad. It's a sizzler! And, forget to count the fat calories on this one.

2 tablespoons vegetable oil

4 candlenuts or macadamia nuts, ground

1 tablespoon shrimp paste

2 shallots, minced

2 tablespoons preserved, salted soybeans, pounded

1 1/4 pounds pork belly, cut into thick strips, lightly sautéed and drained; or substitute thick-cut bacon

1 cup Tamarind Sauce (page 14)

8 fresh green serrano or jalapeño chiles, seeds and stems removed, sliced thinly

6 fresh red serrano or jalapeño chiles, seeds and stems removed, sliced thinly

1 cup chicken stock

2 tablespoons sugar

Heat the oil in a wok or large skillet, add the ground nuts, shrimp paste, and shallots, and sauté until the mixture is light brown. Stir in the soybean paste and stir over low heat for 1 minute.

Add the pork, tamarind sauce, chiles, 1/2 cup of the chicken stock, 1 tablespoon of the sugar, and bring to a boil. Reduce the heat to a simmer, cover half of the wok, and simmer the mixture for 30 minutes, stirring once. If the mixture seems too thick, add a little more stock. Taste the mixture, and if it seems too tart, sprinkle in more of the sugar and simmer a few more minutes.

Serves: 4 to 6

Heat Scale: Extremely Hot

West Sumatran Rendang

(*Rendang*)

Here is the traditional way the Sumatrans cook the often-tough meat of the water buffalo—by slowly simmering it in coconut milk. This recipe takes some time to make, but it's worth it. It keeps for months in the freezer, so make a lot. Serve the *rendang* with any of the rice dishes in Chapter 8.

6 shallots

3 cloves garlic

5 fresh red serrano or jalapeño
    chiles, seeded

1 tablespoon freshly grated ginger

1 teaspoon turmeric

Pinch of salt

8 cups Coconut Milk (page 12)

3 1/2 pounds chuck roast, cut into
    1-inch cubes

Combine the shallots, garlic, chiles, ginger, turmeric, and salt in a blender or food processor and grind to a coarse paste.

    Heat the coconut milk in a large pot, and add the paste and the meat. Cook over low heat, uncovered, for about 1 1/2 to 2 hours, or until the meat is quite tender. Stir the mixture every 15 minutes or so. The sauce will become very thick.

    Raise the heat and, stirring continuously, continue to cook the mixture until all the sauce has been incorporated into the meat and the meat becomes golden brown, about 1/2 hour.

Serves: 6

Heat Scale: Medium

Spicy Mixed Satays

Chile Pepper correspondent Rosemary Ann Ogilvie collected this classic recipe in Bali. She says, "Probably the most well-known of all the Indonesian dishes are the *satays*. They can be served as an appetizer as well as an entrée. Soak the bamboo skewers overnight or for a couple of hours to prevent them from burning while grilling."

Satay Sauce

1/2 cup peanuts, roasted and salted

1 onion, chopped

1/2 cup smooth peanut butter

2 cloves garlic, minced

1/3 cup chutney, as hot as you prefer

1/4 cup peanut oil

1 tablespoon light soy sauce

1/4 cup lemon juice

6 dried bird's eye chiles (chiltepins), stems removed, soaked in water, minced fine; or substitute piquin chiles

The Satays

1 pound rump steak, cut in thin strips

6 large chicken breast fillets, cut in 1- to 1 1/2-inch cubes

1 pound pork fillet or boned pork loin, cut in 1- to 1 1/2-inch cubes

To make the sauce, blend or process the peanuts until finely chopped, but not ground smooth. Add the onion and process for another 20 seconds. Add the peanut butter, garlic, chutney, the oil, soy sauce, lemon juice, and chiles and continue to process until smooth.

Thread the meats onto skewers. Don't combine the meats—use one type of meat on one skewer. Brush the meats well with the *satay* sauce, and grill or barbecue the *satays* until tender, brushing occasionally with the sauce while cooking.

Serve with the remaining *satay* sauce for dipping.

Variation: Serve the *satays* with Indonesian Peanut–Chile Sauce (page 24).

Serves: 4

Heat Scale: Medium

Hot and Spicy Fried Shredded Beef

(*Abon Daging*)

This dish is also known as *dendeng pedas* in Indonesia and *be sampi mesitsit* in Bali. At its most basic, it is one in which beef is boiled, shredded, and then fried with chiles and various spices. In Bali, this dish is served fresh over rice, and it is also deep fried to serve as a finger food appetizer. Research leads us to believe that, in times past, this cooking method was used on cuts of old, tough beef to make something interesting and palatable.

2 pounds beef, topside or arm roast

Water to cover

1 teaspoon salt

4 cloves garlic

2 teaspoons dried shrimp paste

1 tablespoon fresh lime juice

1 teaspoon whole black peppercorns

1 teaspoon coriander seeds

1/4 teaspoon ground coriander

2 teaspoons palm sugar; or substi-tute brown sugar

2 tablespoons sliced galangal; or substitute 1 teaspoon powdered galangal

4 fresh serrano or jalapeño chiles, seeds and stems removed

3 tablespoons oil, preferably peanut

Wash the beef and place it in a heavy pot, with enough water to cover it, and add the salt. Bring the water to a boil and then reduce the heat to a simmer and cover the pot. Cook for 1 1/2 to 2 hours, or until the meat is very tender. Remove the meat from the stock; allow it to drain in a colander until it is cool enough to handle. Shred the meat, using two forks, one in each hand, pulling in opposite directions. Discard the fat.

Combine all of the remaining ingredients, except the oil, in a blender and blend until smooth.

Heat the oil in a large, heavy skillet and add the blended mixture. Sauté the mixture for 1 to 2 minutes over low heat.

Add the shredded beef to the sautéed mixture and stir it in well to coat. Serve immediately over hot cooked rice, with vegetables from Chapter 8 and *sambals* from Chapter 2.

Serves: 6

Heat Scale: Medium

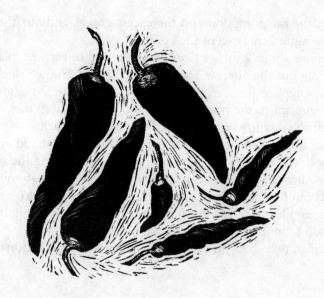

Spicy Pork in Eggplant

(*Bakso Terong*)

This Indonesian recipe illustrates the use of vegetables with meat to make the meat go further. Since the eggplant has such a mild flavor, the use of hot sauce and garlic spices up an otherwise bland dish. Serve the eggplant with one of the side dishes from Chapter 8.

1 pound ground pork
1/2 teaspoon salt
1/4 teaspoon freshly ground black pepper
1 cup chopped onions
2 cloves garlic, minced

1 egg, beaten
2 teaspoons any *sambal* from Chapter 2, or substitute a hot sauce such as Tabasco
2 medium eggplants
2 tablespoons vegetable oil

Quickly sauté the pork, drain off the excess grease, and mix the pork with all remaining ingredients except the eggplant.

Remove about 2 inches from the stem end of each eggplant and then carefully dig out the interior, leaving a shell about 3/4 inch thick. Cube the cored-out eggplant flesh, heat the vegetable oil, sauté the eggplant quickly, add the eggplant to the pork mixture, and toss lightly to mix.

Stuff the mixture into the cored-out eggplant shells.

Place the stuffed eggplants in a deep saucepan and add enough water to come about 3 inches up the sides of the eggplants. Bring the water to a boil, reduce the heat to a rolling simmer, and cook for 30 to 45 minutes, until the eggplants can be easily pierced with a knife. Carefully remove them from the saucepan, and let them rest for 5 minutes. Then cut the eggplants into 1-inch slices, taking care that the filling doesn't fall out.

Arrange two slices on each plate and serve with additional hot sauce.

Serves: 4

Heat Scale: Mild

Indonesian Beef, Prawn, and Noodle Curry

This is a great fork dish for a party. *Chile Pepper* author Rosemary Ann Ogilvie commented: "I was given this recipe twenty-five years ago when I was a teenager just discovering the delights of cooking, and I believe it still takes some beating for sheer taste!"

1 pound tender beef, sliced into thin strips

1/2 pound prawns or shrimp, shelled and deveined

1 cup cooked chicken, sliced into thin strips

2 tablespoons curry powder (preferably freshly made or imported)

2 tablespoons vegetable oil

1 tablespoon chopped celery

1 large onion, chopped

2 cups finely sliced carrots

1 cup shredded cabbage

4 to 6 bird's eye chiles (chiltepins), stems removed, soaked in water, finely minced; or substitute piquin or cayenne chiles

1/2 teaspoon ground black pepper

2 cloves garlic, crushed

1/2 pound thin egg noodles, cooked and rinsed well

1 cup chicken stock

Combine the beef, prawns, chicken, and curry powder in a large bowl. Heat the oil in a large, heavy skillet or wok and stir-fry the mixture for a couple of minutes, or until the beef is almost done. Add the vegetables, chiles, pepper, and garlic, and toss for another 3 minutes.

Add the noodles and chicken stock and simmer for 7 to 10 minutes, stirring occasionally.

Serves: 6 to 8

Heat Scale: Medium

West Sumatra Barbecue

(*Satay Padang* No. 1)

This *satay* recipe is from Padang in west Sumatra. The different kinds of meats create a contrast in textures; we have listed the meats that are traditionally used, but feel free to experiment with your own combinations. The abundant chiles contrast nicely with the spices and lemongrass. Serve the barbecued meats with cubes of fresh cucumber.

2 tablespoons peanut or corn oil

3/4 cup chopped onion

6 garlic cloves, minced

2 beef hearts, cut into 1-inch cubes

2 pounds beef chuck, cut into 1-inch cubes

1 1/2 pounds veal or beef tongue, cut into 1-inch cubes

1 pound beef tripe, cut into 1-inch square pieces

4 fresh serrano or jalapeño chiles, seeds and stems removed, pureed into a paste

2 tablespoons chopped fresh cilantro

1 teaspoon ground cumin

1 teaspoon salt

1 tablespoon turmeric

1 tablespoon finely chopped fresh ginger

1 two-inch piece galangal; or double the amount of fresh ginger

3 square inches of lemon peel or bitter orange

2 *salam* leaves; or substitute 2 bay leaves

1 two-inch stick of cinnamon

1 cup water

2 stalks lemongrass, bulb part only, mashed slightly

3 1/2 cups Coconut Milk (page 12)

The Sauce

1 cup Coconut Milk (page 12)

1/2 cup rice flour

Reserved sauce from meat

1 large tomato, peeled, seeded, and coarsely chopped

Bamboo skewers, soaked in water for 30 minutes

Heat the oil in a large, heavy skillet and sauté the onion for 30 seconds. Add the garlic and sauté lightly, taking care not to burn the garlic.

Add the cubed meats and toss until they are coated with the onion–garlic mixture, adding more oil if necessary. Then add the remaining ingredients, except the 3 1/2 cups coconut milk and the sauce ingredients. Cover the skillet and cook over low heat for 45 minutes to 1 hour, or until the meats are tender. Stir in the 3 1/2 cups coconut milk and simmer for an additional 30 minutes.

Using a slotted spoon, remove the meats to a bowl.

Pour the meat sauce into a saucepan and then measure 2 1/2 cups of the sauce back into the skillet. Bring the sauce to a slow, rolling boil.
Pour the remaining 1 cup coconut milk and the rice flour into a small glass jar with a tight-fitting lid and shake vigorously to blend the ingredients into a thin mixture. Slowly pour the mixture into the boiling meat sauce, stirring constantly until the mixture thickens slightly, and then add the chopped tomato; reduce the heat to a simmer. The mixture should resemble a thick white sauce.

Combine different cuts of meat (five or six kinds) on the soaked bamboo skewers, so that the textures vary. Broil in the oven or charcoal broil the skewers until the meat starts to crisp a little, 2 to 3 minutes per side. Then, dip the skewers into the hot meat sauce and arrange them on a heated platter. Serve the sauce in a warmed bowl for extra dipping pleasure.

Serves: 10 to 12

Heat Scale: Medium

Beef Satay with Spicy Sauce

(*Satay Padang* No. 2)

Anyone who has ever visited Malaysia or Indonesia will find it hard to forget the multitude of *satays* that are served everywhere. *Satay* is practically the national food, and it is served as part of the meal or can be purchased from a street vendor as a snack. Almost every kind of meat and shellfish is used; in Bali, turtle meat is the favorite choice.

1 clove garlic

1 small onion, peeled and quartered

1 cup roasted peanuts

3 fresh serrano or jalapeño chiles, seeds and stems removed

1 teaspoon sugar

1 inch fresh, peeled ginger

3 tablespoons Tamarind Sauce (page 14)

1 tablespoon fresh lime juice

2 tablespoons water

1/4 cup Coconut Milk (page 12)

1 tablespoon soybean sauce

Salt and pepper

1 pound beef fillet, cut into 1-inch cubes

1/2 cup Coconut Milk (page 12)

Bamboo skewers, soaked in water for 30 minutes

Place the garlic, onion, peanuts, chiles, sugar, ginger, and tamarind sauce in a blender and blend until the mixture is smooth.

Fry the blended mixture in a small, heavy skillet for 1 minute. Add the lime juice, water, coconut milk, and soybean sauce and bring the mixture to a quick boil. Reduce the heat to simmer and cook the mixture for 1 minute. Set the mixture aside.

Lightly salt and pepper the beef cubes and toss them to coat. Thread 5 to 6 cubes of beef on each skewer, brush the meat with the coconut milk, and then brush on the chile mixture.

Broil or barbecue the meat, about 3 minutes per side. Place the grilled meat skewers on a heated platter and serve them with the remaining dipping sauce in a small bowl.

Serves: 3 to 4

Heat Scale: Medium

Red Curry Cambogee with Meat and Peanuts

Richard Sterling collected this recipe when he was in Cambodia. It is hot, spicy, and easy to make, as well as being an authentic taste of Cambodia. Serve with a refreshing cucumber salad.

5 cups Red Curry Cambogee
   (page 35)
³/₄ pound diced beef

2 potatoes, peeled and diced
¹/₂ cup chopped peanuts
2 cups bean sprouts

Heat the curry sauce in a large skillet or wok; add the meat and potatoes to the curry sauce. Simmer for 20 to 30 minutes or until the meat and potatoes are done.

   Garnish with the peanuts and serve over the bean sprouts.

Serves: 4

Heat Scale: Medium

Braised Water Buffalo Stew with Chiles

(*Seum Sin Kuai*)

Don't let the use of water buffalo meat in this recipe from Laos prevent you from making it. Simply substitute buffalo meat, which is available from specialty markets and through mail order. Eggplant is often used in Laotian cuisine; it thickens and adds richness to stewed dishes.

2 pounds buffalo meat, cut into
  3/4-inch cubes, or substitute
  beef

7 slices galangal (or substitute 3 tablespoons chopped fresh ginger)

1 onion, sliced

1/2 teaspoon salt

Water to cover

2 tablespoons fish sauce (*nam pla*)

1 eggplant, washed and sliced

1 small head of garlic, roasted,
  peeled, and chopped

1 cup sliced green beans

3 to 4 fresh red serrano or jalapeño
  chiles, seeds and stems removed
  and cut into rings

Juice of 1 fresh lime

1/2 cup chopped green onions,
  white and light green part only

1/4 cup chopped fresh mint or basil

Garnish: chopped fresh cilantro,
  freshly ground black pepper,
  thin slices of cucumber

Place the meat, galangal, onion, and salt in a large, heavy soup pot and cover with water. When the water boils, add the fish sauce and the sliced eggplant. Cook at a rolling simmer for 10 minutes, checking to see when the eggplant is tender. When the eggplant is tender, remove it from the pot, mash it, and set it aside. Cover the meat and continue to simmer until it is tender, about 1 hour.

When the meat is tender, add the mashed eggplants, garlic, green beans, chiles, and lime juice. Boil lightly, uncovered, for 10 minutes until the beans are done, and the sauce has thickened slightly.

Stir in the green onions and mint or basil, and serve in large soup bowls. Garnish with the cilantro, black pepper, and cucumber.

Serves: 6

Heat Scale: Medium

Cambogee Beef

When the aroma of this dish rises up from the cooking fire, it tantalizes the nostrils. For the best results, use a mortar and pestle to combine the ingredients; if you don't have one, use a blender. We thank Richard Sterling for this Cambodian recipe, gathered on one of his extensive Southeast Asian trips.

1 pound beef, cut into thin slices
    and threaded onto skewers

Marinade

2 red serrano or jalapeño chiles,
    stems removed

1/4 cup lemongrass, sliced thin

6 kaffir lime leaves or the peel of
    1 lime

4 cloves garlic

1 slice or teaspoon galangal; or
    substitute ginger

1/2 cup oyster sauce

2 tablespoons sugar

1 pinch salt

1/2 cup water

Mash or blend the chiles, lemongrass, lime leaves, garlic, and galangal together. Combine the mixture with the remaining marinade ingredients. Place the mixture in a saucepan, bring to a boil, and boil for 1 minute. Remove from the heat and let cool. Taste for sweetness—it should be present but not dominant.

    Baste the skewered beef with the marinade; place the skewers in the refrigerator for at least 1 hour.

    Grill the skewers over hot coals, keeping the beef at least 4 inches from the heat (lest the sugar burn), until the desired level of doneness is reached.

    Serve with a salad from Chapter 3 and steamed rice.

Serving suggestion: Before cooking, stick a chunk of fresh pineapple on the end of each skewer.

Yield: 8 skewers

Heat Scale: Medium

Vietnamese Roast Beef with Ginger Sauce

(*Be Thui*)

This tasty northern Vietnamese dish is commonly found at restaurants, but seldom prepared at home. The roasted rice powder adds a unique flavor to the dish, and, if you can't find it at an Asian market, it is easy to make at home (see Note). The *tuong* called for in the recipe is a strong-tasting sauce that can sometimes be found in Asian markets; if not, just substitute fish or squid sauce.

1 tablespoon granulated sugar

2 fresh serrano or jalapeño chiles, stems and seeds removed, quartered

1 two-inch piece of fresh ginger root, peeled and sliced

4 cloves garlic

2 tablespoons *tuong*, or substitute 3 tablespoons fish or squid sauce

2 tablespoons chopped fresh mint

2 to 3 tablespoons water

1 pound tender beef fillet

2 tablespoons roasted rice powder (see Note)

5 green onions, white and tender green parts only, shredded

Preheat the oven to 350°F.

Pour the sugar, chiles, ginger, garlic, *tuong* (or substitute), mint, and water into a blender or food processor and puree the mixture. Set the mixture aside to let the flavors blend.

Put aluminum foil into an 8-inch by 8-inch pyrex-type baking dish and put the beef fillet into the dish. Bake the fillet in the preheated oven for 15 to 20 minutes. Remove the fillet from the oven and allow it to sit for a few minutes before slicing. Quarter the fillet, then slice each quarter into thin slices— they should be about 3-inch by 3-inch or 2-inch by 2-inch pieces. Arrange the slices on a heated platter, overlapping them to form a circular design. Sprinkle the rice powder over the beef slices and arrange shredded green onions over the beef.

Serve a few slices of the meat on each plate and let each diner add as much of the reserved ginger sauce as desired.

Serve with steamed vegetables and hot rice.

Serves: 4 to 6

Heat Scale: Mild

Note: To make your own rice powder, cook 1 cup of long-grain rice in a large, heavy skillet over medium heat until it starts to brown, about 3 to 4 minutes, stirring constantly. Shake the skillet to keep the rice from burning, and continue heating the rice. Some recommend that the pan be removed from the heat at various points, to avoid burning. The total cooking time should be about 8 minutes. Remove the rice from the heat and let it reach room temperature. Then pour the cooled rice into a blender and pulverize it.

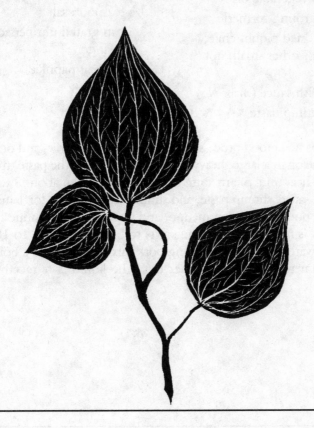

Spiced Burmese Pork with Green Mango

(*Wettha Thayet Thi Chet*)

In Burma, the most popular meat is pork, for a number of reasons. Upper Burma is heavily populated by Chinese, who are traditionally big pork consumers; pork is cheaper than lamb or beef; and pork combines well with a number of diverse ingredients, including the green mango.

2 inches fresh ginger, sliced

3 garlic cloves

1 large onion, cut into eighths

3 tablespoons vegetable oil

1/2 teaspoon ground turmeric

1 tablespoon dried piquin chile, crushed; or other small, hot, dried chile

1/2 teaspoon fish sauce (*nam pla*)

1 teaspoon shrimp paste

1 teaspoon shrimp sauce

2 pounds boneless, lean pork, cut into pieces 2 inches long by 1 inch wide

1/2 teaspoon salt

3/4 cup grated unripened (green) mango

1 teaspoon paprika

3 cups water

In a blender or small food processor, puree the ginger, garlic, and onion to a paste. Heat the oil in a large, heavy skillet and lightly fry the paste, turmeric, and chile over low heat until the mixture becomes red-brown, about 3 to 5 minutes. Stir in the fish sauce, shrimp paste, and shrimp sauce and fry for 1 minute.

Add the pork, salt, green mango, and paprika and continue to stir-fry until the pork is no longer pink and starts to brown, about 8 to 10 minutes.

Stir the water into the simmering pork mixture, bring to a boil, reduce the heat to a simmer, cover, and simmer until the liquid is reduced to 1 cup. It should take about 1 ¹/₄ hours. Check the meat and stir occasionally to prevent sticking and burning. At the end of the cooking period, the sauce should be thick, about the consistency of a thick white sauce.

Serve with steamed rice and stir-fried vegetables.

Serves: 5 to 6

Heat Scale: Medium

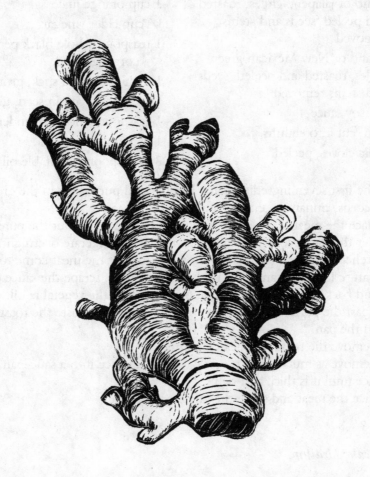

Pork in Adobo

(*Adobong Baboy*)

Adobo is considered the national dish of the Philippines. But it is more than just a dish; it is a style of cooking that has numerous variations and can be made with pork or chicken or fish or vegetables. The one common factor, however, is that a subtle sourness be present. The "sourness" is imparted by the use of vinegar, which also helps to preserve the dish for several days without refrigeration. Note that this recipes requires advance preparation.

3 serrano or jalapeño chiles, roasted and peeled, seeds and stems removed

4 poblano or New Mexican green chiles, roasted and peeled, seeds and stems removed

1/4 cup soy sauce

1 onion, cut into eighths

10 garlic cloves, peeled

1 cup orange juice

1/2 cup cider vinegar

1 teaspoon whole black peppercorns, ground

1 inch cinnamon stick, ground

1/2 teaspoon cumin seed, ground

1 teaspoon whole coriander, ground

1 3-pound pork loin

3 tablespoons vegetable oil

Place the first seven ingredients in a blender and puree. Stir in the ground peppercorns, cinnamon, cumin, and coriander.

Place the meat in a glass (e.g., Pyrex) baking pan. Pour the pureed mixture over the meat, cover with plastic wrap, and refrigerate overnight.

Preheat the oven to 350°F. Before baking, let the meat come to room temperature for about an hour. With a butter knife, scrape the sauce off the roast and back into the pan. Drizzle the pork with the vegetable oil.

Roast the pork for 1 1/2 hours; every 20 minutes, baste the roast with the sauce in the pan.

Remove the roast to a heated platter.

Remove as much fat as possible, pour the sauce into a saucepan, and boil the sauce until it is thick and rich.

Slice the meat and serve the sauce on the side.

Serves: 8

Heat Scale: Medium

Rendang Rituals

❝The prolonged cooking and the spices, especially the chillies, preserve the meat, and it is common for *rendang* to be taken along on long journeys, such as the pilgrimage to Mecca. *Rendang* is then both a reminder of home and a handy dish that saves time—as no [further] cooking is needed apart from boiling the rice to eat with it. Solicitous Sumatran mothers cook, pack, and send it to their children studying or working in the outer islands. If you eat *rendang*—and you should be sure not to miss it—be warned not to put a whole piece in your mouth at once. It is far too rich and spicy to be eaten whole. Break off a small part, then fold it into a spoonful of rice if you want to enjoy it. One should treat all spicy meat dishes with similar respect.**❞**

Yohanni Johns

The Buddhist Egg-Breakers

❝Buddhists cannot slaughter or witness the slaughter of animals; but they can eat animal flesh as long as they are not responsible for the termination of the animal's life. . . As Buddhists grow older they worry a great deal about complying with the ban on killing animals, but they can always get someone else to do the dirty work. In Thailand and Burma, to be truly virtuous, one should never crack an egg. Shopkeepers routinely evade the restraint by keeping a supply of eggs that have been "accidentally" cracked. Wealthy Buddhists ask their servants to break their eggs; the master escapes blame because he didn't do the killing, and the servant escapes blame because he was ordered to do it.**❞**

Marvin Harris

On *Kaeng* Curries

"Like the soups, *kaeng* curries make ingenious use of herbs and aromatic leaves. In fact, some Thai *kaeng* curries contain none of the pungent curry spices at all, relying entirely upon herbs—plus chile, shallots, and sometimes garlic—to provide the zing that a curry should have. Tiny fresh red chiles endow *kaeng phed* with a bright red color and a red-hot power to match—especially if an uncrushed bit of chile finds its way to the tongue. When making their *kaeng* curries, the Thais let the coconut milk boil; this separates the oil from the milk and decorates the sauce with swirls of darker and lighter shades, an effect that is particularly attractive in the red *kaeng phed*. The hot blast of spices and spicy roots in this *kaeng* is tempered by the mellowing presence of basil leaves, but *kaeng phed* is about as far up the scale as most Western visitors want to go."

Rafael Steinberg

And It Didn't Taste Anything Like Chicken

"The Cambodians are great eaters. Their calendar is full of feasts, and any gaps are filled by weddings, births, funerals, and auspicious alignments of the stars. Theirs is a land of abundance. They enjoy regular harvests of rice, wild and cultivated fruits, fresh and saltwater fish, domesticated animals, fowl and game. They love to eat meat. Pork is the most popular and it is excellent, as are all the meats. An English journalist we dined with said of her beefsteak that it was the best she ever had. We didn't tell her it was *luc lac*, water buffalo."

Richard Sterling

Waiter, There's a Centipede in My Soup— And It Has a Raffles Logo on It!

A $160 million restoration of Raffles Hotel in Singapore was completed in 1992. "Yet, her eccentricities are as apparent as ever. The floorboards creak. Virtually no two rooms are exactly alike. Staff whisper of ghostly sightings and new stories have begun to circulate, such as the tale of the centipede. It happened during lunch at the elegant Raffles Grill. When a centipede fell off the chandelier straight into a bowl of soup, the waiter calmly removed the dish, presented a bottle of champagne, and assured the guest that such a visit could only happen at Raffles."

Gretchen Liu

Hot and Herbal Poultry

The old adage "A bird in the hand is worth two in the bush," might well have been the thought of a chef in Southeast Asia. Throughout Asia, birds such as chicken and duck are cooked whole or in parts, cut up, and prepared with the bones in and out. In fact, chicken, which has been domesticated in Asia for many centuries, accounts for a large percentage of the protein consumed by country and urban people alike.

And what perfectly piquant poultry picks we've assembled! We begin with our Vietnamese selections. Please serve these dishes with chopsticks, as Vietnam is the only Southeast Asian country to utilize this Chinese invention. The Vietnamese-Style Beijing Duck (page 162) has a distinct taste enhanced with annatto seeds. Annatto, or achiote, as it is called in Latin America, produces a reddish-orange liquid and becomes flavorful when soaked in hot water.

Clay pot cooking is known to produce meat that will melt in your mouth. We promise our Chicken and Rice in a Clay Pot (page 164) is up to par. Garlic, a vital spice in Asian cooking, is an important part of the Four C's Chicken Curry (page 163). Cinnamon, coriander, cumin, and cayenne are sautéed together to produce an aromatic tour of the Far East. And no tour would be complete without a side trip including lemongrass. We combine chicken with this peppery herb for a spectacular dish, Lemongrass Chicken (page 166). Our final Vietnamese recipe, Fried Chicken with Green Chile (page 167) is the fieriest of our fried chicken specialities. The serrano chiles really add some zip to this dish.

Indonesia consists of nearly 13,700 islands. Each island produces a slightly different version of the highly spiced Indonesian cuisine, the development of which was heavily influenced by Indian and Arab traders. You'll exclaim *"sala-mat makan,"* Indonesian for *bon appetit,* when you taste these island specialties. From our second fried chicken recipe (Not the Colonel's Fried Chicken, page 168), to Santaka Chicken in Lime and Coconut Milk Sauce (page 169), to Spicy Galangal Chicken (page 170), the island fare is fine. The tiny island of Lombok is part of Indonesia and is known for its grilled specialties. Try the Grilled Hot Hen (page 171) for a spicy taste of the islands. Balinese Duck (page 172) is also from that neck of the woods, as is Chicken *Satay* with Spicy Peanut Sauce (page 173) and Chicken-Stuffed Coconut (page 174).

And who could pass up a brush with royalty? His Majesty's Chicken (page 175) is full of pepper, coriander, cardamom, and anise—ingredients that were once reserved for royalty. Chicken and Zucchini Curry (page 176) will turn just about anyone into a squash lover—give it a try!

Thai food has been described in *The Cuisines of Asia,* by Jennifer Brennan, as having "the quality and consistency of Chinese food, the spiciness of Mexican, the lusciousness of Polynesian, and the exact flavors of none of the above." The Thai recipes we've collected are a wonderful blending of all the features Brennan described. Marinated Thai Chicken (page 177) is a perfect example, as is Stir-Fried Minced Chicken with Balsam Leaves (page 178). The Eight-Hour Chicken (page 179) is easily prepared. However, make sure you leave plenty of time to marinate the chicken! Chicken with Chestnuts (page 180) is an interesting Thai dish. This is a good recipe to introduce kids to this exotic cuisine, as it is not particularly hot. Southeast Asian cuisine is as much about the presentation of the food as the taste. Chile Chicken (page 181) will give you a chance to decorate this dish. Chicken Sautéed with Holy Basil (page 182) was collected in Phuket by our friend Jennifer Basye Sander.

Marco Polo wrote about the foods of Burma while on his travels. The Burmese Chicken Curry (page 183) is a good representative of the flavors of this country.

Hot and spicy, tart or sweet, the recipes presented here are sure to please.

Vietnamese-Style Beijing Duck

Duck is quite a delicacy in Southeast Asia. Beijing ducks are bred specially to grow extra plump in the breast area, with a layer of fat growing between the skin and the meat. Serve this dish with Nuoc Cham Dipping Sauce from Chapter 2, and an assortment of vegetables, along with vermicelli rice.

2 1/4 cups water

1 fresh duck, about 5 pounds

1 tablespoon annatto seeds

1/2 cup soy sauce

3 jalapeño chiles, seeded and
    minced

2 cloves garlic, minced

1 teaspoon finely grated ginger

1/4 cup sugar

1/2 cup sliced green onions

Vietnamese Dipping Sauce (*nuoc cham*, page 31)

Preheat the oven to 350°F. Place the water in a pan and bring it to a boil. Place the duck in a deep dish. Pour 2 cups of the boiling water over the duck. Drain the water out of the dish and pat the duck dry. In a small bowl, crush the annatto seeds, and mix them with 1/4 cup boiling water for 15 minutes. When the 15 minutes are over, strain the liquid into another small bowl and mix the liquid with the soy sauce, jalapeños, garlic, ginger, and sugar. Place the duck on a rack over a roasting pan.

Pour some of the marinade into the cavity of the duck, and place the green onions inside the duck also. Close the duck with a skewer, and brush the remaining marinade over the skin of the duck. Place the duck in the oven, and roast it for 45 minutes. When the 45 minutes is up, reduce the temperature to 300°F, brush more of the marinade over the duck, and roast for another 45 minutes. Brush the remaining marinade over the duck and check for doneness, cooking it longer if needed. Slice and serve with a rice dish from Chapter 8 and *nuoc cham*.

Serves: 8

Heat Scale: Mild

Four C's Chicken Curry

Here's an interesting chicken curry from Vietnam. This recipe combines the spices cinnamon, coriander, cumin, and cayenne for a four-way treat. Serve this with rice from Chapter 8 and a dessert from Chapter 9 for a perfect meal.

1 teaspoon corn oil

4 chicken breasts, halved, skin
   removed

2 tablespoons crushed garlic

3 teaspoons fresh turmeric

1 teaspoon ground cinnamon

1 1/2 teaspoons ground cumin

1 teaspoon ground coriander

2 teaspoons cayenne powder

1/4 teaspoon ground black pepper

1 tablespoon minced, fresh lemongrass

1/3 cup plain yogurt

1 cup water

1 teaspoon fish sauce (*nam pla*)

Heat the oil in a large skillet over moderate heat until very hot but not smoking. Add the chicken breasts and sauté, turning until the breasts are golden. Add the garlic, spices, and lemongrass. Continue to sauté until the spices are fragrant, then add the yogurt, water, and fish sauce. Cover the skillet and simmer 10 to 20 minutes, or until the chicken is cooked through. Serve immediately with a rice dish from Chapter 8.

Serves: 4

Heat Scale: Hot

Chicken and Rice in a Clay Pot

(*Com Tay Cam*)

Poultry cooked in a clay pot always seems to turn out wonderfully tender and juicy. This Vietnamese clay pot recipe is no exception. The pot helps the spicy marinade really penetrate the chicken and create a well-spiced, succulent treat.

2 shallots, minced

2 tablespoons minced garlic

1 tablespoon minced ginger

2 pounds chicken parts

1 tablespoon fish sauce (*nam pla*)

1 tablespoon soy sauce

2 tablespoons vegetable oil

1/4 teaspoon ground pepper

3 cups water

3 fresh Thai chiles, seeded and chopped, or substitute other small, hot chiles

8 black mushroom caps, soaked, drained, and halved (retain drained liquid)

2 cups long-grain rice

Vietnamese Dipping Sauce (*nuoc cham*, page 31)

Place the shallots, garlic, and ginger in a mortar and pound into a paste. Disjoint the chicken and place it in a large bowl. Add the paste, the fish sauce, and the soy sauce to the chicken, coat well, and place in the refrigerator to marinate for 1 hour.

Heat the oil in a large skillet over medium heat. Scrape the excess marinade from the chicken and save. Cook a few pieces of the chicken at a time, until browned on all sides, removing them from the pan as they are done.

When all of the chicken is done, add the reserved marinade, ground pepper, water, chiles, and reserved mushroom liquid to the skillet, and bring to a boil. Arrange the chicken pieces in a braising pot, and pour in the mushroom/chile mixture. Cover the pot and simmer until the chicken is tender, about 20 minutes. When the chicken is done, remove it from the pot and allow it to cool. When the chicken is cool enough to handle, remove the skin, cut the meat from the bones, and tear it into thick shreds. Set aside.

Skim the excess fat from the liquid and add the rice and mushrooms to the pot. Bring the mixture to a boil, then reduce the heat, and cook over low heat until the liquid is nearly absorbed. Stir in the chicken, cover, and cook for another 10 minutes. Turn off the heat and let stand for another 15 minutes. Serve the chicken and rice with *nuoc cham*.

Serves: 4

Heat Scale: Medium

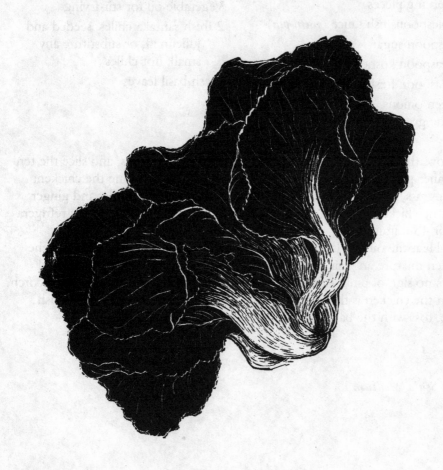

Lemongrass Chicken

(*Ga Xao Sa Ot*)

Vietnamese cuisine is a blending of many cultures, as the country has been invaded by the French, Chinese, and Portuguese. All three of these cultures have left a mark on this recipe—making it truly representative of the best of Southeast Asian cuisine.

2 stalks lemongrass

2 pounds chicken, cut up into
    serving pieces

2 tablespoons fish sauce (*nam pla*)

1 teaspoon sugar

1/2 teaspoon kosher salt

1/4 teaspoon freshly ground pepper

3 green onions, chopped, including
    the greens

1 1/2 tablespoons minced garlic

1 teaspoon powdered ginger

Vegetable oil for stir-frying

2 fresh santaka chiles, seeded and
    julienned, or substitute any
    small, hot chiles

Fresh basil leaves

Remove the tops and tough outer pieces of the lemongrass, and slice the tender inner parts as thinly as possible. In a large bowl, combine the chicken, lemongrass, fish sauce, sugar, salt, pepper, green onions, garlic, and ginger. Toss the chicken in the mixture to coat evenly, then marinate in the refrigerator for 45 minutes.

    Heat the oil in a large pan. Stir-fry the chiles in the pan, then add the chicken mixture and stir-fry it until the chicken is completely cooked and shows no sign of pink. Add a little bit of water if the chicken begins to scorch. When the chicken is thoroughly cooked, sprinkle with any remaining fish sauce, toss with the basil leaves, and transfer to a serving platter.

Serves: 4

Heat Scale: Medium

Fried Chicken with Green Chile

This quick and easy fried chicken is also from Vietnam. Feel free to increase the onions, garlic, and coconut for this meal. Serve with a salad from Chapter 3 for a healthy touch.

1 tablespoon peanut oil

1 chicken, cut into large pieces

2 teaspoons salt

2 teaspoons black pepper

1/2 onion, sliced

1 tablespoon fish sauce (*nam pla*)

2 cups Coconut Milk (page 12)

5 shallots, peeled and sliced

2 cloves garlic, minced

4 serrano or jalapeño chiles, seeded and chopped

14 green onions, white part only, chopped

Chopped cilantro for garnish

Heat the oil in a wok. Rub the chicken with the salt and pepper. When the oil is hot, put in the sliced onion and chicken. Fry the chicken until it is golden brown, then add the fish sauce and enough coconut milk to cover. Cook over low heat until the chicken parts are well done.

In a separate pan, sauté the shallots, garlic, and chiles in the oil until they are fragrant. Next add the green onions. Combine the chicken and seasoning mixtures. Arrange the chicken on a platter and garnish with the cilantro.

Serves: 4

Heat Scale: Hot

Not the Colonel's Fried Chicken

The folks at Kentucky Fried Chicken wouldn't begin to fix their chicken this way. Perhaps this Indonesian recipe will inspire them to new spicy heights.

1 onion, chopped

2 cloves garlic

1 teaspoon fresh ginger

3 fresh cayenne chiles, seeded and chopped; or substitute 5 serranos or jalapeños

4 macadamia nuts

1 tablespoon dark soy sauce

1 3-pound frying chicken

3/4 cup peanut oil

2 teaspoons brown sugar

2 tablespoons lime juice

1/2 teaspoon salt

1 cup Coconut Milk (page 12)

Cilantro leaves for garnish

Place the onion, garlic, ginger, chiles, macadamia nuts, and soy sauce in a food processor and blend until a paste forms. Cut the chicken into quarters, then rinse the pieces and pat dry with paper towels. Heat half a cup of the peanut oil in a frying pan and fry the chicken quickly until brown. Remove the chicken and drain on paper towels. Pour off the oil, leaving only one tablespoon, and fry the paste for a few minutes, stirring constantly. Add the brown sugar, lime juice, salt, and coconut milk, stirring constantly, until the mixture comes to a boil. Return the chicken to the pan and simmer uncovered for 30 minutes. Serve with plain white rice, garnished with the cilantro.

Serves: 4

Heat Scale: Hot

Santaka Chicken in Lime and Coconut Milk Sauce

It is well known in Indonesia that fine cooks add a bit of this and a bit of that from their gardens. As often as not, a dish does not turn out the same twice. Experiment with your own favorite Asian spices to make this your own signature dish.

1 three-pound chicken, cut into pieces, loose skin and fat removed
2 cups Coconut Milk (page 12)
1/2 teaspoon turmeric
4 shallots, chopped
1 clove garlic, minced

1 teaspoon salt
1 stalk lemongrass, chopped
1/2 lime, sliced in rounds
2 dried santaka chiles, seeded and crushed; or substitute other hot, dried red chiles

Place all of the ingredients in a large pan. Cook, covered, over medium heat for 30 minutes, stirring occasionally, until the chicken is tender and the sauce thickens. Serve with white rice and a salad from Chapter 3.

Serves: 6

Heat Scale: Medium

Spicy Galangal Chicken

(*Ayam Masabulu*)

This Indonesian poultry dish features galangal, which is also (and confusingly) known as *laos*. This plant, which is a relative of ginger, grows very well all over Southeast Asia and should be available in Asian markets. However, if you have trouble locating galangal, ginger may be substituted; simply double the amount.

1 tablespoon chopped ripe tomato

1 teaspoon salt

4 fresh piquin chiles, seeded and chopped; or substitute other small, hot chiles

5 shallots, chopped

2 garlic cloves, minced

1 cup plus 1 tablespoon water

1 tablespoon peanut oil

3 *salam* leaves (bay leaves may be substituted)

3 slices galangal

2 stalks lemongrass

1 3-pound chicken, cut into 8 to 10 pieces, giblets included

2 tablespoons fresh lemon or lime juice

In a food processor, blend the tomato, salt, chiles, shallots, garlic, and 1 tablespoon water until the mixture forms a paste. Pour the oil in a wok and stir-fry the paste, with the *salam* leaves, galangal, and lemongrass over medium heat for 2 minutes. Add the chicken parts to the wok and fry for 5 minutes. Add the lemon or lime juice and the remaining water. Cook the chicken, covered, for 30 minutes, or until the chicken is done and the sauce is thickened.

Serves: 4

Heat Scale: Medium

Grilled Hot Hen

(*Ayam Taliwang*)

The small island of Lombok is the home of this recipe. The word *Lombok* translates as "spicy chiles" and is the perfect descriptor of the food on this island next to Bali.

1 two-pound Cornish hen, butter-flied and flattened

1 teaspoon salt

1 tablespoon corn oil

5 shallots, sliced

3 cloves garlic, sliced

1 teaspoon shrimp paste

1/2 teaspoon sugar

1 tablespoon fresh bird's eye chile (chiltepin) or substitute piquin

2 teaspoons pineapple juice

2 cups chopped fresh pineapple

Rub the hen completely with the salt and oil. In a food processor, blend the shallots, garlic, shrimp paste, sugar, chile, pineapple juice, and pineapple to form a paste.

Grill the hen slowly over hot coals, or under a preheated gas or electric broiler, for 5 minutes. Baste the hen well with the paste on both sides, and grill for 3 minutes.

Finally, spread all the remaining paste on the skin side of the hen and grill for 10 minutes, or until done.

Serves: 4

Heat Scale: Medium

Balinese Duck

(*Bebek Bumbu Bali*)

This is the second duck recipe in this chapter; this time we feature the tastes of Bali. Prepare this dish when you're in the mood for a rich and filling meal. A nice fruit salad from Chapter 3 would be an excellent accompanying dish.

1 five-pound duck

10 macadamia nuts, crushed

1/2 teaspoon shrimp paste

1 tablespoon chopped hot chile,
    such as Thai or piquin

1/4 cup sliced onion

5 cloves garlic, chopped

2 tablespoons soy sauce

1/2 teaspoon turmeric

2 teaspoons salt

2 cups water

4 bay leaves

2 pieces galangal, peeled

2 stalks lemongrass

Disjoint the duck and cut it into about 10 pieces. Trim and remove the loose skin and fat. In a food processor, prepare a sauce of the nuts, shrimp paste, chile, onion, garlic, soy sauce, turmeric, salt, and 1/2 cup of the water. Cook the sauce for 3 minutes in a large saucepan that will accommodate the duck.

Add the duck, bay leaves, *laos* (galangal), lemongrass, and the balance of the water (1 1/2 cups). Stir well, and cook over medium heat for about 1 1/2 hours, or until the duck is soft and about half the sauce has evaporated. Should the duck appear to be too dry, 1/2 cup water can be added during the cooking process.

Serves: 6

Heat Scale: Medium

Chicken Satay with Spicy Peanut Sauce

This recipe is provided courtesy of the Equatorial Penang Hotel in Penang, Malaysia. It is a classic Indonesian dish that combines the heat of chiles with the exotic fragrances of the Spice Islands. Note that this recipe requires advance preparation.

4 large pieces ginger, peeled

4 piquins, chopped

5 cloves garlic, peeled

3 shallots, peeled

1 teaspoon cumin seed

1 teaspoon anise seed

1 tablespoon ground turmeric

3 stalks lemongrass

2 teaspoons sugar

1 pound boneless chicken, cut into strips

Indonesian Peanut–Chile Sauce (*katjang saos,* page 24)

Diced cucumbers and onions for garnish

Combine the ginger, chiles, garlic, shallots, cumin, anise, turmeric, lemongrass, and sugar in a food processor and puree, adding water if necessary. Marinate the chicken strips in this mixture for 12 hours in the refrigerator.

Thread the chicken strips onto separate *satay* sticks that have been soaked in water. Grill the *satay* sticks over coals until the meat is done, about 12 minutes, turning often. Serve the *satays* with the sauce on the side and garnished with the diced cucumbers and onions.

Serves: 4

Heat Scale: Medium

Chicken-Stuffed Coconut

(*Ayam Di Batok Kelapa*)

This unusual Indonesian recipe is a specialty on the island of Sulawesi. Covering the coconut with foil allows it to retain all of its hot, sweet flavoring.

1 large young green coconut
1 pound boneless chicken, cut into 1-inch cubes
1 stalk lemongrass, minced
2 green onions, cut into ½-inch slices
2 shallots, sliced

1 teaspoon salt
3 Thai chiles, seeded and minced; or substitute any small, hot chiles
1-inch piece fresh ginger, peeled and minced

Preheat the oven to 325°F. With a sharp knife or a saw, cut a 2-inch-wide plug from the eye end of the coconut, reserving it, and drain and discard the coconut water.

Mix the remaining ingredients together in a bowl, fill the coconut with the mixture, and replace the reserved plug. Wrap the coconut with aluminum foil to seal it further.

Bake the stuffed coconut in the oven for 2 hours. Unseal and unplug the coconut and turn it on its side. Spoon out the chicken stuffing and serve warm.

Serves: 4

Heat Scale: Medium

His Majesty's Chicken

(*Korma Ayam*)

Some of Southeast Asia's most exotic spices are the stars of this Indonesian dish. Ginger, coriander, cardamom, and cloves give it a distinctly rich taste. If you enjoy this recipe, try it next time using lamb. Serve His Majesty's Chicken with a salad from Chapter 3.

4 shallots, sliced

4 serrano or jalapeño chiles, seeded and chopped

2 tablespoons freshly grated ginger

2 cloves garlic

2 teaspoons ground coriander

1 teaspoon ground cumin

1/4 teaspoon black pepper

2 1/2 cups Coconut Milk (page 12)

2 tablespoons corn oil

2-inch piece cinnamon stick

1 teaspoon lemon juice

4 whole cloves

4 cardamom pods

1 teaspoon ground anise

1 three-pound chicken, cut into eight pieces, loose skin and fat removed

1 teaspoon salt

2 ripe tomatoes, sliced

Cilantro leaves for garnish

In a food processor, blend the shallots, chiles, ginger, garlic, coriander, cumin, and pepper with 1/4 cup of the coconut milk to form a paste.

Heat the oil in a skillet, and stir-fry the paste, cinnamon stick, lemon juice, cloves, cardamom pods, and anise over medium heat, for a couple of minutes. Add the chicken and fry it for 5 minutes until browned.

Next add the remaining coconut milk, the salt and tomatoes, and cook over moderate heat. Baste the chicken frequently with the sauce, letting it cook for about 40 minutes. Serve warm, garnishing immediately with the cilantro.

Serves: 4

Heat Scale: Hot

Chicken and Zucchini Curry

We recommend this Indonesian recipe even to folks that don't care for squash. The combination of the zucchini, basil, coconut milk, lemongrass— and, of course, chiles—will convert almost anyone!

4 serrano or jalapeño chiles, seeded
　　and coarsely chopped

1 cup coarsely chopped onion

1 three-inch stalk fresh lemongrass,
　　smashed with the flat of a large
　　knife or cleaver

2 fresh basil leaves

1 teaspoon turmeric

1/4 teaspoon ground galangal
　　powder (*laos*)

1 cup water

1 medium-sized zucchini squash,
　　peeled, cut into 1/2-inch cubes

1 cup Coconut Milk (page 12)

1 pound chicken parts

2 teaspoons lemon juice

1 teaspoon salt

Put the chiles and onions through the finest blade of a meat grinder, or puree them in a food processor. Transfer the puree to a heavy 2- to 3-quart saucepan and stir in the lemongrass, basil, turmeric, *laos,* and 1 cup of water. Bring to a boil over high heat, reduce the heat to low, and simmer uncovered for 5 minutes.

　　Stir in the zucchini and continue cooking for 5 to 6 minutes longer, or until the squash is tender but still crunchy. Add the coconut milk and the chicken, stirring frequently, cooking for 4 to 5 minutes. Do not allow the liquid to boil or it will curdle. Remove the pan from the heat, stir in the lemon juice and salt, and taste for seasoning. Serve at once from a heated bowl, accompanied if you like with hot plain rice.

Serves: 4

Heat Scale: Medium

Marinated Thai Chicken

This interesting main dish mixes elements from both Thai and Chinese cultures. We use yellow rice wine to add an authentic "drunken" recipe touch. The ginger and jalapeños give it spice and zip. Please note that this recipe requires advanced preparation.

2 pounds chicken pieces
Water to cover
1 1/4 cups yellow rice wine
1 teaspoon salt
2 1/2 teaspoons sugar

1 clove garlic, minced
2 teaspoons freshly grated ginger
3 fresh serrano or jalapeño chiles, seeded and minced
Fresh mint leaves for garnish

Rinse the chicken parts well, then place them in a large pan and cover with water. Bring the water to a boil. Cover the pan tightly, reduce the heat, and simmer for 20 minutes. After 20 minutes, drain the chicken, and place it in a deep dish. In a separate bowl, mix the wine, salt, sugar, garlic, ginger, and chiles. Pour the mixture over the chicken. Cover the chicken with plastic wrap, and place in the refrigerator overnight to marinate. When you are ready to serve, drain the liquid from the dish, garnish with mint leaves and serve cold.

Serves: 6

Heat Scale: Medium

Stir-Fried Minced Chicken with Balsam Leaves

This recipe is from the Thai Cooking School at the Oriental Hotel, in Bangkok, Thailand. Balsam is another name for holy basil, and since balsam leaves can be difficult to locate, feel free to substitute basil, mint, or a combination of the two.

10 fresh Thai chiles, chopped; or substitute piquins or other small, hot chiles

1 heaping teaspoon shrimp paste

1 tablespoon salt

1 tablespoon vegetable oil

2 cups chopped chicken breast

1 cup straw mushrooms, halved

1/2 cup ripe tomatoes, blanched, peeled, and roughly chopped

8 cloves garlic, sliced

6 shallots, sliced

1 cup balsam leaves (or substitute basil or mint)

Combine the chiles, shrimp paste, and salt together in a food processor and puree. Heat the cooking oil in a pan and fry the paste in it, stirring well until fragrant; then add the chicken meat and keep stirring until well mixed. Mix in the mushrooms and chopped tomatoes and turn well. In a separate pan, quick-fry the garlic, shallots, and balsam leaves, stirring quickly. Transfer the chicken to a platter, and sprinkle half of the fried shallots and garlic on top of the dish. Arrange the rest of the fried vegetables on the platter.

Serves: 4

Heat Scale: Hot

Eight-Hour Chicken

(*Gai Yang*)

This Thai recipe must be started early in the day, but the extra work is well worth it! Red curry paste is readily available in Asian markets, and is the perfect combination of chiles and spices. Please keep in mind that the chicken should marinate for at least 8 hours for the best results.

1 tablespoon Red Curry Paste (*nam prik gaeng ped*, page 41)

1 cup light soy sauce

2 Thai chiles, seeded and chopped; or substitute piquins or other small, hot chiles

4 cilantro stems with roots, finely chopped

8 garlic cloves, finely chopped

1 carrot, chopped

2 celery stalks, chopped

1 teaspoon lime juice

1 small onion, chopped

1/4 cup vegetable oil

1/4 cup cracked black peppercorns

2 three-pound chicken broilers, halved lengthwise

Pepper Water Sauce (*nam prik*, page 36)

Mix all of the ingredients, except the chicken, in a large mixing bowl. Be sure to blend all of the ingredients well. Place the chicken, skin side down, in a shallow baking dish. Pour the marinade over the chicken. Cover the chicken with plastic wrap, and refrigerate for at least 8 hours (overnight is preferable).

After the chicken has marinated, preheat the oven to 350°F. Bake the chicken, uncovered, in the marinade for 40 to 50 minutes. Just before serving, place the chicken under the broiler for 5 minutes, to crisp it up. Cut the chicken in half and serve it with the Pepper Water Sauce from Chapter 2.

Serves: 4

Heat Scale: Medium

Chicken with Chestnuts

(*Gai Gup Kao Lad*)

Finding chestnuts when they are out of season can be a real burden. So if you have the hankering for this lively Thai dish and can't find the proper nuts, water chestnuts may be substituted. The taste and texture of the dish will be a little different, but the overall flavors will be close enough.

4 cloves garlic, chopped

2 tablespoons cilantro root

1 teaspoon black peppercorns

1 jalapeño chile, seeded and chopped

2 tablespoons vegetable oil

1 pound boned chicken meat, cut into bite-sized pieces

1 1/2 cups chicken stock

4 chicken livers, diced

16 chestnuts, shelled, boiled, and halved; or 1 eight-ounce can water chestnuts, drained and halved

1 teaspoon salt

1 tablespoon palm sugar

In a food processor, puree the garlic, cilantro, black peppercorns, and jalapeño into a paste. In a wok, heat the oil and fry the paste, stirring, for 2 to 3 minutes. Add the chicken pieces (not the livers) and stir-fry until they are just brown. Pour in the chicken stock and add the livers. Adjust the heat and simmer for 5 minutes. Stir in the chestnuts, season with salt, and sprinkle with palm sugar. Cover and simmer until the chicken is tender, about 5 minutes.

Serves: 4 to 6

Heat Scale: Medium

Chile Chicken

(*Panaeng Kruang Don*)

Thai cuisine is known for its beauty as well as its taste. Allow a little extra time to arrange this dish on the platter, and prepare chile flowers for garnish (see Chapter 1). The results of your efforts will be much admired by your guests—and will taste good, too!

8 dried cayenne chiles, seeded, soaked in warm water, finely chopped

2 cloves garlic, chopped

2 shallots, chopped

1 stalk lemongrass, minced

1 teaspoon minced cilantro

1 teaspoon shrimp paste

3 pieces galangal, peeled and chopped

1 teaspoon black peppercorns

1½ cups Coconut Milk (page 12)

1 tablespoon sugar

2 tablespoons fish sauce (*nam pla*)

1 pound chicken meat, cooked and cut into bite-sized pieces

4 fresh red serranos or jalapeños, cut into flowers

2 tablespoons cilantro leaves

Place the cayenne chiles, garlic, shallots, lemongrass, cilantro, and shrimp paste in a food processor and process to a coarse paste. Put the *laos* (galangal) and peppercorns in an electric spice grinder and grind to a powder. Add the powder to the paste and process once more to mix thoroughly.

Pour half of the coconut milk into a wok and bring to a boil. Stir in the curry paste from the processor and cook over medium heat until the mixture is almost dry. Stir in the sugar and fish sauce and remove from the heat. Arrange the chicken pieces on a large, heated platter. Top this with a spoonful of the remaining coconut milk. Decorate with red chile flowers and sprinkle with cilantro leaves. Serve warm.

Serves: 4

Heat Scale: Hot

Chicken Sautéed with Holy Basil

(*Guay Tiew Gai Amanpuri*)

This recipe, from the Amanpuri Resort on Phuket Island, Thailand, is provided courtesy of chef Daniel Lentz. It was collected by Jennifer Basye Sander. The basil in this dish, called *graprao* or sometimes *krapau*, is holy basil (*Ocimum sanctum*), which is revered by Hindus. It has a a more pungent flavor than sweet basil, and that is why mint is sometimes substituted.

4 large lettuce leaves, cut in thin strips with scissors

5 tablespoons vegetable oil

1/2 pound *guay tiew* noodles (thick, flat rice noodles, available in Asian markets)

2 tablespoons minced garlic

4 red serranos or jalapeño chiles, seeded and chopped fine

1 cup ground chicken

2 tablespoons oyster sauce

3 tablespoons fish sauce (*nam pla*)

1/3 cup chicken stock

2 teaspoons sugar

20 leaves *bi graprao,* holy basil, or substitute fresh basil, mint, or a mixture of the two

Arrange the lettuce strips on two plates. Heat 2 tablespoons of the oil in a wok until medium hot; add the noodles and stir-fry until heated through but not browned. Drain the noodles and place them on top of the lettuce.

    Heat the remaining oil in the wok, add the garlic and chiles, and stir-fry for 15 seconds. Add the chicken and stir-fry for another 15 seconds. Add the oyster and fish sauces, stock, and sugar and stir-fry until the chicken is done, about 5 minutes. The mixture should have a saucelike consistency; adjust it by adding more stock, if necessary. Add the basil and stir-fry for 15 seconds. Serve the chicken on top of the noodles.

Serves: 2

Heat Scale: Hot

Burmese Chicken Curry

(*Kyet Tha Sipyan*)

This curry is a favorite all over the world. The fish sauce, tomatoes, and two types of chiles add to the heat level and enjoyment of this dish. Serve with fresh orange slices for a satisfying light meal.

1 3 1/2-pound chicken, cut into eight pieces, loose skin and fat removed

1 teaspoon salt

1/2 teaspoon ground turmeric

4 tablespoons fish sauce (*nam pla*)

2 small onions, sliced

4 garlic cloves, minced

2 tablespoons fresh ginger, sliced

1 teaspoon paprika

1 teaspoon dried red chile flakes

2 tablespoons water

1 jalapeño, stemmed, seeded, and minced

3 tablespoons corn oil

1/4 cup chopped ripe tomatoes

1/2 cup water

Wash the chicken well and pat dry with paper towels. Place the chicken in a deep dish. In a separate bowl, mix the salt, turmeric, and fish sauce. Pour this mixture over the chicken. Marinate the chicken in the refrigerator for 15 minutes. In a food processor, blend the onions, garlic, ginger, paprika, red chile flakes, 2 tablespoons water, and jalapeño. Blend until the ingredients form a coarse paste.

In a large, deep frying pan, pour in the oil and stir-fry the paste over medium heat. Add the chicken and tomatoes and stir-fry for about 15 minutes. The oil will separate and rise to the top of the mixture. Next, add the water, cover the pan, and cook over moderately low heat for about 25 minutes, until the chicken is done and the sauce is nice and thick. Serve with white rice, or over noodles if you prefer.

Serves: 4

Heat Scale: Medium

A Lesson in Pleasurable Pain

"Real Thai food, unlike American versions of it, is one of the wonders of the world. I ate a take-out lunch in my kayak under the shade of a footbridge. I had roast chicken with a hot dipping sauce and an old favorite, *som tam,* a salad of unripe grated papayas in a marinade of lime juice, chile pepper, tamarind sauce, tiny dried shrimp, and peanuts. But I was no more used to the heat of the spices than I was to the heat of the sun. My mouth burned with a fire that teared my eyes. I remembered reading why this pepper pain became so habit forming. The chile causes pain killers to be released by the brain so eating the marinated shrimps became sort of a luncheon high.**"**

Peter Aiken

The Asian-American Pantry

"Two decades ago, Thai cuisine's prerequisite fresh herbs, dried spices, seasoning pastes, and sauces were difficult to obtain in the United States. But as Southeast Asian communities have sprung up or expanded throughout the country, and as immigrants from Cambodia, Laos, Burma, and Vietnam have settled in, the market for the culinary building blocks they share with the Thai kitchen has exploded. Thai food's popularity in restaurants has created an interest among home cooks, bringing shelf-stable ingredients such as fish sauce, coconut milk, and tamarind into gourmet and specialty shops and even upscale supermarkets.**"**

Nancie McDermott

But What if the Husband Gets the Breast?

❝In Central Sumatra . . . there is a custom of 'pulling the fried chicken under yellow rice.' A whole cooked chicken is buried under a cone-shaped heap of rice. The bride and the groom have to seize either end of the chicken and attempt to pull it out at the same time. If the bride gets the thigh bones and the husband the head, then this indicates that in their new life, the husband will be master and protector of his family. Should the wife find herself holding the head, then it is said that the husband will be hen-pecked.❞

Jacqueline M. Piper

Singaporean Signature Dishes

❝A friend's cousin took me to backstreet food bazaars late one evening to try *hoi polloi* versions of Hainanese chicken rice (poached chicken, chicken-flavored rice, and a light soup with Chinese vegetables); fish head curry (a lively, peppery dish traditionally made with snapper); Indonesian satay made of barbecued or grilled beef, lamb, chicken or seafood; and chile crab (crab deep-fried, then stir-fried with sauces and stocks).❞

John Watson

Bali Hot

❝Balinese white rice forms the basis of all meals. The population of Bali is largely Hindu so there are no restrictions on eating pork or any other meats. However, meat dishes comprise only a small part of their diet. *Sates* of small-cubed beef, pork, chicken, and turtle are popular, skewered on bamboo sticks, grilled over hot coals and served with a deliciously spicy peanut sauce. Rice is also the chief constituent of *Nasi Goreng* and *Nasi Padang,* so hot and spicy that some claim it burns your fingers as well as your mouth! Western food is regarded as tasteless by the Balinese, who enjoy highly spiced and peppery dishes containing an abundance of onions, garlic, ginger, white-hot peppers, and fermented fish paste. Oddly, the nutmeg, cloves, and mace that give the 'spice islands' their characteristic name are rarely used, although stretched cloths filled with drying cloves are a common sight in every small village. Coconut milk and ground peanuts impart a rich creaminess to sauces, whilst the rice, along with cucumber and banana taken as side dishes, cool the palate."

Rosemary Ogilvie

At the Eating Meadow in Cambodia

"On several nights we three travelers took the walk north to the festive 'eating meadow.' From each of several sellers we ordered food, then sat down on wooden divans covered with grass mats. As each dish was readied, cook's assistants brought them to us, weaving their way through the visiting crowd. They brought us tangy salads of julienned green mango, tossed with shallots, ground peanuts, chile paste, and lime juice. The seafood kitchen sent steaming dishes of giant prawns in the shell. The girls who delivered them stood by and patiently peeled each one, taking the opportunity to joke and flirt with the three exotic 'Farangis.' Beef, marinated in chile, galangal, and garlic teased our appetites as it sizzled on skewers over hot coals. Little sheaves of asparagus bound up with collars of fish paste, deep fried and drizzled with a piquant sauce, made us ooh and ahh at their cleverness. Runners kept us well supplied with beer."

Richard Sterling

"The Pig of the Sea"
Southeast Asian Seafood

In true Southeast Asian cuisine, only fresh ingredients are used. This is especially true of their fruits of the sea. While "catch of the day" in most countries translates to "here's the fish we have," the opposite is true in most Southeast Asian countries. Just as freshness is the rule, chances are also good that the fish will be cooked into a wonderful meal the same day.

Indonesia and Malaysia have abundant waterways as well as a veritable treasure trove of indigenous spices. This has allowed us to offer the fieriest of fish dishes, such as Malaysian Seafood with Noodles and Coconut Sauce (page 190) and Prawns in Chile-Bean Sauce (page 192). Hot and Sour Flounder (page 193) is an unusual Indonesian dish, in which cayenne chiles, mustard, and vinegar blend to create a unique pungency. While there may not be many Cajuns in Indonesia, cayenne chiles are quite evident in their cuisine, as demonstrated again in Tuna in Brown Bean Sauce with Stir-Fried Vegetables (page 194).

Thai food is often described as the most Asian of Asian foods. This has been attributed to the fact that Thailand has never been colonized; thus their cuisine has never been subjected to western influence. Thai food is prepared in a variety of ways: fried, as in the Thai Crab Fried Rice (page 196) and Deep-Fried Curried Fish Patties (page 197); and stuffed and baked, as with the Thai Baked Stuffed Chile Peppers (page 198). And you certainly don't want to miss the last of our Thai dishes—Sour Seafood Pot (page 199), Spicy Anchovy Fish Pot (page 200), and Spicy Steamed Mussels with Coconut (*Haw Mog Hoy*, page 202) are steamed and wonderful!

Singapore sizzles! We guarantee a hot time with this trio of temptations. We begin with a recipe featuring hard shell crabs. Singapore Chile Crab (page 204) is a relatively simple dish that is fantastic when one can find these crustaceans in season! Singapore Fried Prawns with Dried Chile (page 206), guarantees the spiciest fried shrimp you'll ever have the pleasure of eating. The batter contains those little red devils, piquins, and the sauce has twelve—that's right, twelve—cayenne chiles. Save this recipe for a heat-worshiping friend! And not to be outdone, Prawns in Chile-Garlic Sauce (page 205), offers the power of serranos, ginger, and garlic for a mighty pungent punch.

Cambodian cuisine has been significantly affected by India. Unlike other Southeast Asian countries, these influences came by way of trade rather than war and domination. David Karp highlights a Cambodian catfish dish with the favorite aromatic spice, kaffir lime leaves, in Lemongrass-Enrobed Catfish Fillets (page 208). We've also included the Cambodian classic Curried Shrimp and Cucumbers (page 210) and another catfish dish, Tantalizing Catfish (page 212).

Our first Vietnamese recipe, Fish with Ginger Salsa (page 211) comes to us by way of *Chile Pepper* magazine Contributing Editor Richard Sterling, who always enjoyed a good meal or two with every adventure. And we would be remiss if we didn't include a Steamed Spicy Fish (page 214) recipe from Vietnam. The dish includes pickled plums and celery, which adds a lot of textural excitement to the meal.

And of course, we have collected a curried fish dish from Burma, and it's certainly an interesting one. If only pigs could swim—and maybe they do! Our curried fish dish, Pigfish Curry (page 215), is made with grouper, which the Burmese refer to as the "pig of the sea."

Borneo is yet another island founded on trade. Spice trading posts were set up on Borneo so that ships could wait there until the north-blowing monsoon winds would propel them to China. We like to think our Tangy Marinated Fish (page 216) recipe would have kept the ships' crews happy while they waited.

While Bali is, of course, a region of Indonesia, we've listed its recipe (Fiery Party Snapper, page 217) separately because of its unique ingredients—snapper and tamarind sauce. It is in Bali that Indonesian ceremonial foods are said to attain their most ornate and complicated form.

And who wouldn't make a meal of Fried Fish with Tomatoes and Eggs (page 218)? The Filipinos certainly would! Add a few chiles and the possibilities are endless!

Malaysian Seafood with Noodles and Coconut Sauce

(*Laksa Lemak Melaka*)

The Malaysian people hold chile peppers in the highest esteem, picking them out carefully at the market, and incorporating a bit of heat into most recipes. This dish features serranos, but piquins may be substituted if you would like to experience a little more heat.

1 pound shrimp, peeled and deveined

1 pound halibut or other white fish, cut into 3/4-inch chunks

1 cup water

8 candlenuts, or substitute Brazil nuts

3 serrano or jalapeño chiles, seeded and chopped

1 1/2 teaspoons ground turmeric

3/4 teaspoon ground ginger

Pinch ground cinnamon

2 large cloves garlic

1 teaspoon grated lemon peel

1/4 cup vegetable oil

2 cups minced onion

2 cups Coconut Milk (page 12)

2 cups water

2 tablespoons lime juice

1 pound bean sprouts

1 pound vermicelli or spaghetti

1 cucumber, peeled, seeded, and cut into strips

Fresh or dried mint (optional)

Place the shrimp and fish in a pan; add the water and simmer for about 5 minutes. Remove from the heat and let cool.

In a food processor, process the nuts, chiles, turmeric, ginger, cinnamon, garlic, and lemon peel to a paste. Heat the vegetable oil in a skillet, add the onions and paste, and stir-fry until the onions are soft (about 3-5 minutes). Add the coconut milk, water, and lime juice to the onion mixture and simmer uncovered for 8 minutes, stirring occasionally.

Add the cooked shrimp, fish, and fish broth. Simmer over low heat for 10 minutes. Blanch the bean sprouts for 1 minute in rapidly boiling water. Cook the noodles as noted on the package and drain. In individual bowls, divide the noodles and bean sprouts equally. Pour the shrimp, fish, and sauce over each serving and garnish with cucumber and mint.

Serves: 6 to 8

Heat Scale: Medium

Prawns in Chile-Bean Sauce

This Malaysian recipe features the plentiful seafood of the area, as well as the many spices available. Chinese rice wine may be substituted for the dry sherry if you would like a sweeter and most authentic taste. Serve this with a favorite hot rice dish from Chapter 8.

1 pound raw prawns or large shrimp, shelled and deveined

1 clove garlic, crushed

1/2 teaspoon salt

1/2 teaspoon finely grated fresh ginger

2 teaspoons dry sherry

2 fresh Thai chiles, seeded and chopped; or substitute piquins or other small, hot chiles

1 serrano or jalapeño chile, seeded and chopped

1 tablespoon canned salted black beans

1 to 2 teaspoons commercial Chinese chile sauce; or substitute commercial Sriracha sauce

2 teaspoons *hoisin* sauce

2 tablespoons peanut oil

Green onion tops for garnish

Place the prawns in a bowl and mix in the garlic and salt. Add the ginger and sherry, mix well, and allow to marinate while you prepare the rest of the recipe.

Place the chiles in a bowl. Rinse the black beans and drain, then crush or chop them finely and place in the bowl with the chiles. Add the chile sauce and *hoisin* sauce. Set aside.

Next, pour the oil into a heated wok. Stir-fry the chile mixture for 2 minutes, then move it to the side of the wok and add the prawns. Fry the prawns over high heat until they turn pink, about 2 minutes. Move the prawns to one side and add a little more oil, about half a tablespoon. Return the chile-black bean mixture to the oil and stir-fry for 30 seconds, then mix the prawns into the sauce and fry for a few seconds until coated with the black bean mixture. Garnish with green onion and serve at once.

Serves: 3

Heat Scale: Medium

Hot and Sour Flounder

(*Acar Ikan*)

Jeff Corydon collected this recipe in Indonesia. He found the area to be rich with coastal waters, lakes, and rivers. *Acar* refers to the pungent sweet and sour vegetables or relish typical of the region.

1 two-pound whole flounder	3 macadamia nuts
1 teaspoon salt	1 teaspoon ground ginger
1 teaspoon ground cayenne	1 teaspoon ground cumin
4 dried cayenne chiles, seeded, soaked in water until soft, and chopped	1/2 cup vegetable oil
	1/2 cup cider vinegar
3 cloves garlic, chopped	1 teaspoon dry mustard
1 large onion, chopped	1 teaspoon sugar
	1 cup water

Clean the fish, remove the head, but leave the skin on. Firmly rub some salt and cayenne pepper into both sides of the fish.

Place the chiles, garlic, onion, nuts, ginger, and cumin in a blender or food processor and process to a paste.

Heat 2 tablespoons of the oil in a large skillet or wok, and fry the chile paste over low heat for 2 to 3 minutes, stirring constantly. Add the vinegar, mustard, sugar, and water and simmer, uncovered, for 15 minutes.

In the meantime, heat the rest of the oil in another skillet and fry the fish over medium heat until both sides are golden brown.

Combine the fish with the sauce in the large skillet and simmer 2 to 3 minutes over low heat, basting frequently with the sauce. Serve immediately.

Serves: 4 to 6

Heat Scale: Hot

Tuna in Brown Bean Sauce with Stir-Fried Vegetables

(*Tauco Ikan*)

Indonesian cuisine often combines fish with vegetables and herbs for spectacular results. We highly recommend experimenting with different chiles in this dish to experience different heat levels and tastes. Serve this with a salad from Chapter 3 and a side dish from Chapter 8.

1 1/2 pounds tuna steaks

Salt

1 small onion, peeled, cut into
1/8-inch-thick rings, and then
the rings cut in half

1 fresh cayenne chile, seeded and
cut into strips; or substitute 2
serrano or jalapeño chiles

1 cup thinly sliced fresh green beans

1 cup sliced bamboo shoots

1 small onion, chopped

2 cloves garlic, finely chopped

1 1/2 teaspoons finely grated fresh
ginger

2 tablespoons brown bean sauce

4 tablespoons peanut oil

1 teaspoon shrimp paste

1 tablespoon soy sauce

2/3 cup water

Cut the fish into serving pieces, sprinkle with salt, and set aside.

Set the halved onion rings, chile, green beans, and bamboo shoots on separate plates. Combine the chopped onion with the garlic, ginger, and brown bean sauce in a bowl.

Wipe the fish with paper towels to remove excess moisture. Heat the peanut oil in a wok or frying pan and fry the fish on high heat until the pieces are browned on all sides. Remove them from the pan.

Pour all but 2 tablespoons of oil out of the wok. Add the onion-bean sauce mixture and fry, stirring constantly, over medium heat until the onions are soft. Add the shrimp paste and green beans and stir-fry for 2 minutes. Add the chiles and halved onion rings and stir-fry for 1 minute. Add the bamboo shoots, soy sauce, and water, stir well, and cover and simmer for 3 minutes. Add the fish to the mixture and heat through. Serve with white rice.

Serves: 6

Heat Scale: Medium

Thai Crab Fried Rice

Chile Pepper correspondent Peter Aiken paddled a kayak to the floating markets of Bangkok. There, he discovered that while white rice in the region is eaten with meals, fried rice is a meal in itself; it's often made from leftover rice and other ingredients and is cooked and served with *nam prik* sauce. It is quite salty, high in vitamins, and takes some getting used to.

2 tablespoons peanut oil

1 medium onion, minced

1 jalapeño chile, seeded and minced

2 cloves garlic, minced

3 cups cooked white rice

1 cup crab meat

2 eggs

3 green onions, sliced

Lime wedges

Pepper Water Sauce (*nam prik*, page 36)

Heat the oil in a wok, add the onion, chile, and garlic, and stir-fry for a minute on high heat. Add the rice and crab meat and heat. Push the rice mixture to the side of the wok. Crack the eggs into the center and, while stirring continuously, cook until the eggs are half done; then stir the rice into the eggs. Add the green onions just before removing the mixture from the heat. The cooking should not take more than 5 minutes.

  Squeeze fresh lime over the finished product and add pepper water sauce as desired to individual plates.

Serves: 4 to 6

Heat Scale: Varies according to sauce added

Deep-Fried Curried Fish Patties
(*Thod Mun Pla*)

What exciting foods are in this recipe! The smokiness of trout and the complexity of red curry offer an aromatic and pungent Thai delight.

2 cups minced sea trout or other
    white fish
2 tablespoons Red Curry Paste
    (*nam prik gaeng ped*, page 41)
1 tablespoon finely shredded kaffir
    lime leaves
5 fresh Thai chiles, seeded and
    chopped; or substitute piquins
    or other small, hot chiles

3 tablespoons fish sauce (*nam pla*)
1 teaspoon brown sugar
1/4 teaspoon ground black pepper
1 egg
1 cup sliced string beans
1 cup basil leaves
2 tablespoons peanut oil

In a large bowl, combine everything but the cooking oil, until the ingredients are pasty and well mixed. Form the mixture into small, flat patties.

Heat the oil. Fry the patties until they turn golden brown. Remove them from the hot oil and drain well on paper towels. Serve hot with a sampling of hot sauces from Chapter 2.

Serves: 4

Heat Scale: Hot

Thai Baked Stuffed Chile Peppers

(*Prik Chee Sy Moo*)

This low-calorie dish is from Thailand. This recipe reminds one of chile rellenos, the stuffed green chile dish of the American Southwest. The Bean Curd, Vegetable, and Peanut Salad in Chapter 3 would be a great accompaniment to this meal.

3/4 pound fresh or frozen snapper
   fillets, minced
1/3 cup water chestnuts, finely
   chopped
1 egg white, lightly beaten

2 green onions, minced
2 teaspoons peanut oil
2 teaspoons soy sauce
8 New Mexican green chiles, stems
   on, roasted, and peeled

In a bowl, combine the fish with the water chestnuts, egg white, green onions, 1 teaspoon oil, and soy sauce. Mix well.

Slit the roasted chiles along one side and remove the seeds. Fill the chiles by carefully spooning the fish filling through the slits. Place the stuffed chiles in a baking dish sprayed with nonstick vegetable coating; brush the chiles lightly with oil.

Bake at 350°F for 30 minutes, or until the chiles are tender and the filling is cooked.

Serves: 4

Heat Scale: Mild

Sour Seafood Pot

(*Po Taek*)

It is easy to understand why fish, next to rice, is the main food consumed in Thailand: more than 60 percent of Thai people who live in the country catch their own fish for their meals. And although we don't use it in this recipe, one of their favorite fresh fish is the carp, a true delicacy in much of Asia.

8 fresh mussels

1 small fresh crab

4 large fresh shrimp

1 small squid

6-ounce fillet of sea bass or other
    white fish

4 1/3 cups chicken stock

2 pickled plums with juice

1/4 cup fish sauce (*nam pla*)

Salt to taste

Freshly ground white pepper

5 dried bird's eye chiles (chiltepins),
    crushed; or substitute piquins

3 tablespoons fresh orange juice

2 tablespoons lemon juice

Freshly chopped cilantro leaves

Scrub the mussels with a stiff wire brush and rinse in salted cold water. Cook the crab in rapidly boiling water for 2 minutes, then cut into four pieces. Shell and devein the shrimp, leaving the tails intact. Clean the squid and cut into four pieces. Cut the sea bass into bite-size pieces.

Pour the chicken stock into a large pot and bring to a boil. Add the pickled plums, with juice, the fish sauce, salt, and white pepper. Reduce the heat and simmer gently for 10 minutes, then add all the seafood and the chiles, orange juice, and lemon juice. Cook over medium heat until the seafood is completely cooked (discarding any mussels that fail to open), then garnish with the fresh cilantro leaves and serve.

Serves: 4

Heat Scale: Medium

Spicy Anchovy Fish Pot

(*Lap Pa*)

This Thai recipe features *Stolephorus heterolobus,* better known as the anchovy. The anchovy is fished extensively in Asian waters, and is eaten fresh, marinated, salted, and dried. It is also one of the main ingredients used in fish sauce.

4 cups water

1 rib celery with leaves

1 sprig parsley

1 carrot, chopped

1 lemon, halved

1 two-pound perch or other white fish, cleaned and filleted; reserve the head and trimmings

1/4 cup glutinous rice

3 anchovy fillets packed in oil, drained, but 1 tablespoon oil reserved

4 dried cayenne chiles, seeded and reduced to a powder in a blender or mortar

2 serrano or jalapeño chiles, seeded and minced

3 green onions with tops, thinly sliced

1 slice (1/8 inch) peeled fresh ginger, finely chopped

1 tablespoon fresh mint leaves

1 tablespoon fish sauce (*nam pla*), or to taste

Lime wedges for garnish

Combine the water, celery, parsley, carrot, and lemon in a large saucepan and heat to boiling over medium high heat. Add fish head and trimmings, reheat to boiling, and skim the foam from the top. Cover the saucepan, reduce the heat, and simmer for 20 minutes. Strain the fish broth through a sieve lined with a double thickness of dampened cheesecloth. Set the broth aside.

Heat the rice in a dry, heavy skillet over medium heat, stirring constantly until lightly toasted, about 4 minutes. Remove from the heat. Pour the rice into a blender or food processor and grind as fine as possible. Or, grind into a powder with mortar and pestle. Reserve.

Heat the anchovy fillets and the 1 tablespoon reserved oil in a large, heavy saucepan over low heat; mash the anchovy fillets to a paste with the back of a fork. Stir the reserved fish broth into the anchovy paste and keep warm over low heat.

Cut the fish fillets into 1-inch pieces. Process the fish pieces in a food processor until they are reduced almost to a paste; or, place them on a cutting board and chop them fine, using a large, heavy knife. Add the reserved ground rice and the ground dried chiles and blend thoroughly.

Just before serving, heat the fish stock mixture to boiling. Place the fish mixture, fresh chiles, green onions, ginger, and mint in a large serving bowl. Pour the boiling fish stock mixture over the contents of the bowl and stir well. Serve at once in warmed individual bowls, seasoned with fish sauce and garnished with lime wedges.

Serves: 6 to 8

Heat Scale: Medium

Spicy Steamed Mussels with Coconut

(*Haw Mog Hoy*)

The coconut plays an important part in Thai cuisine. The tradition in upper-class households in this region says that coconut should be the first solid food to pass through the lips of any Thai baby. This is accomplished at the age of one month, when the infant is bathed in water containing coconut, and is fed three spoonfuls of soft, young coconut by a priest.

2 pounds fresh mussels

2 tablespoons vegetable oil

1 shallot, chopped

1 clove garlic, chopped

4 fresh serrano or jalapeño chiles, seeded and chopped

1 teaspoon chopped cilantro root (or stems)

1 teaspoon chopped fresh ginger

1 teaspoon chopped lemongrass

$1/2$ teaspoon minced lemon peel

2 teaspoons shrimp paste

$3/4$ cup Coconut Milk (page 12)

1 large egg, lightly whisked

2 tablespoons rice flour

Salt to taste

Freshly ground black pepper

$1/4$ cup basil leaves

Scrub the mussels with a stiff wire brush and rinse in salted cold water. Cook in a steamer until they open, discarding any that fail to do so. Remove the mussels from the shells, retaining the larger shells.

Heat the oil in a pan and sauté the shallot and garlic for 3 to 4 minutes, then add the chiles, cilantro, ginger, lemongrass, lemon peel, and shrimp paste. Continue to cook, stirring frequently, until the mixture gives off a fragrant aroma, then remove from the pan and place in a mixing bowl. Add the coconut milk, egg, rice flour, salt and freshly ground black pepper and stir to combine thoroughly.

Blanch the basil leaves in boiling water and arrange on the bottom of the retained mussel shells. Place three mussels in each shell and spoon a little sauce on top of each. Place in a steamer or in the oven and cook until heated through, then serve immediately.

Serves: 4

Heat Scale: Medium

Singapore Chile Crab

Here is a classic hot and spicy dish from the island nation of Singapore. It is
said there is an endless supply of chiles in Singapore, and also a huge assortment of chile pastes and hot sauces of every heat level. If you can't make it to
Singapore right away, this dish will give you the inspiration needed to buy
your ticket!

2 tablespoons sugar

1 tablespoon salt

2 tablespoons tomato paste

1 1/2 teaspoons fresh ginger, peeled
    and chopped

2 garlic cloves, chopped

4 serrano or jalapeño chiles, seeded
    and chopped

2 pounds live hard-shelled crabs

1/2 cup vegetable oil

2 large eggs, beaten lightly

In a small bowl, stir together the sugar, salt, and tomato paste. In a mortar
with a pestle, mash to a paste the ginger, garlic, and chiles.

In a pot, blanch the crabs in boiling water for 2 minutes, drain them,
and let them cool until they can be handled. Discard the top shells, the
aprons, gills, sand sacs, mouths, and mandibles, and break the bodies in half,
reserving the claws for other use.

In a large, heavy skillet heat the oil over moderately high heat until it is
hot but not smoking. Fry the crabs in the oil, turning them, for 4 minutes.
Transfer the crabs with a slotted spoon to a platter. In the oil remaining in the
skillet, fry the ginger mixture, stirring, for 2 minutes. Stir in the tomato paste
mixture, stirring until well combined. Add the crabs and cook, stirring, until
the crabs are coated. Add the eggs and cook, stirring about 1 minute, or until
the eggs are just set. Serve with a spicy rice dish from Chapter 8.

Serves: 4

Heat Scale: Medium

Prawns in Chile-Garlic Sauce

(*Udang Goreng Chilli*)

This simple recipe is a *Nonya* favorite. The garlic combined with the chile makes for a spicy Singapore extravaganza. The Fried Coconut Triangles (page 77) in Chapter 3 are a nice addition to this meal.

1/2 pound large prawns, peeled and deveined; or substitute large shrimp

10 serrano or jalapeño chiles, seeded

10 cloves garlic

1 teaspoon minced ginger

1/4 cup vegetable oil

2 tablespoons soy sauce

Trim the heads of the prawns by removing the feelers, but leave the heads on. Wash the prawns and pat dry with paper towels.

In a food processor, puree the chiles, garlic, and ginger to make a rough paste.

Heat the oil in a wok and, when it smokes, add the chile-garlic paste and stir-fry until fragrant. Add the prawns and stir-fry for about 5 minutes. Add the soy sauce and stir-fry until well mixed, about 1 minute.

Serve with hot steamed rice.

Serves: 2

Heat Scale: Hot

Singapore Fried Prawns with Dried Chile

Here is another Singapore classic, this time featuring prawns. Prawns are used extensively in Asian cooking, and are dried, ground, and processed into various types of pungent pastes. The twelve cayenne chiles in this recipe's sauce will definitely give your guests a thrill!

The Sauce

12 dried cayenne peppers, seeded and crushed

1/4 cup rice wine

1 tablespoon vegetable oil

2 teaspoons sugar

1 teaspoon soy sauce

4 thin slices fresh ginger

4 diagonal thin slices green onion

1 garlic clove, minced

1/4 teaspooon cornstarch mixed with 1/2 teaspoon cold water

Dash of dark soy sauce

The Prawns

1 tablespoon cornstarch

1 teaspoon light soy sauce

2 eggs, beaten

2 tablespoons flour

1/2 teaspoon salt

3 piquin chiles, seeded and crushed; or substitute other small, hot dried chiles

Freshly ground black pepper

Vegetable oil for deep frying

1 pound large prawns or shrimp, shelled and deveined

For the sauce, combine all of the ingredients in a small saucepan over high heat and stir until the mixture thickens slightly. Remove from heat.

For the prawns, combine the cornstarch and soy sauce in a small bowl and blend until smooth. Add the eggs, flour, salt, piquins, and pepper and blend thoroughly.

Heat the oil in large saucepan or deep-fat fryer to 400°F. Meanwhile, pat the prawns dry with paper towels. Dip the prawns into the batter, then drop gently into the oil and fry for 15 to 20 seconds. Remove them with a slotted spoon and drain well on paper towels.

Reheat the sauce. Add the prawns to the sauce in batches, stirring just enough to coat. Transfer to a platter and serve immediately with rice.

Serves: 3 to 4

Heat Scale: Extremely Hot

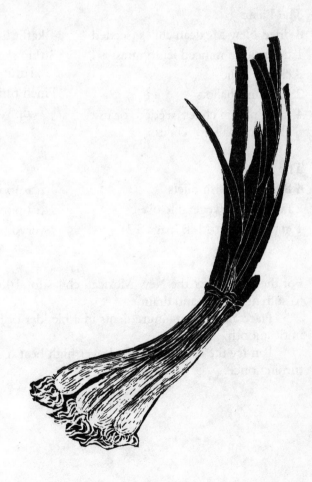

Lemongrass-Enrobed Catfish Fillets

(*Trey Trung Kroeung*)

This Cambodian recipe was collected by David Karp, from the Elephant Walk Restaurant in Somerville, Massachusetts. The chef features catfish in this recipe, as it is close in flavor and texture to some of the freshwater fish found in Cambodia.

The Paste

3 dried New Mexican chiles, seeded

1 tablespoon minced lemongrass

3 cloves garlic

2 medium shallots

4 dried piquin chiles, seeded; or use other small hot chiles

4 kaffir lime leaves

3 thin slices peeled galangal; or substitute ginger

Pinch turmeric powder

1/2 cup water

The Fish

4 8-ounce catfish fillets

2 tablespoons vegetable oil

1 cup Coconut Milk (page 12)

1 teaspoon salt

2 teaspoons sugar

4 very finely julienned kaffir lime leaves for garnish

For the paste, soak the New Mexican chiles for 10 minutes in lukewarm water to soften; remove and drain.

Place all the paste ingredients in a blender or food processor and puree until smooth.

Pan fry the catfish in the oil over high heat until firm, but not browned, turning once.

Using a separate pan, cook the paste over medium heat for about 2 minutes, stirring constantly, until the aroma is released. Add the coconut milk, salt, and sugar. Add the fish to the sauce and cook 5 more minutes. If the paste is too thick, add more water until the desired consistency is achieved.

Garnish with julienned kaffir lime leaves, and serve with jasmine rice.

Serves: 4

Heat Scale: Medium

Curried Shrimp and Cucumbers

(*Kari Bongkong Lasak*)

One of Cambodia's most popular recipes, this dish offers a twist on the usual use of coconut milk by spiking it with lemon juice. The cuisine of this region offers many unique and wonderful culinary contributions.

2 cloves garlic, crushed

2 green onions, chopped

1 1/2-inch piece ginger, peeled and chopped

1 teaspoon ground fennel

2 teaspoons ground coriander

1/2 teaspoon turmeric

2 teaspoons cayenne powder

4 tablespoons peanut oil

1 pound medium shrimp, shelled

2 cups Coconut Milk (page 12)

1 cucumber, quartered lengthwise, deseeded, and cut into thick slices

2 teaspoons grated lemon peel

Juice of 1 lemon

1 teaspoon sugar

1 tablespoon fish sauce (*nam pla*)

Place the garlic, green onions, and ginger into a food processor and blend to a puree. Scrape the mixture from the blender and transfer to a mixing bowl. Stir in the fennel, coriander, turmeric, and cayenne powder.

Heat the oil in a deep frying pan. When hot, add the spice puree and fry for 3 minutes. Add the shrimp and stir-fry for 5 minutes. Stir in the coconut milk and bring to the boil. Reduce the heat to low, add the cucumber and remaining ingredients, and simmer gently for 5 minutes, or until the cucumber is soft. Serve at once with rice or noodles.

Serves: 4

Heat Scale: Medium

Fish with Ginger Salsa

This recipe is from *Chile Pepper* Contributing Editor Richard Sterling. Richard has spent many years in Southeast Asia, and collected this recipe on one of his trips back to Vietnam.

1/4 teaspoon salt

1/2 teaspoon ground black pepper

1 teaspoon sugar

4 teaspoons fish sauce (*nam pla*)

1 whole fish, snapper recommended, about 2 pounds, cleaned, head and tail left on

12 large basil leaves

4 cloves garlic, minced

1 tablespoon grated ginger

1 serrano or jalapeño chile, seeded and minced

Juice of 1 lime

Vietnamese Dipping Sauce (*nuoc cham*, page 31)

Bamboo steamer

Combine the salt, pepper, sugar, and fish sauce, and sprinkle it over the fish. Marinate for 30 minutes on a plate covered with the basil leaves.

Combine the garlic, ginger, chile, and lime juice and spread evenly over the top of the fish. Transfer the fish and the plate to a steamer and cook for 30 minutes.

Serve with *nuoc cham*.

Serves: 4

Heat Scale: Mild

Tantalizing Catfish

(*Amok*)

Cambodian cooking is very similar to Thai cooking, which also shares the influence of Vietnam, China, and Indonesia. It can be characterized by its use of lemongrass, galangal, ginger, garlic, and many freshwater fish, most of which are not available in the United States. We have used catfish in this recipe, as it bears a close resemblance to its Vietnamese counterparts. This recipe requires advance preparation.

1 teaspoon galangal, peeled and sliced thinly

1 clove garlic, peeled

1 1/2 tablespoons kaffir lime leaves, very finely julienned

1/4 teaspoon turmeric powder

4 tablespoons fresh lemongrass, minced

5 dried santaka or piquin chiles, seeded and soaked 10 minutes in lukewarm water, chopped fine

2 tablespoons fish sauce (*nam pla*)

1 egg, well beaten

2 tablespoons sugar

2 cups Coconut Milk (page 12)

1 1/2 pounds catfish fillets, sliced into strips 1/4 inch thick

8 pieces of banana leaves, cut 14 inches by 10 inches

1/2 pound fresh spinach leaves

Toothpicks

9- or 10-inch bamboo steamer

In a blender or food processor, combine the galangal, garlic, 1 teaspoon of julienned kaffir lime leaves, turmeric, lemongrass, chiles, fish sauce, egg, sugar, and coconut milk. Process, scraping the sides of the container occasionally, until ingredients are pureed.

Combine the contents of the blender and the catfish in a glass bowl, coating the fish thoroughly. Cover and refrigerate overnight, or at least for 5 hours.

Put one piece of banana leaf atop another, to make a double thickness. Place one quarter of the spinach leaves into the center and top with one quarter of the fish mixture (about 1 cup). Garnish with a pinch of julienned kaffir lime leaves. Fold the two layers of banana leaves lengthwise in thirds, then fold the ends up to the top and secure with toothpicks. Keep the sides up to prevent leaking. Repeat the procedure, making four packages.

Place the bottom rack of a 9- or 10-inch bamboo steamer in a wok and pour in water to about an inch below the steamer. Put two fish packages on the bottom rack. Fit a second rack above it and place the remaining two packages on it. Cover the steamers, heat the water to boiling, and cook for about 5 minutes. Reduce the heat to medium low and cook for 45 minutes. To serve, remove the toothpicks and open the packages.

Serves: 4

Heat Scale: Medium

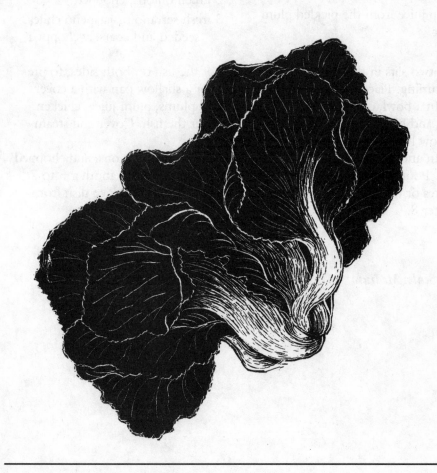

Steamed Spicy Fish

(*Pla Nuang*)

Vietnam is also the origin of this steamed fish recipe. The pickled plums can be found in Asian markets and offer a tart taste. Pickled mangoes can also be used, if you would like a sweeter flavor.

1 three-pound whole grouper or
    snapper, cleaned and scaled,
    head and tail left on
3 pickled plums, coarsely chopped
¹/₄ cup juice from the pickled plum
    jar

¹/₂ cup chicken stock
¹/₄ teaspoon ground black pepper
¹/₄ cup celery leaves
2 green onions, chopped
3 fresh serrano or jalapeño chiles,
    seeded and coarsely chopped

Make two slits in the skin across the width of the fish on both sides, to prevent curling. Place the fish in a fish poacher or a shallow pan with a cover.

In a bowl, combine the chopped pickled plums, plum juice, chicken stock, and black pepper. Pour this mixture over the fish. Cover and steam over low heat for 15 minutes.

In another bowl, combine the celery leaves, green onions, and chopped chiles. Pour this mixture over the fish, cover, and steam for another 5 to 7 minutes or until the fish is completely cooked. Serve with a rice dish from Chapter 8.

Serves: 4

Heat Scale: Medium

Pigfish Curry
(*Nga Wetma*)

The Burmese call the grouper the "pig of the sea," referring to its meaty texture and large size. A grouper may grow to more than 700 pounds. This curry is sweet, hot, and smooth all at the same time.

1-pound grouper fillets, cut into
    1-inch cubes
1 teaspoon paprika
1/4 teaspoon turmeric
1/2 teaspoon salt
3 teaspoons fish sauce (*nam pla*)
2 tablespoons corn oil
2 tablespoons finely chopped onion

1 tablespoon minced fresh ginger
2 garlic cloves, minced
1 cup diced tomatoes, fresh or
    canned
2/3 cup water
2 tablespoons chopped cilantro
2 serrano or jalapeño chiles, seeded
    and sliced thin

In a large dish, marinate the fish with 1/2 teaspoon paprika, 1/8 teaspoon turmeric, the salt, and 1 teaspoon fish sauce for 15 minutes.

Heat the oil in a pan and fry the onion, ginger, garlic, and the rest of the turmeric and paprika over moderate heat for 2 minutes. Add the tomatoes and remaining fish sauce and stir-fry for 3 minutes to reduce the mixture to a thick puree.

Add the fish and stir-fry it and the sauce for 5 minutes. Add the water, stir a moment, cover the pan, and cook over low heat for 20 minutes to evaporate the liquid and create a thick sauce.

Sprinkle the curry with the cilantro and chiles and serve with rice or noodles.

Serves: 4

Heat Scale: Medium

Tangy Marinated Fish

(*Umai*)

The key to this recipe from Borneo is to use the freshest fish possible. The Latin American version of this dish would be ceviche, which also involves the cooking of fish with lime juice. Fresh scallops or shrimp can be substituted for an interesting change.

½ cup freshly squeezed lime juice
    (or more if needed)

1 pound very fresh fish fillets
    (Spanish mackerel preferred),
    cut into thin slices

3 serrano or jalapeño chiles, seeded
    and chopped

1 teaspoon salt

8 shallots, thinly sliced

1 two-inch piece ginger, peeled and
    grated

2 sprigs cilantro, chopped

2 sprigs celery leaves, chopped

Reserve 2 tablespoons of lime juice; marinate the fish in the remaining juice for at least 30 minutes, stirring once or twice, until the fish turns white. Drain and discard the lime juice marinade.

    While the fish is marinating, pound the chiles with the salt until a paste is formed. When the fish is ready, mix it with the chile paste, shallots, ginger, fresh cilantro, celery, and reserved lime juice. Taste and add more salt if desired. Serve immediately with any fried rice dish from Chapter 8.

Serves: 3 to 4

Heat Scale: Medium

Fiery Party Snapper

(*Ikan Bandeng*)

This fish makes a truly elegant entrée for a dinner party when unwrapped at the table, says Rosemary Ogilvie, who collected this fine recipe in Bali for *Chile Pepper* magazine.

1 whole snapper or grouper, about 3 to 4 pounds, cleaned but head and tail left on

1 medium onion, chopped

2 cloves garlic, minced

1 teaspoon minced ginger

¼ cup Tamarind Sauce (page 14)

1 tablespoon dark soy sauce

1 tablespoon vegetable oil

1 teaspoon turmeric

2 teaspoons Basic Spice Islands Chile Paste (*sambalan*, page 18), or more to taste

1 teaspoon salt

3 tablespoons finely chopped cilantro

Aluminum foil

Preheat the oven to 350°F.

Wash the fish, dry well with paper towels, and score the flesh diagonally on each side.

Place the onion, garlic, ginger, tamarind sauce, soy sauce, oil, turmeric, *sambalan*, and salt into a blender and puree until smooth. Rub the mixture well into the fish on both sides and put the remaining mixture inside the body cavity.

Line a baking dish with aluminum foil. Place the fish on the foil, sprinkle with the cilantro, and fold the foil over to enclose the fish.

Bake for 35 to 40 minutes. When cooked, the flesh of the fish will appear milky white and be easy to flake with a fork.

Lift the fish onto a serving platter and open the foil at the table.

Serves: 6

Heat Scale: Mild

Fried Fish with Tomatoes and Eggs

(*Cardillo*)

This Filipino recipe illustrates the spread of chiles into the Far East. This entrée is especially good with halibut fillets.

1 pound white fish fillets, halibut recommended, cut into thin strips

Salt

2 tablespoons olive oil

1 clove garlic, crushed

1 medium onion, sliced

2 fresh piquin chiles, seeded and chopped; or substitute other small, hot chiles

2 tomatoes, sliced

1/2 cup water

2 eggs, beaten

Place the fish strips on a platter and rub a little salt into them. Heat the olive oil in a frying pan and fry the fish strips until golden brown. Remove and set aside.

Fry the garlic in the olive oil remaining in the pan and when it turns golden, add the onion, chiles, and tomatoes. Cook until the tomato is soft and pulpy, then add the water and simmer for 3 to 5 minutes. Place the fried fish into the sauce, add the eggs, and cook briefly, about 1 to 2 minutes. Serve immediately.

Serves: 4

Heat Scale: Medium

The Monster of the Mekong

“Restaurants in Chiang Khlong occasionally serve *pla buk*, a monstrous type of catfish considered the largest of its kind in the world. *Pla buk* can grow up to 3 meters in length and weigh over 300 kilograms, making it the undisputed monster of the Mekong. The fish is praised for its white, succulent meat, which tastes like milk-fed veal and guarantees long life to all who eat it.

“The process of catching *pla buk* begins when local priests invoke dockside prayers to summon the spirits of the legendary fish and bring good luck to the fishermen. Fishermen then set out in sleek pirogues on 24-hour fishing shifts, only returning after a successful catch . . . which can pay for a new boat or provide for the children's education.

“Sadly, the *pla buk* is an endangered species. Earlier this century, *pla buk* were plentiful and could be captured from Tonle Sap in Cambodia to Th Li Lake in Southern China. Overfishing, however, has severely reduced their numbers to the point where just a few dozen are being caught during the April–June spawning season. The Thai Fisheries Department has recently taken steps to save the fish by initiating a strict quota system and conducted an ambitious breeding program.**”**

Carl Parkes

Don't Bother to Ask for the Snapper Special

“On Bali the presence over several decades of a tourist market has resulted in a plethora of reasonably priced restaurants of various foreign persuasions. Predictably enough, it has also produced restaurants with Indonesian food far more complicated than that cooked in the Balinese home. Probably the greatest surprise is that few of the restaurants offer dishes that involve fish; the Balinese traditionally consider the sea impure, full of danger and demons, whereas the land and its produce are sacred."

Anthony Weller

Curries as Panacea

"This is the famous Java curry; and if you have taken plenty of the pepper and chutney, and other hot things, your mouth will burn for half an hour as though you had drunk from a kettle of boiling water. And when you have eaten freely of curry, you don't want any other breakfast. Everybody eats curry here daily, because it is said to be good for the health by keeping the liver active, and preventing fevers."

A wonderful description of the effects of Indonesian
curries appeared in a nineteenth century travel book,
The Boy Travelers in the Far East, by Thomas Knox

Filipino Fish Farms

"In addition to the bountiful resource of the ocean, the Filipinos have another source of protein—freshwater fish ponds. Though aquaculture, the raising of fish and shellfish under controlled conditions, may be new in some areas of the world, that activity has been going on in the Philippines for at least a thousand years. Fish ponds supply the population with over twenty varieties of fish, crabs, shrimps, oysters, and other shellfish. The milkfish, *bangus,* is one of the most popular fish raised in ponds in the Philippines, and with good reason. Its flesh is white, solid, and delicious, and it lends itself to many satisfying meals."

Reynaldo Alejandro

Khmer Cookery

❝Hot peppers, lemongrass, mint, and ginger add flavor to many Khmer dishes; sugar is added to many foods. Several kinds of noodles are eaten. The basic diet is supplemented by vegetables and by fruits—bananas, mangoes, papayas, rambutan, and palm fruit—both wild and cultivated, which grow abundantly throughout the country. Beef, pork, poultry, and eggs are added to meals on special occasions, or, if the family can afford it, daily. In the cities, the diet has been affected by many Western items of food. French, Chinese, Vietnamese, and Indian cuisine were available in Phnom Penh in pre-Khmer Rouge days.❞

Robert K. Headly, Jr.

Mexican–Filipino Trade

❝The venerable galleon trade between the Philippines and New Spain continued as a government monopoly until 1815, when the last official galleon from Acapulco docked at Manila. The Royal Company of the Philippines, chartered by the Spanish king in 1785, promoted direct trade between the islands and Spain. All Philippine goods were given tariff-free status, and the company, hand in hand with Basco y Vargas' Economic Society, encouraged the growth of a cash-crop economy by investing a portion of its early profits in the cultivation of sugar, indigo, peppers, and mulberry trees for silk, as well as in textile factories.❞

Frederica M. Bunge

Rijsttafel

Rice and Other Side Dishes

S ide dishes are as important to a Southeast Asian meal as the main course itself, whether it be meat, fish, or vegetable. There are several rice side dishes included in this chapter to accommodate the Western way of eating; however, this would not be the case in Southeast Asia, where rice would at the forefront of every meal, including breakfast.

An incredible variety of different types of rice exists, and they all differ in color, flavor, and aroma. Each country has its own particular favorites, as well as its own standard of quality. Even the methods of cooking vary. Rice is also subject to many customs, superstitions, and religious beliefs; in Thailand, the Thai rice goddess, Mother Posop, reigns supreme.

The rice recipes presented here will seem unique to Western palates; for example The Spicy Rice Medley (page 226) from Malaysia has the interesting addition of roasted fish. The Thai recipe for Piquant Pineapple Fried Rice (page 227) combines fruit and chiles. Jasmine rice is the preferred rice to use in Chile Fried Rice (page 228), a hearty side dish from Thailand. One recipe is given here for Yellow Festive Rice (page 230), although there are many variations, according to Devagi Shanmugan of Singapore. Two versions of Indonesian Rice (*nasi goreng*) are given here; this rice dish is another one that has many permutations, depending on what the cook happens to have on hand. The first recipe, Indonesian Spicy Fried Rice (page 231), has the tasty additions of shrimp paste and *sambalan*. The next variation, Indonesian Savory Rice (page 232), contains more herbs and spices, such as coriander and cinnamon. Laotians eat only glutinous rice, or sticky rice, and the recipe for Glutinous Rice with Chiles, Carrots, and Tofu (page 234) makes an exciting and unusual side dish.

Because rice is the predominant starch in Southeast Asian cuisine, potatoes play only a minor role. Since potatoes are so easy to grow and require little maintenance, farmers simply plant them along with the other vegetables in the garden. These two recipes are a great way to use up leftover cooked potatoes because thrifty, frugal cooks throw nothing away. Perkadels (page 236) hail from Bali, and, very simply, are deep-fried spicy mashed potato balls. The Potato *Sambal* (page 237) from Indonesia resembles a spicy, cold mashed potato salad.

All kinds of noodles play a major role in Southeast Asian cuisine; they show up in soups, stews, and as side dishes, some hot from the frying pan. The most common kind of noodle used is made with rice flour, rather than the wheat flour noodles we are used to in the West. Noodles are also made from agar gelatin, bean curd, bean curd skin, mung bean flour, and rice flour vermicelli. A recipe from Thailand, Herbed Crispy Vermicelli (page 238), is enlivened by the addition of garlic and chile powder. Another Thai recipe, Spicy Thai Noodles (page 240), is one that has many variations; in this particular *pad Thai* recipe, roasted peanuts add some crunch. Vegetarian Fried Noodles (page 242) could be a complete meal in itself. The flavors of the chiles, shrimp paste (*blacan*), and bean curd blend well with the otherwise bland noodles.

In Southeast Asia, the flowers, hearts, leaves, and shoots of the banana are all utilized in some manner. Bananas are also battered, fried, baked, and sun-dried. And, in Malaysia, bananas are also curried, as in the recipe for Malaysian Banana Curry (page 244). Here, unripe bananas are combined with chiles, spices, and coconut milk to make this delectable curry. Another unusual and tasty side dish is from Vietnam; Happy Pancakes (page 246) are rich with vegetables and are served with a hot and spicy dipping sauce.

Vegetable side dishes become gourmet creations with the deft touch of Southeast Asian ingredients. Moms in this part of the world never have to bribe their children to eat the vegetables. Vegetables, both raw and cooked, are an important component in the diet. Even the most jaded "cucumber avoider" will never think of cucumbers as uninteresting after trying the Chile and Coconut Braised Cucumbers (page 245) from Bali. The shallots, chiles, and coconut milk make this a special vegetable dish. Coconut milk is also used in Spicy Vegetables and Coconut Milk (page 248), giving it a rich flavor as well as blending well with the shrimp paste and the chile.

Cabbage takes on new meaning in Spicy Stir-Fried Cabbage (page 249); it is crisp, delicious, and spicy. Even cauliflower gets a special treatment in Chile Fried Cauliflower (page 250), which is jazzed up with garlic and chiles. For those of you who love smoky flavors, then Smoky Eggplant, Country Style (page 251) is a recipe to try. This Cambodian recipe is spiced with three sauces as well as the addition of some powerful chile. Another unusual Cambodian vegetable dish is Asparagus Sheaves Kambu (page 252), which is sure to leave you wanting more. Three or four asparagus spears are bound together with a spicy paste and then deep fried. It could be as addictive as the Stuffed Chile Peppers (page 254) from Laos. The chiles are stuffed with an unusual variety of ingredients—a little fish, garlic, and fresh ginger—but frugal cooks will also add anything that they happen to have. But, remember to eat your vegetables because they are good for you!

Spicy Rice Medley with Roasted Fish

(*Nasi Kerabu*)

This Malaysian rice dish has just a touch of roasted fish added to give it a different flavor dimension, and it contrasts nicely with the coconut and chiles. Serve the rice at room temperature with one of the meat recipes from Chapter 5 or one of the poultry recipes from Chapter 6.

2 cups cooked white rice, chilled
   slightly

1 teaspoon whole black pepper,
   crushed

1/2 cup fish, roasted and chopped;
   grouper preferred

1 cup chopped red onion

1/4 cup shredded coconut

1/4 cup sliced and cooked long
   beans; or substitute green beans

3/4 cup sliced cucumber

1/4 cup bean sprouts

1/4 cup wild ginger flower or ginger
   buds (*bunga kantan*), finely
   sliced; or substitute 1/8 cup
   grated fresh ginger

3 fresh serrano or jalapeño chiles,
   seeds and stems removed,
   minced

Garnishes

2 tablespoons chopped fresh mint
   leaves

5 scallions, sliced

In a large bowl, toss together all of the ingredients except the garnishes. Place the rice in a serving bowl decorated with sliced scallions and fresh mint leaves.

Serves: 5 to 6

Heat Scale: Medium

Piquant Pineapple Fried Rice

(*Khow Pat Prik Sapbhalot*)

This rice dish makes a spectacular show piece at a buffet or a special dinner; the decoratively cut pineapple is one of those lovely Thai touches, as the Thais create the most gorgeous designs for fruit and vegetables. At the Royal Sheraton in Bangkok, we watched a master create some unforgetable flowers out of fresh vegetables. However, this dish also tastes wonderful with just the pineapple, chiles, and rice.

1 large ripe pineapple

2 to 3 tablespoons vegetable oil

3 fresh prawns, shelled, cleaned, and finely chopped

1/4 pound Chinese sausage, chopped, or browned ground pork

1 shallot, finely chopped

1 clove garlic, minced

2 fresh red serrano or jalapeño chiles, seeds and stems removed and sliced into rings

2 cups cooked and cooled rice

1/4 teaspoon freshly ground black pepper

1 tablespoon fish sauce (*nam pla*)

1 tablespoon soy sauce

1/2 teaspoon lemon zest

1 teaspoon sugar

3/4 cup pineapple pulp, set in a colander to drain

Cut the pineapple in half lengthwise, using a decorative zigzag cut. Carefully remove the flesh, measure out 3/4 cup, and place it in a colander to drain; set aside. Cut a very small slice from the bottom of each half of the pineapple, so that they will lay flat without tipping.

Heat the oil in a wok or large skillet and add the prawns, sausage, shallot, garlic, and chile rings and sauté for 2 minutes.

Add the remaining ingredients and toss them until they are blended and heated through. Serve immediately or keep warm in a 350°F oven for a few minutes until serving.

Serves: 4

Heat Scale: Mild

Chile Fried Rice

(*Kao Pad Prik*)

This spicy Thai side dish is not for the faint-hearted! It is rich in chiles and makes a great accompaniment for hearty meat dishes. The preferred rice to use is jasmine, but ordinary white rice is transformed when it is cooked in this manner. Chilling the rice first helps to keep the grains separated when it is mixed with all of the other ingredients.

2 tablespoons vegetable oil

1/2 cup onion, finely chopped

3 fresh serrano of jalapeño chiles, seeds and stems removed, minced

1 tablespoon Red Curry Paste (page 41)

2 cloves garlic, minced

1/4 cup finely minced pork or ham

4 cups cooked rice, chilled

2 eggs, beaten

1 tablespoon fish sauce (*nam pla*)

2 teaspoons sweet soy sauce

Salt and ground white pepper to taste

1/4 cup green onions, finely chopped

Garnishes

1/3 cup thinly sliced cucumber

3 tablespoons cilantro, minced

Heat the oil in a wok or large skillet and fry the onion and the chiles until the onion starts to wilt, about 1 to 2 minutes. Then, add the red curry paste and fry for 2 minutes, until the oil starts to separate.

Add the garlic and the pork and fry, stirring, for 2 minutes.

Stir in the rice and toss until it is coated with the chile paste mixture.

Make a deep well in the center of the rice mixture and add the beaten eggs, and allow them to cook, undisturbed, for about 20 seconds, then start to mix them throughout the rice.

Add the fish sauce, sweet soy sauce, salt and pepper, and green onions and toss into the rice.

Place the rice on a heated platter and garnish with the cucumber and cilantro.

Serves: 4

Heat Scale: Hot

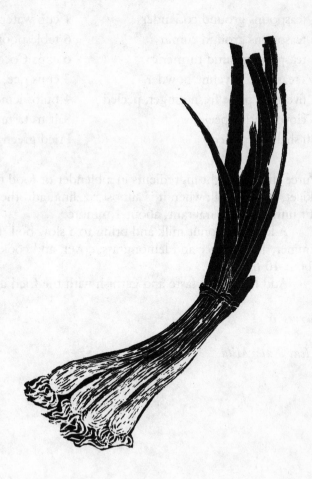

Yellow Festive Rice

(*Nasi Kunyit*)

We thank Devagi Shanmugan, who runs the Thomson Cooking School in Singapore, for this rice recipe that makes a very colorful, fragrant dish that goes well with meat dishes. If you ever get to Singapore, be sure to take some of her classes. Remember to use coconut milk, not canned coconut cream, which is too sweet.

4 teaspoons ground coriander

2 teaspoons ground cumin

1 teaspoon ground turmeric

1/2 teaspoon cayenne powder

1 five-inch piece fresh ginger, peeled

3 cloves garlic, peeled

20 shallots, peeled

1 cup water

6 tablespoons vegetable oil

6 cups Coconut Milk (page 12)

3 cups rice, washed and drained

4 bulbs lemongrass

Salt to taste

Fried green onion rings

Puree the first eight ingredients in a blender or food processor. In a heavy skillet, heat the oil; when it is almost sizzling, add the pureed ingredients and stir until they are fragrant, about 1 minute.

Add the coconut milk and bring to a slow boil. Reduce the heat to a simmer, add the rice and lemongrass, cover, and cook until the rice is done—about 40 minutes.

Add the salt to taste and garnish with the fried green onion rings.

Serves: 6

Heat Scale: Mild

Indonesian Spicy Fried Rice

(*Nasi Goreng* No. 1)

This Balinese specialty comes from *Chile Pepper* magazine correspondent Rosemary Ann Ogilvie. She comments: "*Nasi goreng* is the Indonesian term for fried rice. Recipes will vary, as no two dishes are ever quite the same—it depends on what combinations of seemingly endless ingredients are used. *Sambal ulek* is a paste made of ground chiles and salt and can be found in Asian markets."

3 eggs, lightly beaten

2 medium onions, coarsely chopped

2 cloves garlic

1/2 teaspoon shrimp paste

2 tablespoons vegetable oil

1 pound boneless pork or lean beef, cut in thin strips

1 pound medium prawns or shrimp, shelled and deveined

6 cups cold cooked rice

2 cups firmly packed mung bean sprouts

2 tablespoons light soy sauce

1 tablespoon prepared *sambal oelek* or substitute *sambalan* (page 18)

1 cucumber, thinly sliced

3 tablespoons dried onion flakes, fried in hot oil until golden brown, and drained

Pour the eggs into a large frying pan that has been sprayed with cooking spray and cook until the omelette is set. Remove and cut it into strips.

Combine the onions, garlic, and shrimp paste and blend to a paste. If no blender is available, finely chop the onions, crush the garlic, dissolve the shrimp paste in a little hot water, and combine the three ingredients.

Back to the frying pan: fry the paste in the oil for a minute. Add the meat to the pan and stir-fry for a couple more minutes, until cooked. Add the shrimp and cook until they are almost done. Stir in the rice, bean sprouts, soy sauce, and *sambal oelek,* tossing until it is well mixed and heated through.

Decorate with the cucumber, the strips of omelette, and the fried onion flakes and serve.

Serves: 6 to 8

Heat Scale: Mild

Indonesian Savory Rice

(*Nasi Goreng* No. 2)

The owners of the Golden Dragon Restaurant in Colorado Springs, Colorado, collected this recipe on one of their Southeast Asian trips and currently serve it in their restaurant. This dish is an attractive, tasty side dish that is easy to make.

4 tablespoons vegetable oil

1 cup onions, chopped

1 tablespoon garlic, chopped

1 tablespoon AiKan Sweet & Spicy Master Sauce (or see note below for substitution)

1 teaspoon ground coriander

1/2 teaspoon cinnamon

2 quarts cooked rice

4 eggs

2 tablespoons water

3/4 pound shrimp, cooked and peeled

1/2 pound ham, cut into strips

Heat 2 tablespoons of the oil in a heavy skillet and sauté the onion and garlic until the onion is wilted, about 1 to 2 minutes. Stir in the AiKan (or the substitution), coriander, and cinnamon; reduce the heat and cook, stirring, for about 20 seconds. Stir in the rice, mix well, and keep warm.

Combine the eggs and the water in a bowl and whisk until frothy. In a skillet, heat the remaining 2 tablespoons of oil, pour in the eggs, and cook; carefully pull the edges away from the side of the skillet, and allow the uncooked eggs to slide down to the bottom, as when cooking an omelette. Slide the eggs from the pan, roll up, and slice into pinwheels.

To serve, heap the rice in a large bowl and garnish the top with the shrimp. Create runners down the rice with the ham. Place the egg pinwheels around the edge.

Note   If AiKan sauces are not available in your area, they can be ordered (see Mail-Order Sources), or use this substitution:

    1 tablespoon ground coriander
    1 teaspoon ground turmeric
    1 tablespoon ground cumin
    1/2 teaspoon hot red ground chile
    1/2 teaspoon ground ginger

Serves: 8 to 10

Heat Scale: Mild

Glutinous Rice with Chiles, Carrots, and Tofu

This hot and spicy Laotian recipe is a good accompaniment to grilled meats or poultry. The pureed carrots not only add color, they also add a unique flavor to this rice dish. Although this dish takes some prior preparation and planning (because of the soaking of the rice), it is easily prepared after that stage. While it is baking, you are free to prepare that terrific dinner that is to follow.

1 cup glutinous rice, soaked overnight and then drained

3 large carrots, cooked

2 cups tofu, excess water squeezed out

1 fresh green serrano or jalapeño chile, seeds and stem removed

Sprinkling of fresh nutmeg

1 egg, beaten

1 1/2 tablespoons flour

1 to 2 tablespoons olive oil

1/3 cup breadcrumbs

Preheat the oven to 375°F.

Steam the rice for 20 minutes and then divide it into two portions. Line an 8-inch square pan with aluminum foil, with the foil extending over the edge of the pan; add the rice, packing it down tightly to make a thin layer. Allow the rice to sit for a few minutes. Remove the rice from the pan, using the foil to lift it out. Cut the mixture in half and set aside.

Puree the carrots, tofu, and chile and pour the mixture into a bowl. Stir in the nutmeg, egg, and flour and blend.

Lightly oil the 8-inch square pan and sprinkle in half of the breadcrumbs. Carefully pour in the carrot puree and spread it out evenly. Sprinkle the remaining breadcrumbs on top and drizzle 1 tablespoon of the oil over the top. Bake the puree for 15 minutes, or until it is firm.

After the puree has cooled, remove it from the pan, cut it in half, and place the two slices between the rice, pushing down a little.

Serve warm or at room temperature.

Serves: 3 to 4

Heat Scale: Mild

Perkadels

This Balinese recipe is from Rosemary Ann Ogilvie, who says, "What an unusual way to rework leftover mashed potatoes! Serve them as an accompaniment to both meats and poultry."

1 small onion, chopped

2 cloves garlic, minced

2 tablespoons butter or margarine

1/4 pound ground beef

3 small fresh hot red chiles, such as
serranos or jalapeños, stems
removed, minced

1/2 teaspoon nutmeg

6 shallots or green onions, chopped

2 eggs, separated

Vegetable oil for frying

3 cups cooked, mashed potatoes

Sauté the onion and garlic in the butter until golden brown. Add the beef, chiles, and nutmeg and toss over medium heat until the meat browns well. Stir in the shallots and cook for three more minutes.

Combine the meat mixture with the potatoes and add the egg yolks. Beat until well combined. Cool and refrigerate for 30 minutes.

Roll into balls the size and shape of an egg.

Beat the egg whites until just frothy and dip the balls into the egg whites. Deep fry in 350 to 375°F oil until the balls are golden brown. Drain the fried balls on paper towels.

Yield: 6 to 8

Heat Scale: Mild

Potato Sambal

(*Sambal Ubi Kentang*)

Although many people think of *sambals* as a spicy condiment or sauce that is added to other dishes, *sambals* also include side dishes that range in heat from mild to wild, particularly in Indonesia and Malaysia. This particular Indonesian recipe is a good example of a spicy side dish that is labeled a *"sambal."* Serve these spicy, chilled potatoes with a meat dish from Chapter 5.

1/2 pound potatoes (all approximately the same size)

1/4 teaspoon salt

2 serrano or jalapeño chiles, seeds and stems removed, minced

1/4 cup green onions, finely chopped

2 teaspoons fresh lime juice

2 tablespoons Coconut Cream (page 12)

1/4 teaspoon freshly grated nutmeg

2 tablespoons chopped cilantro

Put the scrubbed potatoes in a large pot and cover them with water. Bring the water to a boil and boil the potatoes, in their skins, for 15 to 20 minutes, or until a fork can easily pierce the potato. Drain the potatoes, let them cool, and then peel them.

Place the potatoes in a bowl and add the remaining ingredients, except the cilantro, and mash the potatoes very coarsely.

Mound the potato mixture in a serving bowl, sprinkle with the cilantro, and chill in the refrigerator until serving time.

Serves: 4

Heat Scale: Medium

Herbed Crispy Vermicelli

(*Mee Grob*)

This recipe was given to us at the Thai Cooking School at the Oriental Hotel in Bangkok, where we visited, inhaled the delightful aromas, and interviewed the chef. What a treat to the senses and the palate! Serve this with meat, chicken, or fish with the addition of bean sprouts on the side. It will lend some contrast in texture. Meat could also be added to the noodles to make a one-dish meal.

1 pound rice vermicelli

Enough vegetable oil for deep frying

4 tablespoons vegetable oil

1/2 cup chopped shallots

4 garlic cloves

1 cup yellow bean curd, cut into 3/4-inch cubes

1 teaspoon salt

5 eggs, beaten

1/4 cup vinegar

1/4 cup fish sauce (*nam pla*)

5 tablespoons sugar

1 teaspoon hot red chile powder

Garnishes

Sliced pickled garlic

Fresh serrano or Thai chiles, minced

Chopped cilantro

Sprinkle the noodles with cold water and allow them to soften for a few minutes. If they are not uniformly soft or are too dry, sprinkle more water on them. Keep them moist until frying time.

Heat the oil in a deep fat fryer and deep-fry the noodles in the hot oil until they are golden. Remove the noodles from the oil and keep them warm by wrapping them in paper towels so they remain crisp until they are needed.

Heat several tablespoons of the oil in a large skillet and fry the shallots and garlic. Push the mixture to one side of the pan and add the cubed bean curd; fry the curd until it is crisp, turning it carefully in the pan.

Add the salt and more oil if necessary. Add the eggs next, turning the contents continuously until the eggs are almost done.

Sprinkle the eggs with the vinegar, *nam pla*, sugar, and chile powder and stir until the ingredients are blended. Mix the crisp-fried noodles and the egg mixture and heat gently.

Serve the finished dish with any or all of the garnishes.

Serves: 6 to 8

Heat Scale: Mild

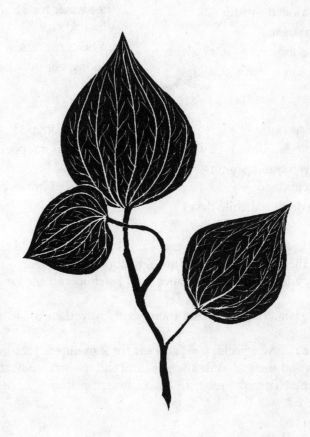

Spicy Thai Noodles

(*Pad Thai*)

When we were guests at the famous Mohonk Mountain House in New Paltz, New York, enjoying a hot and spicy Asian weekend, Gloria Zimmerman was one of the guest chefs, and she prepared her recipe for *pad Thai*. Gloria has studied Thai cuisine extensively and is a true master at preparing almost any Thai dish. We thank Gloria for truly tingling our taste buds at the Mohonk!

1/2 cup vegetable oil

6 cloves garlic, finely chopped

1 cup small cooked shrimp

1 tablespoon sugar

3 tablespoons fish sauce (*nam pla*)

1 1/2 tablespoons tomato ketchup

2 eggs, beaten

1/2 pound rice vermicelli, soaked in hot water for 15 minutes and drained

1 cup bean sprouts

2 scallions, cut into 1-inch lengths

Garnishes

1/2 cup bean sprouts

1 tablespoon dried shrimp powder

2 tablespoons roasted peanuts, coarsely chopped

1/2 teaspoon dried red chile flakes

2 scallions, chopped

2 tablespoons chopped cilantro leaves

2 limes, sliced into 1/8-inch circles

Heat the oil in a wok and fry the garlic until it is golden. Add the shrimp and stir-fry until the shrimp is heated through, about 2 minutes.

Quickly add the sugar, fish sauce, and ketchup and stir until the sugar dissolves.

Add the beaten eggs, letting them set slightly, then stir to scramble them.

Add the rice vermicelli, toss, and stir for 2 minutes. Toss in the 1 cup of bean sprouts and the scallions, and stir until the sprouts are heated through, about 1 minute. Turn the mixture onto a heated platter.

Place the 1/2 cup of bean sprouts along one side of the vermicelli mixture and sprinkle the noodles with the garnish ingredients, in the order given in the recipe. Ring the platter with the rounds of sliced lime and serve.

Serves: 4 to 6

Heat Scale: Mild

Vegetarian Fried Noodles

(*Sayur Mee Goreng*)

Serve this unusual and delicious dish from Malaysia with a curry from Chapter 5. The turmeric powder gives the noodles a lovely yellow hue that contrasts nicely with the red chiles.

2 teaspoons cayenne powder or piquin chile powder

1 teaspoon powdered turmeric

2 potatoes, peeled, boiled, and chopped into 1/8-inch cubes

1/2 teaspoon cayenne powder or piquin chile powder

1/4 teaspoon powdered turmeric

4 tablespoons vegetable oil

1 cup finely sliced onion

1/2 teaspoon prawn or shrimp paste (*blacan*)

2 fresh red serrano or jalapeño chiles, seeds and stems removed, sliced into rings

1 tablespoon soy sauce

1/2 pound bean sprouts, washed and drained

4 pieces fried bean curd, fried and sliced

12 ounces egg noodles, cooked and drained

2 eggs, beaten

Mix the chile powder and the turmeric with a little water to make a thick paste and set aside.

Mix the chopped potatoes with the 1/2 teaspoon chile powder and the 1/4 teaspoon turmeric. Set aside.

Heat 3 tablespoons of the oil in a wok or large skillet, add the onion, and sauté the onion until it is soft. Then add the *blacan,* the reserved chile paste, the fresh chiles, and soy sauce and stir-fry for 2 minutes.

Add the reserved potatoes, and toss them in the pan for 1 minute. Then add the bean sprouts, bean curd slices, and the cooked noodles and gently toss the ingredients until the noodles are coated with the stir-fry mixture.

Make a well in the center of the noodles, add 1 more tablespoon of oil (if necessary), and pour in the beaten eggs. Allow the eggs to cook undisturbed for a few seconds, and when they start to set, mix them in with the noodle mixture, gently tossing and stirring until the eggs are cooked.

Serves: 6

Heat Scale: Medium

Malaysian Banana Curry
(*Pisang Kari*)

Malaysia is believed to be the original home of the banana, or *pisang*, cultivated there for more than 4,000 years. Banana leaves are often used as plates
for curry—at the Banana Leaf Apolo Restaurant in Singapore, for example.
Do not use ripe bananas in this recipe.

4 large, unripe bananas
1 teaspoon salt
½ teaspoon turmeric powder
3 tablespoons *ghee* or vegetable oil
2 cups Coconut Milk (page 12)
2 small, fresh, hot green chiles, such
    as serranos or jalapeño, stems
    and seeds removed, chopped

2 teaspoons pounded Bombay duck
    (optional)
½ teaspoon fenugreek powder
½ teaspoon crushed fennel seed
1-inch stick cinnamon
3 curry leaves, crushed (or substi-
    tute 1 bay leaf)
½ cup minced onion

Peel the bananas, cut them in half lengthwise, and sprinkle them with the salt
and turmeric powder. Fry the bananas in the oil for 2 minutes on each side.

In another pan, combine the coconut milk, chiles, Bombay duck, fenugreek, fennel, cinnamon, curry leaves, and onion. Cook over medium heat for
30 minutes, then add the bananas and cook, uncovered, over low heat for 10
minutes.

Serves: 4 to 6

Heat Scale: Medium

Chile and Coconut Braised Cucumbers

(*Timun Mesanten*)

Serve this tasty recipe from Bali with some spicy grilled fish or *satay*. The spices jazz up the bland cucumber, and the coconut milk adds a touch of richness. Because the dish tends to be rather soupy, make sure that you serve a rice dish to help soak up some of the delicious sauce. Shallots are used frequently in Bali, rather than the sharper yellow onions that are so prevalent in North America.

3 tablespoons vegetable oil

3 shallots, peeled and chopped

3 cloves garlic, minced

3 red serrano or jalapeño chiles, seeds and stems removed, minced

1/2 teaspoon shrimp paste

2 cups Coconut Milk (page 12)

1/2 teaspoon white peppercorns, crushed

3 cucumbers, peeled, seeded, and cut into 1/2-inch slices

Fried shallots (optional)

Heat the oil in a heavy skillet and when it is hot, add the chopped shallots, garlic, and chiles; reduce the heat and sauté the mixture for 2 minutes over low heat. Mix in the shrimp paste and simmer for 1 minute.

Pour in the coconut milk and bring the mixture to a boil, and then reduce the heat and simmer for 3 minutes.

Add the white pepper and the cucumbers and simmer, uncovered, until the cucumbers are tender and the sauce starts to thicken slightly, about 5 to 7 minutes.

Garnish with fried shallots, if desired, and serve immediately.

Serves: 4 to 6

Heat Scale: Medium

Happy Pancakes with Vietnamese Dipping Sauce

This interesting Vietnamese dish was first presented to us by cookbook author Binh Duong at the Mohonk Mountain House's hot and spicy weekend. When we asked Binh why they are called "happy pancakes," he replied, logically: "Because they make people happy when they eat them!" Both the dipping sauce and the batter will keep in the refrigerator for up to three days. Serve the pancakes with Vietnamese Dipping Sauce (*nuoc cham*, page 31).

1¼ cups rice flour

2 cups water

¼ teaspoon ground turmeric

1 green onion, thinly sliced

¼ cup plus 2 tablespoons vegetable oil

1 pound lean pork shoulder or loin, cut into ¼-inch slices

1 pound medium shrimp, peeled and deveined

21 small onions, thinly sliced

10 medium mushrooms, sliced

1¼ teaspoons freshly ground black pepper

2½ cups mung bean sprouts

Vietnamese Dipping Sauce (*nuoc cham*, page 31)

Whisk together the rice flour and water. Add the turmeric and green onion and mix well. Set the batter aside.

In a large, nonstick skillet, heat 1½ tablespoons of the oil over high heat. Add three slices of pork, three shrimp, a few slices of onion, and one sliced mushroom. Lightly sprinkle the black pepper and cook until the onion starts to brown slightly, about 1 minute. Ladle ⅓ cup of the batter into the skillet and tilt the pan to distribute the batter evenly. Keep the heat on high, cover the skillet, and cook until the sides of the pancake turn deep brown and curl up, about 3 to 4 minutes.

Scatter ¼ cup of mung bean sprouts over the pancake, fold it in half, and slide it onto a warm platter. Keep the pancake warm in the oven while making pancakes with the remaining ingredients.

Sprinkle the pancakes with the dipping sauce before serving, or serve it on the side.

Serves: 10 (as a side dish)

Heat Scale: Mild

Spicy Vegetables and Coconut Milk

(*Sajur Lodeh*)

This simple and unusual Indonesian vegetable dish is a great way to use up the small amounts of fresh vegetables that always seem to accumulate in your refrigerator. Since it is rich and soupy, you might consider serving it in small bowls. Traditionally, three or four different types of vegetables are included, such as bamboo shoots, eggplant, green beans, cabbage, or zucchini.

2 tablespoons vegetable oil

1 medium onion, sliced

2 cloves garlic, minced

1 teaspoon shrimp paste

2 teaspoons crushed cayenne, dried piquin chile, or any *sambal* from Chapter 2

1 large tomato, peeled, seeded, and chopped

2 cups Coconut Milk (page 12)

4 cups mixed vegetables, cut into bite-size pieces

1 teaspoon brown sugar

Heat the oil in a large skillet and sauté the onion, garlic, shrimp paste, and crushed chile. When the onion starts to wilt a little (about 1 to 2 minutes), add the tomato and coconut milk and bring to a slow boil. Next, add the vegetables and the brown sugar. Bring the mixture to a second slow boil and then reduce the heat to a simmer and cook, covered, for 5 to 8 minutes, or until the vegetables are crisp-tender.

Serves: 6

Heat Scale: Mild

Spicy Stir-Fried Cabbage

Don't turn up your nose because it's cabbage—this recipe from Malaysia will please even those of you who hate the thought of cabbage. It is infused with chiles, ginger, and a little coconut cream that smooths outs the flavor. Serve the cabbage with one of the meat dishes from Chapter 5.

3 tablespoons vegetable oil

1 garlic clove, minced

1 onion, sliced

4 serrano or jalapeño chiles, seeds and stems removed, and minced

1 tablespoon fresh ginger, minced

1 pound Chinese cabbage, shredded; or use white cabbage

2 teaspoons soy sauce

2 tablespoons Coconut Cream (page 12)

Freshly ground black pepper

Heat the oil in a large skillet or wok. When the oil is sizzling, add the garlic, onion, chiles, and ginger and stir-fry for 30 seconds.

Add the cabbage and stir-fry for 1 minute. Then add the soy sauce, coconut milk, and black pepper. Cook for 3 to 5 minutes over medium low heat, stirring occasionally to avoid burning the cream. Serve immediately.

Serves: 6

Heat Scale: Hot

Chile Fried Cauliflower

(*Sambal Goreng Kembang*)

The favorite method of preparing vegetables in Malaysia is to stir-fry them to bring out the flavor; if the vegetables have a low water content, a few tablespoons of stock are added. This spicy side dish would be an interesting addition to a meat or poultry dish from Chapter 5 or 6.

3 tablespoons vegetable oil

3 cloves garlic, minced

1 cup chopped onion

4 fresh red serrano or jalapeño
  chiles, seeds and stems removed,
  cut into rings

1 teaspoon dried shrimp paste

1 pound cauliflower, separated into
  small florets

3 tablespoons warm chicken stock
  or hot water

Heat the oil in a large frying pan or wok and fry the garlic, onion, and chiles over low heat, stirring often, until the onion is soft, about 1 to 2 minutes. Add the dried shrimp paste, using a fork to mash it into the onion mixture, and sauté for 1 minute.

Stir the cauliflower into the sautéed mixture, making sure that the cauliflower is thoroughly coated. Add the chicken stock or water. Cover the skillet and cook over low heat for 8 to 10 minutes, until the cauliflower is tender.

Serves: 6

Heat Scale: Hot

Smoky Eggplant, Country Style

Our traveling culinary adventurer and recipe collector, Richard Sterling, discovered this unique dish in Cambodia. As he says, "This is a very typical Cambodian dish. People who roast their own chiles will appreciate its distinctive, smoky flavor. When I tasted it near the town of Udong, I was unable to get the recipe, but Sidney and Bopah Ke were kind enough to provide it." We suggest serving it with Three Cambodian Condiments (page 32).

1 large eggplant

1/2 pound ground lean pork

1 scallion, chopped

1 clove garlic, minced

1 tablespoon fish sauce

1 tablespoon oyster sauce

1 tablespoon soy sauce

4 large cooked shrimp, peeled and chopped

Salt and pepper to taste

1 scallion, sliced

3 serrano or jalapeño chiles, stems and seeds removed, coarsely chopped

Pierce the eggplant several times with a fork, to prevent it from exploding. Hold the stem with tongs or a long fork, and stand it up over hot coals (or a gas flame) until the skin on the bottom is thoroughly charred. Lay it down and continue cooking in this manner, turning when necessary, to char the entire eggplant on the outside and cook it through on the inside. Wash the black crust off under cool running water. Tear the eggplant apart into manageable pieces and place them on a warm platter; set aside.

Combine the pork, chopped scallion, and garlic in a large pan or wok and quickly brown the pork. Stir in the fish, oyster, and soy sauces, and bring the mixture to a quick boil. Add the shrimp and heat through; add salt and pepper to taste. Pour this mixture over the eggplant. Garnish with the sliced scallion and chopped chiles.

Serves: 6 (as a side dish)

Heat Scale: Medium

Asparagus Sheaves Kambu

This recipe was also collected by Richard Sterling when he was in Cambodia. Richard says, "Use slender, tender spears, with the lower third removed. If you don't want to make your own fish paste, you can buy it from any Chinese supermarket or fish monger. It is important that the chile paste have enough sugar content to taste. Thai style is good."

The Fish Paste

1 pound ling cod or other firm
    white fish
1 tablespoon light soy sauce
1 tablespoon dry sherry

1 teaspoon fresh ginger
1/2 cup sliced scallions
2 egg whites
4 tablespoons cornstarch

The Asparagus

2 cups vegetable oil
1 pound asparagus
1 cup fish paste
4 teaspoons Red Chile and Tomato
    Dip (page 38)

For the fish paste, place all of the ingredients in a blender or food processor and reduce to a paste. It should have the consistency of cookie dough. If it is not dry enough, add more cornstarch.

Heat the oil in a wok or other deep, heavy vessel to medium heat. Take 3 or 4 asparagus spears in one hand and about 2 or 3 tablespoons of fish paste in the other. Wrap the fish paste around the middle of the sheaf to bind it together. Drop it into the hot oil and deep fry for about 3 minutes, or until the fish paste is set and just beginning to brown. Remove and drain. Repeat, cooking three or four sheaves at a time. Combine the remaining fish sauce and chile paste and drizzle over the cooked sheaves.

Variation: To reduce calories, cook the sheaves in boiling clarified chicken or fish stock. You could also use green beans, or bell peppers cut into thin strips lengthwise.

Yield: About 8 sheaves

Heat Scale: Mild

Stuffed Chile Peppers
(*Mawk Mak Phet*)

These stuffed chiles are steamed in banana leaves in Laos, but sometimes the leaves are hard to find in the United States. We have had success in finding them in both Asian and Latin American markets, even here in Albuquerque. If you can't find them in your area, steam the chiles in foil. Experiment with a variety of fillings such as ground pork, ground beef, and rice.

8 poblano or fresh New Mexican green chiles

3/4 pound flounder, snapper, or any white fish fillets, flaked

1/2 cup cooked rice

4 green onions, chopped, including the green portions

2 cloves garlic, minced

1 tablespoon fish sauce (*nam pla*)

1 teaspoon minced fresh ginger

Juice of 1 lemon

Banana leaves or aluminum foil

Slit each chile from the stem to the tip, being careful not to cut completely through the chile to the other side. Remove the membrane and the seeds.

Combine the remaining ingredients and toss until thoroughly mixed.

Stuff each chile with the mixture and wrap the chiles, two to a package, tightly in aluminum foil.

Place the packets in a bamboo steamer or colander over boiling water. Cover and steam for 20 to 25 minutes.

Serve the chiles with any juices from the foil poured over the top.

Serves: 4

Heat Scale: Mild

Durian Quotes, Part 2

❝What makes the durian so famous, or notorious, is the combination of its taste and its smell. Most Europeans say that its smell is nauseating but the taste, if you can nerve yourself, is exquisite and indescribable. . . . The smell of durian I do not find disgusting, and nor do European friends of mine who have become accustomed to it, but it does become a tiresome smell if you have too much of it.❞

Sri Owen

❝Overripe cheese, rotting fish, unwashed socks, or a city dump on a hot summer's day.❞

Local Singapore description

❝It has the smell from hell and a taste from heaven.❞

Local Singapore saying

King Rice

❝But rice is more than just a commodity to the Thai people. Symbolically, it represents a gift to be respected and shared. Rice grains are not to be intentionally thrown on the floor and, if seen on the ground, should not be stepped over. The Thai words 'to eat,' *geen cow,* literally mean 'to eat rice.' Eight out of every ten Thais are rice farmers. As of 1986, more than twenty million tons of rice were produced a year.❞

Alan Rabinowitz

Symbolic Supper

"A Malay who has baited a trap for crocodiles, and is awaiting results, is careful in eating his curry always to begin by swallowing three lumps of rice successively; for this helps the bait to slide more easily down the crocodile's throat. He is equally scrupulous not to take any bones out of his curry; for, if he did, it seems clear that the sharp-pointed stick on which the bait is skewered would simply work itself loose, and the crocodile would get off with the bait. Hence in these circumstances it is prudent for the hunter, before he begins his meal, to get somebody else to take the bones out of his curry, otherwise he may at any moment have to choose between swallowing a bone and losing the crocodile."

Sir James George Frazer

A Filipino Food Riddle

Walay ba-ba apan dunay ngipon;
Walay kamot apan dunay bukton;
Walay tiil apan dunay lawas.
Kagoran.

No mouth but it has teeth;
No hands but it has an arm;
No feet but it has a body.
A coconut shredder.

Donn V. Hart

A Market in Kuala Lumpur

"Another experience I will not forget was an early morning visit to an open air market. Oh, the baskets piled high with fresh, shiny chiles of all shapes and sizes and ranging from bright green through yellow and orange to vivid scarlet; the bundles of white lemongrass and other herbs; the dark green edible fern fronds in bundles; the eggplants in amazing variety—green, purple, white, large, small, round, or long, and one variety only as large as a pea."

Charmaine Solomon

Thai Heat, Part 3

"Some specialties of the region [south Thailand] reflect the influences of foreign cultures: among them an Indian-style curry known as *kaeng massaman,* involving cardamom, cloves, and cinnamon and either chicken or beef (never pork); several Malayan fish curries, often with a garnish of fresh fruits and salted peanuts; and satay, marinated pieces of meat on skewers with a spicy peanut sauce, which originally came from Indonesia and is now a popular snack all over Thailand. On the whole, southerners like their food hot—hotter, perhaps than any other region with the possible exception of the northeast—and liberally season it with the most pungent chiles."

William Warren

From Zi-Thi to Dadar

Beverages and Sweets

Since this is our cool-down chapter, we have resisted the impulse to add chiles to these recipes—although there are some other pungent ingredients. Interestingly enough, although chiles are commonly added to drinks and sweets in other parts of the world, we have yet to see that combination in Southeast Asia.

Because of the numerous culinary influences on the region, it is not surprising that some of the beverages served in Southeast Asia have foreign origins; a good example is the presence of chocolate in Filipino drinks. We begin with *Zi-Thi* Plum Syrup Drink (page 262), a popular refresher in Myanmar, with the *zi-thi* plums probably descended from Chinese imports. It certainly is a great way to use up excess plums, if you have them.

Two of our drinks prominantly feature ginger. Javanese Ginger Java (page 263) is a delicious combination of the pungent rhizome with another of Java's favorite products, coffee. Indonesia's *bandrek*, or Ginger Tea (page 264), is also simple to make and both sweet and slightly spicy at the same time.

Teas are represented by only a small fraction of the number of variations on that sipping subject. Iced Thai Tea (page 265), a beverage also served in American Thai restaurants, is another sweet drink but it is countered by Lemongrass Mint Tea (page 266), a much tarter treat.

Chocolate was introduced to the Philippines from Mexico, and its influence is illustrated in Spanish–Filipino Hot Chocolate (page 267), a thick, hearty, after-dinner drink that can be topped with nutmeg, if desired.

Ah, a beverage steeped in history and lore is the famous Singapore Sling (page 268), still served at the Long Bar in the beautifully remodeled Raffles Hotel in Singapore, where Mary Jane downed several while Dave stuck to the famous Tiger Beer. Another variation on the sling, the Penang Gin Sling (page 269), is served in Malaysian bars. Our final alcoholic drink is the Oriental Hotel Delight (page 270), served at the famous hotel in Bangkok.

We had often heard that desserts were not popular in Southeast Asia, but a trip to Singapore proved that not always to be the case. Why, in Mrs. Leong Yee Soo's landmark cookbook, *The Best of Singapore Cooking*, there are nearly seventy recipes for desserts, *kueh* candies, and cakes, besides fifteen more for cookies and pastries. While it is true that fruits usually finish the meal in most countries, sweets that resemble desserts are eaten as snacks and for special celebrations.

Filipino Kalamansi Pie (page 271) is a great example of European influence on Southeast Asia, as it is a transformed Key lime pie.

If this is Southeast Asia, there must be bananas and coconuts everywhere, including in the sweets. Fried Green Sesame Bananas (page 272) is a Thai street sweet, while Baked Singapore Ginger Bananas (page 273) is a more elegant and fruity formal dessert.

We've uncovered a pudding and a custard to rival any we have ever tasted. Malacca Pudding with Jaggery–Ginger Sauce (page 274) is spiked with ginger and garnished with mangoes, while Coconut Custards in Shells (page 275), a Laotian delicacy, features custard served in coconut shells. Speaking of coconuts, the Burmese treat called *dohl-dohl*, or Coconut-Almond Rice Candy (page 276), is difficult to resist.

Not only is fresh fruit served before and after meals in Southeast Asia, it is combined with other native foods of the region with stunning effect. Fresh Mangoes and Sticky Rice with Coconut Cream (page 277) is a classic and simple Thai dessert using glutinous rice, while another Thai favorite, Chilled Mixed Fruit in Scented Syrup (page 278), combines fruit with flower petals for a truly exotic effect. The interesting Fruit Fool (page 279) shows the British influence in Malaysia and gives the cook the advantage of choosing the fruit to use.

Coconut lovers will love the next two desserts. Malaysian Coconut Crepes (page 280) are topped with a coconut sauce and garnished with toasted coconut, while Balinese Coconut Pancakes (page 282) feature a filling of coconut and bananas.

Our final three desserts illustrate the wide range of sweets in Southeast Asia. Mango Dessert Jellies (page 283) is a gelatin-based sweet that makes an attractively wiggling dessert. Deep-Fried Pineapple Slices (page 284), from Indonesia, are served when (and if) you tire of unadorned fresh fruit. And just to prove that cakes are alive and well in the tropics, we present Farina Cardamom Cake with Tropical Fruits (page 285). This cake shows how the Burmese appropriated cake-baking techniques from the British, but substituted their own ingredients and flavorings.

All and all, an eclectic—and refreshing—ending to a frenetically fiery collection of Southeast Asian recipes!

Zi-Thi Plum Syrup Drink

One of the most refreshing drinks served in Myanmar (Burma) is this plum syrup concoction. Simply add 2 teaspoons of the syrup to a tall glass filled with ice and add carbonated water. Garnish with a slice of pomelo (grapefruit) and you've got an instant, nonalcoholic fruit drink. Feel free to add gin for an authentically British tropical touch.

30 ripe plums, *zi-thi* preferred
Water
Sugar

In a stockpot, combine the plums and water to cover and cook over medium heat until the fruit is tender and easily mashed. Strain the plums and liquid through a sieve and reserve the liquid.

Measure out 1 cup of sugar for each cup of plum liquid. Add the plum liquid to a saucepan, bring to a boil, and skim off any foam. When clear, add the sugar and boil rapidly for 20 minutes. It can then be sealed in sterilized bottles and kept for months or placed in the refrigerator, where it will last two weeks. It can also be placed in ice cube trays and frozen.

Note: Other fruits, such as peaches or mangoes, can be substituted for the plums.

Yield: 3 cups or more

Javanese Ginger Java

(*Kopi Jahe*)

Indonesia became so famous for its coffee that the slang word "java" entered the English language. Coffee is quite popular in the country, where it is served in *kopi warungs,* or small coffeehouses. This after-dinner coffee is traditionally served quite sweet.

4 one-inch slices fresh ginger,
    peeled
4 cups water
4 teaspoons instant coffee
Sugar to taste

Combine the ginger and water and bring to a boil. Reduce the heat and simmer for 15 minutes. Remove the ginger and discard.

    Add 1 teaspoon instant coffee to each of four cups. Pour the ginger water into the cups and stir. Add sugar to taste and stir again.

Serves: 4

Ginger Tea

(*Bandrek*)

This simple recipe makes one of the most popular beverages in Indonesia, especially in the mountain regions. *Bandrek* is usually served hot.

4 cups water
1 cup brown sugar
6 one-inch slices ginger, peeled

Combine the ingredients in a pan and cook over low heat for 40 minutes, stirring occasionally. Strain and pour into cups.

Serves: 4

Iced Thai Tea

(*Cha Yen*)

This very popular tea is made from a tea, grown in northern Thailand, that is flavored with vanilla and corn, so you'll have to visit an Asian market to find it. Take note that this tea is quite rich and sweet. However, the tea can be adjusted by replacing some of the sweetened condensed milk and the half-and-half with regular (or even lowfat) milk.

3 cups water
1/2 cup Thai tea
14-ounce can (1 3/4 cups) sweetened condensed milk
1 1/2 cups half-and-half or milk

In a pan, heat the water to boiling. Put the tea in a coffee drip filter in its holder, placed over a pitcher. Pour the water over the tea and, when drained through, repeat the procedure four or five times until the tea is very strong and dark orange in color.

Add the condensed milk to the tea, stir, and cool to room temperature. Pour the tea over ice cubes in individual glasses until half full. Add half-and-half or milk and stir well.

Serves: 4 to 6

Lemongrass Mint Tea

The British tea tradition is influenced by Asian ingredients in this snappy tea from Myanmar, where it is usually served with lime slices and honey rather than with sugar and cream.

4 teaspoons green tea
1 teaspoon minced mint leaves
6 two-inch stalks lemongrass
4 cups boiling water

Combine the tea, mint, and lemongrass in an earthenware teapot and pour the water over them. Allow to steep for 3 minutes. Strain and serve.

Serves: 4

Spanish–Filipino Hot Chocolate

Cacao was imported into the Philippines from Mexico during the Spanish occupation of the islands and turned into a status symbol because it was so difficult to grow. Chinese merchants dominated the trade in cacao, and mixed the chocolate with various other ingredients, such as sugar, peanuts, spices, and even corn. We recommend the use of Mexican chocolate in after-dinner drinks since the traditional Filipino *tableyas* of chocolate are difficult to find in North America. This is chocolate *espeso,* or thick hot chocolate.

2 cups water
2 bricks Mexican chocolate, such as
    Ybarra, crushed
4 cups milk
3 egg yolks

In a saucepan, bring the water to a boil and add the chocolate. Stir well until the chocolate is dissolved. In a bowl, beat together the milk and egg yolks. Add this mixture to the chocolate, remove from the heat, and pour into cups.

Serves: 6 to 8

Singapore Sling

This famous drink was invented in 1903 (some say 1915) by Raffles Hotel bartender Ngiam Tong Boon. There are many variations on this potent potable, but this one seems to be the most authentic. We tested it thoroughly, of course, in the bar at Raffles, where they serve about 2,000 per day.

1/3 cup gin

1/8 cup lime juice

1/2 cup pineapple juice

1/8 cup Cherry Heering or cherry brandy

1 drop Angostura Bitters

1 dash Bendictine liqueur

1 dash Cointreau

Pineapple wedges and cherries for garnish

Combine all ingredients in a cocktail shaker with five or six ice cubes and shake well. Strain into tall glasses and add ice cubes if desired. Thread a pineapple wedge and a cherry on a toothpick for garnish.

Serves: 2

Penang Gin Sling

In Penang, Malaysia, this version of the sling is served with two gins and two brandies as the major ingredients.

¹/₈ cup sloe gin

1 tablespoon dry gin

1 tablespoon apricot brandy

1 tablespoon cherry brandy

1 teaspoon sugar

Juice of ¹/₂ lime

Ice cubes

Seltzer water

1 cherry for garnish

1 slice pineapple for garnish

1 slice orange for garnish

Combine the sloe gin, dry gin, apricot brandy, cherry brandy, sugar, and lime juice in a 12-ounce glass and stir well to dissolve the sugar. Add ice cubes and top off with seltzer water. Stir slightly, add the garnishes, and serve.

Serves: 1

Oriental Hotel Delight

(*Sook*)

Here is another classic Asian mixed drink that we tried at the Oriental Hotel along the Chao Phraya River in Bangkok. Note the prominence of gin once again.

¹/₂ cup gin
¹/₂ cup light rum
¹/₂ cup cream of coconut (sweetened coconut syrup) or
    Coconut Cream (page 12) plus
    1 tablespoon sugar

¹/₃ cup lime juice
¹/₃ cup pomelo or grapefruit juice; or substitute orange juice
¹/₃ cup pineapple juice
Ice cubes
Mint leaves for garnish

Combine the liquids in a cocktail shaker, add about six ice cubes, and shake well. Strain into cocktail glasses and garnish with the mint leaves.

Serves: 4 to 6

Filipino Kalamansi Pie

The Philippines were heavily influenced by the Americans as well as the Spanish. After the Americans arrived, pies, cakes, and ice cream were added to the desserts of Filipino cuisine. In this recipe, Key lime pie is recreated in modified form in Manila with the *kalamansi*, the native lime of the islands. The best substitute is the Key lime, sometimes available in Latin markets, but any lime—or lemon—will do.

1 packet unflavored gelatin	1/4 cup water
1/8 teaspoon salt	2 teaspoons grated lime rind
1 cup sugar	1 baked 9-inch pie crust in pan
4 eggs, separated	1 cup cream, whipped
1/3 cup *kalamansi* (lime) juice	Grated toasted coconut for garnish

Combine the gelatin, salt, and 1/2 cup of sugar in a double boiler and mix. Add the egg yolks, lime juice, and water and heat, stirring constantly, until the gelatin and sugar are dissolved. Remove from the heat and stir in the rind. Allow to cool at room temperature for 10 minutes.

Whip the egg whites until stiff and add the remaining sugar. Fold the egg white mixture into the lime juice mixture and pour into the baked pie crust. Top with the whipped cream and refrigerate for at least 2 hours before serving. Sprinkle with toasted coconut just before serving.

Serves: 8

Fried Green Sesame Bananas

(*Gluay Kaeg*)

Here is a street-food delicacy, one that is commonly devoured on the streets of major Thai cities as a sweet snack as well as a dessert.

1 cup rice flour
1 cup flour
1 teaspoon baking powder
1 cup water
1/2 cup Coconut Milk (page 12)
1/4 cup sesame seeds

2 tablespoons sugar
3/4 cup freshly grated coconut
Vegetable oil for deep-frying
6 small green bananas, sliced in half
   lengthwise

In a bowl, combine all of the ingredients except the bananas and oil and mix well to make a batter.

    Heat the oil in a wok. Dip the banana slices in the batter and deep-fry until golden brown. Remove from the oil and drain on paper towels.

Serves: 4

Baked Singapore Ginger Bananas

The orange and lime juices plus the slightly hot ginger give this banana dessert an "edge" that most others lack.

1/4 cup butter
1/3 cup dark brown sugar
1/4 teaspoon ground cloves
2 tablespoons orange juice
2 teaspoons lime juice

1 one-inch piece ginger, peeled and minced
6 bananas, sliced in half lengthwise
Ground cinnamon for garnish

Preheat the oven to 375°F. Cream the butter and sugar together and then mix in the cloves, orange juice, lime juice, and ginger.

Place the bananas cut side down in a greased glass casserole dish and spread the butter mixture over them. Bake for 10 to 15 minues or until the bananas are tender. Remove from the oven and serve, sprinkled with the cinnamon and accompanied by ice cream.

Serves: 6

Malacca Pudding with Jaggery–Ginger Sauce

(*Goula Malacca*)

This dessert has ever-so-slight "heat" because of the ginger, which is boiled with *jaggery*, the dark brown palm sugar found in Southeast Asia. Below is the recipe that was served at the Prome Road Nursing Home in Rangoon, Burma in the 1960s.

$3/4$ cup pearl tapioca

$1\,1/2$ cups milk

1 cup water

$1/4$ cup sugar

Whites of 2 eggs, whipped until stiff

3 drops vanilla

1 cup dark brown sugar

3 slices fresh ginger, peeled

4 teaspoons Coconut Cream (page 12) at room temperature

Sliced mangoes for accompaniment

Combine the tapioca, milk, water, and sugar in a saucepan and bring to a boil. Boil until the tapioca and sugar are dissolved. Remove from the heat, allow to reach room temperature, and fold in the egg whites and vanilla. Transfer to a baking dish, cover with plastic wrap, and place in the refrigerator.

In a saucepan, melt the brown sugar over low heat. Add the ginger slices and heat over medium heat until sugar thickens and begins to caramelize. Remove from the heat and allow to reach room temperature.

To serve, transfer the pudding to four shallow bowls. Spoon a little coconut cream over the puddings and top with the ginger-sugar sauce. Garnish with the mango slices.

Serves: 4

Coconut Custards in Shells

(*Sankhagnaa Mak Phao*)

This Laotian dessert is as dramatic as it is tasty. Since coconuts are round, it will be necessary to trim the bottoms flat or place each in a round "collar" so they will stand upright.

4 fresh, young, small coconuts,
    outer husks removed
8 eggs, lightly beaten
1 1/2 cups sugar
1 1/2 cups thick Coconut Milk
    (page 12)

Cut the tops off the coconuts with a saw. Pour out the coconut water and reserve it for mixing rum drinks.

    Combine the eggs, sugar, and coconut milk in a bowl and mix well. Pour the mixture into the four coconuts and top with the sawed-off shells. Place in a steamer and steam for 30 minutes.

Serves: 4

Coconut-Almond Rice Candy

(*Dohl-Dohl*)

Of Portuguese origin, this sweet was transferred from Goa, India to Burma (now Myanmar). It is a Christmas festival sweet, especially among the Catholics of the country.

4 cups brown *putoo* rice, or substitute any brown, sticky rice

1 cup sesame oil

4 cups sugar

8 cups coconut milk

1 teaspoon salt

2 cups slivered almonds

Wash and drain the rice, then pound it with a mortar and pestle into a coarse, grainy mixture.

In a large skillet, boil the sesame oil and add the sugar, coconut milk, salt, and pounded rice. Cook, uncovered, over medium heat, until all the milk is absorbed and only oil is left. Add most of the almonds, stir well, and remove from the heat. Pour into a shallow dish, sprinkle the remaining almonds over, and cool. Slice into diamond shapes for serving.

Yield: 40 or more candies

Fresh Mangoes and Sticky Rice with Coconut Cream

(*Khao Neow Ma-Maung*)

During the mango season in Thailand, this is the dessert of choice. It is extremely easy to make and uses up a lot of the fast-ripening mangoes.

1 1/2 cups Coconut Cream (page 12)

1/2 cup sugar

1/2 teaspoon salt

1 1/2 cups glutinous rice, soaked overnight, drained, and steamed for 15 minutes

4 ripe mangoes, peeled and cut into large slices

Sesame seeds for garnish

In a bowl, combine 1 cup of the coconut cream, sugar, and salt. Stir until the sugar is dissolved. Stir in the cooked rice and set aside for 10 to 15 minutes.

Simmer the remaining coconut cream, uncovered, for 10 minutes, stirring occasionally.

Place the rice in mounds on four dessert plates, arrange the mango slices over the mounds, and drizzle the remaining coconut cream over them. Garnish with sesame seeds.

Note: This recipe requires advance preparation.

Serves: 4

Chilled Mixed Fruit in Scented Syrup

(*Loy Gaew*)

Here is a truly elegant Thai dessert. The cook helps create the flavor by choosing which fruit to include.

3 cups water

20 fresh jasmine flowers, or substitute a few drops of jasmine essence

10 fresh rose petals, or substitute a few drops of rose essence

3 screwpine leaves, or substitute 1/4 teaspoon vanilla extract

1/2 cup sugar

2 cups diced mixed fresh fruit, such as oranges, pineapples, payapas, starfruit, mangoes, bananas, and melons

Fresh mint leaves for garnish

Bring the water to a boil, remove from the heat, and add the jasmine flowers, rose petals, and screwpine leaves (or vanilla). Allow to sit for an hour to blend the flavors.

Heat the water, add the sugar, and boil until reduced and slightly thick. Remove from the heat and chill in the refrigerator.

When cold, add the fruit, stir, and serve garnished with mint leaves.

Serves: 4

Fruit Fool

The term "fool" in this recipe title is curiously connected to another fruit dessert—trifle. The connection is that both refer to confections containing fruit and cream, which were considered to be mere trifles, small desserts to "fool with." The British influence survives today in Malaysia with this trifle, which can be made with your choice of fruit.

1 cup Coconut Milk (page 12)
3 egg yolks
3 pounds fruit, (papaya, mango, or
    banana, or a combination),
    peeled, seeded, and chopped

2 tablespoons lime juice
3 egg whites
1/4 cup sugar
Slivers of fresh fruit for garnish
Fresh spearmint leaves for garnish

In a saucepan, heat the coconut milk, add the egg yolks, and bring to a boil, stirring constantly. Remove from the heat, allow to cool, and beat well until frothy.

Combine the fruit and the lime juice and puree in a blender until smooth. Beat the egg whites until peaks form.

In a bowl, combine the beaten egg yolk mixture, the fruit puree, and sugar and stir well. Fold in the egg whites. Transfer the fool to parfait glasses and chill. Serve garnished with fruit slivers and spearmint leaves.

Serves: 8 to 10

Malaysian Coconut Crepes

(*Ketayap*)

For true coconut lovers, here are crepes stuffed with coconut, topped with a coconut sauce, and garnished with toasted coconut!

The Filling
2 cups freshly grated coconut
1 cup water
1/2 cup dark brown sugar
Ground cinnamon and nutmeg,
    pinch each

The Sauce
1 cup Coconut Milk (page 12)
2 tablespoons sugar
1 tablespoon cornstarch

The Crepes
1 1/4 cups water
1 cup all-purpose flour
1 large egg
Vegetable oil
2 tablespoons coconut, grated and
    browned

For the filling, combine all ingredients in a skillet. Cook and stir over medium heat until the mixture is dry, 10 to 15 minutes. Remove from the heat and let cool.

For the sauce, combine all ingredients in a saucepan. Cook and stir over medium heat until thickened, about 2 minutes. Remove from the heat and keep warm.

For the crepes, combine all ingredients in a bowl and whisk until smooth. Heat an 8-inch nonstick skillet or crepe pan until hot. Brush the pan lightly with oil, then add 3 tablespoons of crepe batter. Swirl the batter to cover the bottom of the pan. Cook for about 1 minute, then flip and cook the other side of the crepe for about 30 seconds. Remove to a plate and use wax paper to separate the crepes. Repeat until all the batter is used, about eight crepes.

Place 3 tablespoons of filling in a crepe and roll it up. Repeat with all crepes. Place two crepes on each dessert plate, top with the warm sauce, and garnish with the grated coconut.

Serves: 4

Balinese Coconut Pancakes

(*Dadar*)

These light and delightful pancakes (actually, rice crepes) have a coconut filling (*unti*) that traditionally consists of coconut and palm sugar syrup. Regular cane sugar syrup can be substituted. The pancakes are also eaten as a snack and sometimes for breakfast.

The Filling
1 cup freshly grated coconut
1/2 banana, diced
1/2 cup sugar syrup
1 screwpine leaf, or substitute
    1/2 teaspoon vanilla extract

The Pancakes

1 cup rice flour	3 eggs
2 tablespoons sugar	1 cup fresh Coconut Milk (page 12)
1/4 teaspoon salt	2 tablespoons peanut oil

Combine all filling ingredients in a skillet and cook over low heat for about 2 to 3 minutes until browned. Remove from the heat and use at room temperature.

Combine all pancake ingredients in a bowl and stir well with a whisk until smooth. The batter should be quite liquid in consistency.

Heat a nonstick skillet over low heat and spread about 1/4 cup batter in a circle and fry, turning once. Remove the pancake and cool. Repeat until all the batter is used.

Spread 1 tablespoon of filling on each pancake and roll tightly into a tube shape.

Serves: 6

Mango Dessert Jellies

This Singaporean favorite is simple to make and its orange color makes a spectacular presentation on the dessert plate.

4 cups water	2 eggs, beaten
1 cup sugar	1 cup mango pulp
6 teaspoons gelatin	1 large mango, seeded and diced
1 cup Coconut Milk (page 12)	Fresh mint for garnish
1/2 cup evaporated milk	

Combine the water and sugar in a saucepan over low heat and cook, stirring, until the sugar dissolves. Add the gelatin and continue to cook until it is dissolved. Add all of the remaining ingredients except the diced mango, turn off the heat, and stir. Add the diced mango and stir well.

Pour the mixture into individual molds and refrigerate until set, at least an hour. Garnish with mint and serve.

Serves: 6

Deep-Fried Pineapple Slices

(*Goreng Nenas*)

Once again fruit is favored in this dessert from Indonesia. Fresh pineapple is preferred here, although canned slices can be used if they are well drained.

1/3 cup flour

1 teaspoon cinnamon

3 eggs, lightly beaten

1 tablespoon brown sugar

Pinch salt

Vegetable oil for deep frying

6 slices fresh, peeled pineapple (about 1/2 inch thick), well drained

Powdered sugar (optional)

Vanilla ice cream (optional)

In a bowl, combine the flour, cinnamon, eggs, brown sugar, and salt to make a batter. Beat the batter lightly with a whisk to remove any lumps.

Heat the oil in a saucepan or a deep-fryer until it is quite hot but not smoking. One at a time, dip each pineapple slice in the batter and deep-fry it in the oil until golden brown, turning once with tongs. Drain on paper towels.

Sprinkle each slice with powdered sugar, or serve each slice with a small scoop of vanilla ice cream in the center.

Serves: 6

Farina Cardamom Cake with Tropical Fruits

(*Sin We Makin*)

The Burmese serve this cake during their New Year's celebrations rather than at the end of a meal, but don't let that stop you from serving it after one of our hot and spicy entrées. Serve it with whipped cream and the usual tropical fruit slices.

2 tablespoons sesame seeds

1 cup farina

2 cups Coconut Milk (page 12)

1 cup half-and-half

1/2 cup sugar

1/2 cup butter, cut into small pieces

1/2 teaspoon ground cardamom

3 eggs, separated, whites beaten stiff

Freshly sliced ripe mangoes, pineapple, papaya, and banana

Whipped cream

In a large skillet, toast the sesame seeds over medium heat, shaking frequently, until they are toasted, about 6 minutes. Transfer the seeds to a bowl, wipe out the skillet, and repeat the process with the farina until it turns a light yellow-brown, about 8 minutes.

Preheat the oven to 325°F. In a saucepan, combine the coconut milk, half-and-half, sugar, and butter and heat to boiling. Reduce the heat to medium and add the farina. Cook the mixture, stirring constantly, until it is very thick, about 5 minutes. Add the cardamom and the egg yolks, one at a time, stirring well. Fold the egg whites into the batter. Transfer the batter to a greased, 8-inch cake pan, sprinkle with the sesame seeds, and bake at 325°F until a toothpick inserted into the cake comes out clean, about 1 hour. Remove the cake from the oven and cool on a wire rack.

Serve thin slices of cake surrounded by the fruit slices and topped with a dollop of whipped cream.

Serves: 8 to 10

Your Bathtub Will Work Fine for This

❝Alcohol made from rice is used to celebrate marriages and annual rituals. Various types of rice wine are made across the region by steeping glutinous rice in water, together with herbs and a cake made from very old, dry, finely ground rice containing fungi, yeasts, and spices. The mixture is left in open tubs whilst the desired alcoholic strength is reached (about a month); then it is decanted into vessels which are closed and stored for several months. Steady fermentation of sticky rice may achieve an alcohol content of around twenty percent.❞

Jacqueline M. Piper

Yes, We Have Some Bananas

❝At least 100 kinds of bananas are known, but there is considerable confusion because different names are used for the same variety in different places. Botanists assign the banana to a genus, *Musa,* but do not bother listing any species. The many varieties are simply called cultivars. The name 'banana,' of limited use worldwide, is of East African origin. There are about as many names for the plant as there are areas where it grows. The Balinese call the banana *biu,* or *biyu,* but that won't get you too far because there are so many kinds of *biu* that you will immediately be asked which one you want. There is a variety in Bali called *biu batu* (stone banana) that is full of seeds—a favorite joke in Bali is to give a foreign friend a *biu batu* to chomp on. It is difficult to tell the difference on the outside, and the shock is considerable after years of seedless bananas.❞

Fred B. Eiseman, Jr.

Southeast Asian Slings, Part 1

❝It was Penang, at the hour of the gin sling, which is not the Malayan equivalent for cocktail time, but the morning break at the hour when people begin to weary of their offices. . . .❞

Alec Waugh, *Hot Countries,* 1930

❝A few moments later we were seated in an immense lounge and I was initiated into the mysteries of the gin sling, the most seductive and powerful of the many potent drinks brewed in the tropics. It is a delicious concoction, as pleasant to the eye as to the palate, but beware of it! The first glass makes the whole world seem as roseate as its own crystal pinkness. The second is a siesta. The third is a knock out, and will reduce the proudest spine to an invertebrate condition.❞

Ambrose Pratt, *Magical Malaya,* 1931

Southeast Asian Slings, Part 2

❝It is one of tourism's great rites of passage to have a Singapore Sling at Raffles.❞

Australian Weekend Review

❝It is said that Raffles is the largest consumer of gin in the world: 20,160 bottles are required per year. In 1985, 131 Singapore Slings were drunk by five gentlemen in two hours, which makes 26.2 per head and is one Sling every 4.6 minutes. ❞

Ruth Law

A Shower of Sweets

"The Burmese do not have a tradition of serving a dessert at the end of a meal, although occasionally they do have fruits. However, they make many lovely sweets, cakes, and candy-like concoctions using ingredients such as agar, coconut milk, farina, palm sugar, and sesame seeds. These sweetmeats do not form part of regular meals; they are traditionally served on important occasions such as a wedding ceremony or the birth of a child. They are particularly associated with the spring water festival that introduces the Burmese New Year—a joyous holiday during which people douse themselves with buckets of water to commemorate the resurrection of a slain god through the life-giving power of water. "

Julie Sahni

How About a Durian Dessert?

"Desserts in both Balinese homes and restaurants almost always consist of fruit: mangoes, papayas, guavas, grapes, pineapple, or several others rarely, if ever, found outside of Indonesia. *Salak* tastes like an apple—but appears to be covered in snakeskin. *Sawo* tastes a little like a pear but looks a lot like a potato. Durians may be one of the smelliest fruits on earth, but most who can overcome their initial repugnance learn to love it. Balinese coffee, with the grounds afloat on the surface, usually follows, as strong as jet fuel. "

Anthony Weller

Mail-Order Sources

Many of the ingredients mentioned in the recipes are carried by the companies listed below.

Chile Pepper Magazine
P.O. Box 80780
Albuquerque, NM 87198
(800) 359-1483

Source for Southeast Asian food suppliers

Blake's Natural Herbs and Spices
505 North Railroad
Ellensburg, WA 98926
(800) 932-HERB

Prepared curry powders and spice blends

Cinnabar
1134 W. Haining St.
Prescott, AZ 86301
(602) 778-3687

Specialty foods and seasonings from India, Thailand, and the Caribbean

Colorado Spice Company
5030 Nome St., Unit A
Denver, CO 80239
(303) 373-0141

Curry spices and prepared curry mixes

Cosmopolitan Foods, Inc.
138 Essex Ave.
Glen Ridge, NJ 07028
(201) 680-4560

Indonesian sauces and spices

Dean and DeLuca
Mail Order Department
560 Broadway
New York, NY 10012
(212) 431-1691

Exotic herbs and spices from around the world

DeWildt Imports
R.D. 3
Bangor, PA 18013
(215) 588-0600

Spices and ingredients from Indonesia, Malaysia, Vietnam, and Thailand

Enchanted Seeds
P.O. Box 6087
Las Cruces, NM 88006
(505) 233-3033

Exotic chile seeds

Frieda's, Inc.
4465 Corporate Center Dr.
Los Alamitos, CA 90720-2561
(800) 241-1771

Shipper of fresh and dried habaneros and other exotic chiles

Golden Bow Gift Baskets
P.O. Box 27778
Honolulu, HI 96827

Curry pastes from Thailand

House of Spices
76-17 Broadway
Jackson Heights, NY 11373
(718) 476-1577

Curry spices and other Indian and Pakistani foodstuffs

Le Saucier
Faneuil Hall Marketplace
Boston, MA 02109
(617) 227-9649

Curry pastes, oils, powders, and sauces

Nancy's Specialty Market
P.O. Box 327
Wye Mills, MD 21679
(800) 462-6291

Spices, herbs, hot sauces, coconut extract, coconut milk, curry pastes, Indian pickles and chutneys

Nature's Key Products
P.O. Box 1146
New Hyde Park, NY 11040
(516) 775-5279

Various packaged Sri Lankan curries and curry pastes, including black curries for fish

Old Southwest Trading Company
P.O. Box 7545
Albuquerque, NM 87194
(505) 836-0168

Chiles from all over the world, plus sauces and salsas

G.B. Ratto & Co.
821 Washington St.
Oakland, CA 94607
(510) 836-2250

Spices and foods from India, Indonesia, and Africa; Curry spices and mixes

Spices of Vermont
Rt. 7, P.O. Box 18
North Ferrisburg, VT 05473
(802) 425-2555

Glossary

Note: Most of the ingredients listed here can be found in Asian markets all over North America, and by mail (see Mail-Order Sources, page 289).

Atjar: A pickled Indonesian relish.

Annatto: The orange-colored seeds of the annatto tree; used as a coloring agent and seasoning. Also called achiote.

Balsam: *See* Basil.

Basil (*Ocimum basilicum*): A common herb native to Central Asia. Fresh basil is an ingredient in curries from the Malaysian state of Selangor. Holy basil, also called balsam and *krapau,* is *Ocimum sanctum.*

Blacan: See Prawn paste. Also, *blachan* and *belacan.*

Black pepper (*Piper nigrum*): The pungent berry that is perhaps the most famous spice in the world.

Brown bean sauce: Called *tauco* in Indonesia and *mor see jeng* in China, it is made with fermented soybeans.

Cabe: Also, *cabai.* General term for chile peppers in Indonesia and Malaysia. *Cabe hijau* means green chiles; *cabe merah,* red chiles; *cabe rawit,* bird's eye chiles (*Capsicum frutescens*). An alternative word for chiles is *lombok.*

Candlenut (*Aleurites moluccana*): A fleshy nut of the candleberry tree of Southeast Asia. Substitute macadamia nuts, Brazil nuts, almonds, or cashews.

Capsicum: In Southeast Asian recipes, this means bell pepper.

Cardamom (*Elettaria cardamomum*): The seeds of a relative of ginger, primarily grown in India and Guatemala. Unripe (green or white) cardamom pods are also sold; the seeds must be removed before using. A common ingredient in home and commercial curry powders.

Cashew nut (*Anacardium occidentale*): Nut of a small evergreen tree (cashew apple) that is laden with fat, up to 48 percent.

Cassia (*Cinnamomom cassia*): The scraped, dried bark of a relative of cinnamon. It is often used in place of cinnamon in the curries of Southeast Asia and Malaysia.

Cayenne (*Capsicum annuum*): One of the hotter dried chiles; its powder commonly appears in curries worldwide. *See* Chile peppers.

Celery seed (*Apium graveolens* var. *dulce*): The seed of the common salad vegetable. An ingredient in some commercial curry powders.

Cilantro (*Eryngium foetidum*): Coriander leaf, often used as a garnish for curries, or chopped and sprinkled over them. An ingredient in some curry pastes.

Chile peppers (*Capsicum species*): The fruits of members of the genus *Capsicum*. They are found all over the world and are used dried in commercial and home powders and both fresh and dried in Southeast Asian dishes. We have suggested appropriate chiles and substitutions in the recipes. *See Prik and Cabe.*

Cili: Alternate Malaysian term for chiles. *Cili padi* are apparently the same as *cabe rawit*, the small bird's eye chiles, while dried red chiles are *cili kering*. Chile powder is *serbuk cili*. Compare with *Sili*.

Cinnamon (*Cinnamomum zeylanicum*): The bark of an evergreen tree that grows in western India and in Sri Lanka. It is a common ingredient in curry powders and pastes from all over the world.

Cloves (*Eugenia caryophyllata*): The dried, unopened flower buds of an evergreen tree native to the Moluccas; the spice is now grown extensively in Zanzibar. Cloves are a common ingredient in curry powders and in curry pastes from Southeast Asia, Malaysia, and Indonesia.

Coconut (*Cocos nucifera*): The fruit of the *Cocos* genus of palms, found in tropical regions. The grated flesh, and milk extracted from it, appear in many Southeast Asian dishes.

Coriander (*Eryngium foetidum*): The seed of a Mediterranean herb; one of the most common ingredients in curry powders. The fresh leaves, cilantro, are a common ingredient in Southeast Asian dishes.

Cumin (*Cuminum cyminum*): The seed of a common annual herb native to Egypt; another common ingredient in curry powders.

Curry leaf (*Murraya koenigii*): The aromatic leaf of the curry leaf tree, which grows on the Indian subcontinent and is used throughout Southeast Asia.

Durian (*Durio zibethinus*): A large fruit related to jackfruit with a strong, nauseating odor.

Farangi: Thai for foreigner.

Fenugreek (*Trigonella foenumgraecum*): The seeds of an annual herb native to the Mediterranean area and India. A common ingredient in curry powders.

Fish sauce: Called *nam pla* in Thailand and *nuoc cham* in Vietnam, this salty, fermented fish sauce is a very common condiment. Prepared fish sauces can be obtained in Asian markets.

Five-spice powder: A blend of star anise, fagara (Chinese prickly ash), cassia, fennel, and cloves; popular in Southeast Asia, it occasionally appears in curries.

Galangal (*Alpinia galanga*): A close relative of ginger, this rhizome appears in many Southeast Asian dishes. *Laos* powder is a dried spice made from galangal.

Garlic (*Allium sativum*): A perennial herb used in many curries and curry pastes.

Ginger (*Zingiber officiale*): A rhizome that appears in curries, curry powders, and pastes.

Gulai: An Indonesian soup or stew.

Jackfruit (*Artocarpus herterophyllus*): A tropical fruit whose seeds and flesh are cooked, pickled, and roasted. The jackfruit flesh is also ground with rice and turned into fritters.

Jaggery: Dark brown palm sugar.

Kaffir lime leaves (*Citrus hystrix*): Leaves of a Southeast Asian citrus tree; used in curries and many other dishes of the region.

Kasmiri: A popular chile in Thailand that is also grown in Kasmir, India.

Katjang: Malay term for beans.

Kencur: See Galangal.

La lot: Vietnamese term for a relative of black pepper; the crinkly leaf is used in soups and as a wrapper for grilled meats.

Ladyfinger: Okra.

Laos: See Galangal.

Lemongrass (*Cymbopogon citratus*): The bulbs and lower stalk of this perennial plant have a strong citrus flavor. It is used in Southeast Asian dishes and curry pastes. If fresh lemongrass is used, cooks should remove the upper two-thirds of the stalks and cut the rest, including the bulb, into small bits. In the case of dried lemongrass, it should be soaked in warm water for 90 minutes before use, drained, and chopped. It is called *serai* in Malaysia, *sereh* in Indonesia.

Lombok: Alternate Indonesian term for chile peppers.

Mace (*Myristica fragrans*): The outer, fibrous covering of the nutmeg seed; occasionally appears in curry powders.

Mak phet: A Laotian term for chile peppers. *Mak phet dip* are fresh green chiles; *mak phet deng,* fresh red chiles; *mak phet nyai,* large chiles; *mak phet kuntsi,* small chiles; *mak phet kinou,* tiny, "rat-dropping" chiles; *mak phet haeng,* dried red chiles; *mak phet pung,* ground red chiles.

Mango (*Mangifera indica*): A tropical fruit that is often eaten as a dessert in Southeast Asia.

Mint (*Mentha arvensis*): A common perennial herb and an ingredient in some Singaporean curries.

Nam pla: See Fish sauce.

Nasi: Malay term for cooked rice.

Nga yut thee: Burmese term for chiles.

Nuoc cham: A spicier, Vietnamese version of *nam pla*.

Nutmeg (*Myristica fragrans*): The seed of an evergreen tree native to the Moluccas; a common ingredient in curry powders and pastes.

Okra (*Hibiscus esculentus*): The pods of an annual vegetable; an occasional ingredient in Malaysian curries, often used as a thickening agent. It is widely used in curries and soups (*sambhar*) in southern India.

Onion (*Allium cepa*): A common ingredient in curry pastes and dishes. It appears in some commercial curry pastes.

Ot: General Vietnamese term for chile peppers. Dried chiles are *ot kho* and chile sauces are *tuong ot*.

Pandan: See Screwpine.

Papaya (*Carica papaya*): A tropical fruit. Green papayas are widely used in curries in India; the ripe papayas are used as desserts.

Patis: Filipino term for fish sauce.

Petis: Malay term for prawn paste.

Petjili: Indonesian sweet relishes with chiles.

Pisang: Malay word for banana.

Pla buk: Giant Mekong River catfish.

Prawn paste: Called *blacan* in Malay, this strong-smelling paste is made with fermented prawns and salt. The fishy odor dissipates during cooking. It is sold in blocks and cakes in Asian markets. Substitute shrimp paste, or fish paste, as a last resort.

Prik: The Thai word for chile peppers. *Prik khee noo* are the tiny, slender chiles often labeled as "Thai chiles" or "bird's eye pepper." (Sometimes spelled *prik khee noo suan.*) *Prik leuang* is a yellow, medium-length, slender chile used in southern Thailand. *Prik khee fah* (sometimes *prik chee far*) is a term used to refer to cayenne chiles, while *prik yuak* is the yellow wax hot variety. The long, green, New Mexican types are *prik num*. Dried red chiles are *prik haeng*, while *prik pon* is red chile powder. *Prik bod* is chile paste.

Rau ram: Vietnamese term for polygonum; also called Vietnamese mint or Vietnamese basil, and it tastes like a combination of mint and basil.

Rendang: An Indonesian curry.

Rijsttafel: Dutch, literally meaning rice table. A series of contrasting and complementary dishes served together at a complete Indonesian meal.

Salam (*Eugeneia polyanza*): A laurel leaf that dries to a very dark color, almost black; used in Malaysian curries. It is not a bay leaf, but bay leaves may be substituted.

Sambal: A Malaysian and Indonesian chile paste.

Santan: Malay for coconut milk.

Satay or **sate:** Grilled meat or poultry served on skewers.

Screwpine (*Pandanus odoratissimus*): Leaves used to flavor rice in India and Malaysia. Available in leaf form or essence in some Asian markets. Called *pandan* in Malay and pandanus leaves in English.

Sesame seeds (*Sesamum indicum*): The seed of an annual herb indigenous to Indonesia; an occasional ingredient in Indonesian and Malaysian curries.

Shallots (*Allium ascalonicum*): This onion-like bulb is an ingredient in Malaysian, Thai, and Singaporean curries, curry pastes, and many other dishes.

Shrimp paste: Called *hei-ko* in Chinese, *petis* in Malay, *kapi* in Thai, and *trassi* in Indonesian, this paste combines shrimp and salt, which are allowed to ferment. It is milder than prawn paste and is an ingredient in some commercial Thai curry pastes

Sili: The Filipino (Tagalog) word for capsicums in general. *Siling bilog* is bell pepper; *siling haba* is the long green or red chile; *siling labuyo* is the bird's eye pepper, very small and very hot.

Tabia: Balinese word for chile peppers. The *Tabia lombok* (sometimes called *tabia jawa*) is finger-length and resembles cayenne; *tabia Bali* is about an inch long and is the most popular chile in Bali; *tabia kerinyi* are the "bird's eye" chiles, or piquins. *Tabia gede* is bell pepper.

Tamarind (*Tamarindus indica*): The five-inch pods of this tree contain seeds and a sour pulp. The pulp and seeds can be rehydrated in hot water and then strained. Tamarind can also be found in specialty markets in a variety of forms: pastes, concentrates of pulp, and whole pods dried into bricks or ground into powders.

Tempeh: Fermented vegetable protein, usually made from cultured soybeans.

Tuong: Also called Vietnamese soy sauce, this strong, fermented sauce is not read-ily available in North America except in specialized markets; substitute fish sauce.

Turmeric (*Curcuma longa*): The yellow rhizome of a relative of ginger; one of the most common ingredients in curry powder and curry pastes.

Bibliography

Aiken, Peter. "Paddling to the Peppers." *Chile Pepper* (November–December, 1993): 18.

Alejandro, Reynaldo. *The Philippine Cookbook*. New York: Perigee Books, 1982.

Alejandro, Reynaldo. "A Philippine Festival." *Cuisine* (January, 1983): 46.

Alford, Jeffrey. "Hanoi's Amazing Graze." *Food Arts* (July–August, 1994): 38.

Amatyakul, Chalie. *The Best of Thai Cooking*. Hong Kong: Travel Publishing Asia, Ltd., 1987.

Andrews, Jean. *Red Hot Peppers*. New York: Macmillan, 1993.

Anson, Robert Sam. "City of the Sixth Sense." *Condé Nast Traveler* (June, 1988): 88.

Bhumichitr, Vatcharin. *The Taste of Thailand*. Bangkok: Asia Books Co, Ltd., 1988.

Brennan, Jennifer. *The Original Thai Cookbook*. New York: Richard Marek Publishers, 1981.

Brennan, Jennifer. *The Cuisines of Asia*. London: Macdonald, 1984.

Brissenden, Rosemary. *Joys and Subtleties: South East Asian Cooking*. New York: Pantheon Books, 1970.

Bunge, Frederica M. *Philippines: A Country Study*. Washington, D.C.: Department of the Army, 1983.

Burt, Elinor. *Far Eastern Cookery*. Boston: Little, Brown & Co., 1947.

Campbell, Dawn and Janet Smith. *The Coffee Book*. Gretna, La.: Pelican Publishing Co., 1993.

Cordero-Fernando, Gilda. *The Culinary Culture of the Philippines*. Manila, Philippines: Bancom Audiovision Corp., 1976.

Corydon, Jeff. "The Peppery Palates of Padang." *Chile Pepper* (November–December, 1992): 23.

Crawford, William and Kamolmal Pootoraksa. *Thai Home Cooking from Kamolmal's Kitchen*. New York: New American Library, 1985.

Davidson, Alan. "The Traditions of Laos." *Cuisine* (May, 1982): 43.

Day, Harvey with Sarojini Mudnani. *Curries of India*. Bombay: Jaico Publishing House, 1962.

DeWit, Antoinette and Anita Borghese. *The Complete Book of Indonesian Cooking*. New York: Bobbs-Merrill, 1973.

DeWitt, Dave. "Singapore Fling." *Chile Pepper* (May–June, 1992):22.

DeWitt, Dave and Nancy Gerlach. *The Whole Chile Pepper Book*. Boston: Little, Brown & Co., 1990.

DeWitt, Dave and Arthur Pais. *A World of Curries*. Boston: Little, Brown & Co., 1994.

Donovan, Marie Kozslik. *The Far Eastern Epicure*. Garden City, NY: Doubleday & Co., 1958.

Duong, Binh and Marcia Kiesel. *Simple Art of Vietnamese Cooking*. New York: Prentice Hall, 1991.

Eiseman, Fred B. *Bali: Sekala & Niskala*. Singapore: Periplus Editions, 1990.

Falkner, Elizabeth. "Indonesia Sambals: Heat with Good Taste." *Chile Pepper* (July–August 1991): 37.

Farah, Adelaide. "Subtle Fire." *Health* (April, 1986): 35.

Fernandez, Rafi. *Malaysian Cookery*. London: Penguin Books, 1985.

Ferretti, Fred. "The Nonya Kitchen of Singapore." *Gourmet* (September, 1986): 50.

Ferretti, Fred. "In Search of the Indonesian Rijsttafel." *Gourmet* (April, 1990): 87.

Frazer, Sir James George. *The Golden Bough*. New York: The Macmillan Co., 1963.

Gader, June R. "A Taste of Thailand." *Bon Appetit* (October, 1982): 79.

Greeley, Alexandra. *Asian Grills*. New York: Doubleday, 1993.

Harris, Marvin. *The Sacred Cow and the Abominable Pig*. New York: Touchstone Books, 1985.

Hart, Donn V. *Riddles in Filipino Folklore: An Anthropological Analysis*. Syracuse, NY: Syracuse University Press, 1964.

Headly, Robert K., Jr. *Cambodia, A Country Study*. Washington, D.C.: Department of the Army, 1987.

Herklots, G. A. C. *Vegetables in South-East Asia*. London: George Allen & Unwin, Ltd., 1972.

Hiang, Lie Sek. *Indonesian Cooking*. New York: Crown Publishers, 1963.

Hooi, James. *The Guide to Singapore Hawker Food*. Singapore: Hospitality Host, 1985.

Hutton, Wendy, ed. *The Food of Malaysia*. Singapore: Periplus Editions, 1994.

Hutton, Wendy, ed. *The Food of Singapore*. Singapore: Periplus Editions, 1994.

Hynan, Gwenda. *Cuisines of Southeast Asia*. New York: John Wiley & Sons, 1993.

Johns, Yohanni. *Dishes from Indonesia*. Philadelphia: Chilton Book Company, 1971.

Johns, Yohanni. "The Art of Sumatran Cooking." In *Sumatra*, ed. by Eric M. Oey. Singapore: Periplus Editions, 1991.

Karp, David. "Where Cambodians Traveled to Study and Cook," *New York Times*, March 30, 1994, C3.

Karp, David. "The Elephant Walk." *Chile Pepper* (July–August, 1994): 44.

Kongpan, Sisamon and Pinyo Srisawat. *The Elegant Taste of Thailand*. Berkeley, CA: SLG Books, 1989.

Law, Ruth. *The Southeast Asia Cookbook*. New York: Donald I. Fine, 1990.

Liu, Gretchen. *Raffles Hotel*. Singapore: Landmark Books, 1992.

Marks, Copeland. "Indonesian Cookery." *Gourmet* (November, 1979): 50.

Marks, Copeland. *The Exotic Kitchens of Indonesia*. New York: M. Evans & Co., 1989.

Marks, Copeland and Aung Thein. *The Burmese Kitchen*. New York: M. Evans & Co., 1987.

McDermott, Nancie. *Real Thai*. San Francisco: Chronicle Books, 1992.

McDermott, Nancie. "The Triumph of Thai." *Food Arts* (June, 1993): 70.

Minifie, Kemp M. "A Cooking School in Bangkok." In *Travelers' Tales Thailand*, ed. by James O'Reilly and Larry Habegger. San Francisco: O'Reilly & Associates, Inc., 1993.

Ngo, Bach and Gloria Zimmerman. *The Classic Cuisine of Vietnam*. Woodbury, NY: Barron's, 1979.

Nikorpun, Manee and Pibob Lumyong. "Tomato and Pepper Production and Improvement in Thailand." In *Tomato and Pepper Production in the Tropics,* ed. by T. D. Griggs and B. T. McLean. Taipei, Taiwan: Asian Vegetable Research and Development Center, 1989.

Ogilvie, Rosemary Ann. "Beautiful, Bountiful Bali." *Chile Pepper* (March–April, 1994): 24.

Owen, Sri. *Indonesian Food and Cookery*. London: Prospect Books, 1986.

Owen, Sri. *The Rice Book*. New York: St. Martin's Press, 1993.

Parkes, Carl. *Southeast Asian Handbook*. Chico, CA: Moon Publications, 1990.

Parkes, Carl. *Thailand Handbook*. Chico, CA: Moon Publications, 1992.

Passmore, Jacki. *The Letts Companion to Asian Food and Cooking*. London: Charles Letts & Co., 1991.

Permadi, Anggoro Hadi. "Tomato and Pepper Production in Indonesia: Problems, Research, and Progress." In *Tomato and Pepper Production in the Tropics,* ed. by T. D. Griggs and B. T. McLean. Taipei, Taiwan: Asian Vegetable Research and Development Center, 1989.

Piper, Jacqueline M. *Rice in South-East Asia: Cultures and Landscapes*. Kuala Lumpur, Malaysia: Oxford University Press, 1993.

Poladitmontri, Panurat, Judy Lew, and William Warren. *Thailand: The Beautiful Cookbook*. San Francisco: Collins Publishers, 1992.

Rabonowitz, Alan. " 'To Eat' Means to Eat Rice." In *Travelers' Tales Thailand,* ed. by James O'Reilly and Larry Habegger. San Francisco: O'Reilly & Associates, Inc., 1993.

Ramirez, Orlando. "Vietnamese Food Influenced by Other Countries." Copely News Service, December 29, 1993.

Roces, Irene Pineda. "*Anong Ulam?*" In *The Culinary Culture of the Philippines,* (Gilda Cordero-Fernando, ed.) Manila, Philippines: Bancom Audiovision Corp., 1976.

Root, Waverly. *Food*. New York: Simon & Schuster, 1980.

Sahni, Julie. "Welcome Fall with a Burmese Buffet." *Cuisine* (October, 1982): 42.

Sanders, Joanne, ed. *1963 Y.W.C.A. Cookbook*. Bangkok: Chatra Press, Ltd., 1963.

Scott, David L. and Kristiaan Inwood. *A Taste of Thailand*. London: Rider, 1986.

Sheridan, Dan. "New Cuisine in Town." *Chicago Tribune,* June 22, 1989, 7-3.

Shukor, N. M., et al. "Tomato and Chili Pepper Growing in Malaysia." In *Tomato and Pepper Production in the Tropics,* ed. by T. D. Griggs and B. T. McLean. Taipei, Taiwan: Asian Vegetable Research and Development Center, 1989.

Sing, Phia. *Traditional Recipes of Laos*. London: Prospect Books, 1981.

Singapore Tourist Promotion Board. *Singapore: 101 Meals*. Singapore: Singapore Tourist Promotion Board, circa 1990.

Solomon, Charmaine. *The Complete Asian Cookbook*. New York: McGraw-Hill Book Company, 1976.

Soo, Leong Yee. *The Best of Singapore Cooking*. Singapore: Times Books International, 1988.

Steinberg, Rafael. *Pacific and Southeast Asian Cooking*. New York: Time-Life Books, 1970.

Sterling, Richard. "Nothing Beats a Bug." *Chile Pepper* (November–December, 1992): 46.

Sterling, Richard. "Secrets Shared: A Cambodian Journey." *Chile Pepper* (May–June, 1993): 20.

Sterling, Richard. "Return to the Land of the Ascending Dragon." *Chile Pepper* (November–December, 1993): 30.

Sterling, Richard. *Jungle Feasts*. Freedom, CA: The Crossing Press, 1995.

Taik, Aung. *The Best of Burmese Cooking*. San Francisco: Chronicle Books, 1993.

Tiruchelvam, Sharmini. *Foods of the Orient: South-East Asia*. London: Marshall Cavendish, Ltd., 1978.

Vatanapan, Pojanee. *Pojanee Vatanapan's Thai Cookbook*. New York: Harmony Books, 1986.

von Holzen, Heinz and Lother Arsana. *The Food of Bali*. Singapore: Periplus Editions, 1993.

Watson, John. "Singapore Fling." *Food Arts* (November, 1994): 54.

Weller, Anthony. "Gourmet Holidays—Bali." *Gourmet* (April, 1991): 66.

Woman's Society of Christian Service. *Rangoon International Cook Book*. Rangoon, Burma: Methodist English Church, 1962.

Yan, Martin. *A Simple Guide to Chinese Ingredients and Other Asian Specialties*. Foster City, CA: Yan Can Cook, Inc., n.d.

Zainu'ddin, A. G. Thompson. *How to Cook Indonesian Food*. Melbourne, Australia: Australian Indonesian Association of Victoria, 1982.

Index